Baudelaire's World

Baudelaire's World

ROSEMARY LLOYD

CORNELL UNIVERSITY PRESS
Ithaca & London

First published 2002 by Cornell University Press

Printed in the United States of America

Library of Congress Cataloging-in-Publication Data

Lloyd, Rosemary.
  Baudelaire's world / Rosemary Lloyd.
    p. cm.
Includes bibliographical references and index.
  ISBN 0-8014-4026-2 (cloth : alk. paper)
  1. Baudelaire, Charles, 1821–1867.   I. Title.
  PW2191.Z5 L59 2002
  841'.8—dc21

                                                    2002007299

Cloth printing   10 9 8 7 6 5 4 3 2 1

For Elizabeth

Contents

Illustrations

Acknowledgments

I started reading Baudelaire in the northern spring of 1968, when I had gone to Paris to spend part of my year between school and university. My command of French was minimal, but his poetry elated and moved me with an unforgettable intensity. I vividly remember walking along the Seine and reciting to myself "Elévation," "Correspondances," and "L'Héautontimorouménos." While in Paris during those months I attended lectures by the ebullient Baudelaire scholar Antoine Adam, known for bouncing on his feet at crucial moments and exclaiming: *Voyez-Vous? Bon!* In my undergraduate study at Adelaide University I had the great good fortune of being taught by an impassioned Baudelaire scholar, Peter Hambly, whose exploration of the secret architecture of *Les Fleurs du mal* taught me to see shapes and patterns between and among poems, where before I had focused on them each in isolation. At the University of Cambridge my Ph.D. supervisor was that wonderfully sensitive and demanding reader of Baudelaire, Alison Fairlie, whose advice and delicately expressed but intellectually probing criticism I greatly miss. Lloyd and Jeannot Austin were not just great sources of knowledge about Baudelaire but wise and generous friends. Since those days I have had the good fortune to count among my friends many Baudelaire specialists whose work and thinking has guided mine. My thanks, therefore, to Ross Chambers, Graham Chesters, Michele Hannoosh, Jim Hiddelston, Jim Lawler, Margaret Miner, Steve Murphy, Claude and Vincenette Pichois, Graham Robb, and Sonya Stephens. I'm also indebted to Jane Fulcher for her insights into the music world of Baudelaire's time. I'm deeply grateful to all those Baudelaireans whose studies have helped me in my thinking, even if I haven't been able to mention them all in bibliographies and footnotes. William Gass's *Reading Rilke* was inspirational in the preparation of this study, despite the enormous differences between the two poets. My thanks, as always, go to the librarians in Indiana University's Lilly and Main libraries. I am grateful to the University of Chicago Press for permission to quote from *Selected Letters of Charles Baudelaire: The Conquest of Solitude* (© 1986 by The University of Chicago. All rights reserved). Oxford University Press for permission to quote from my translation of *The Prose Poems and La Fanfarlo* © 1991 by Oxford University Press. All rights reserved. "Recitative by

Death" copyright © 1976 by Edward Mendelson, William Meredith and Monroe K. Spears, Executers of the Estate of W. H. Auden, and "Have a Good Time" copyright © 1976 Edward Mendelson, William Meredith and Monroe K. Spears, Executers of the Estate of W. H. Auden, from *W. H. Auden: Collected Poems* by W. H. Auden are used by permission of Random House, Inc. "Baudelaire's Music" by Robert Fitzgerald from *Spring Shade: Poems 1931–1970* copyright © 1969 by Robert Fitzgerald, reprinted by permission of New Directions Publishing Corp. "The Digging Skeleton" from *North* by Seamus Heaney, reprinted by permission of Faber and Faber.

This book is dedicated to an inspiring teacher and a dear friend, Elizabeth Warburton.

R. L.

Brief Chronology

1759 Birth at La Neuville-au-Pont of Joseph-François Baudelaire, father of Charles.

1793 Birth in London of Caroline Archenbault Defayis, poet's mother.

1819 Marriage of Joseph-François Baudelaire and Caroline Defayis.

1821 9 April: birth of Charles-Pierre Baudelaire.

1827 Death of Charles Baudelaire's (CB's) father.

1828 Caroline Baudelaire marries Lieutenant-Colonel Jacques Aupick.

1832 CB and his mother go to Lyon where Aupick is stationed.

1836 Return to Paris. CB attends the College Louis-le-Grand.

1839 Expulsion from the lycée Louis-le-Grand.

1841 CB sets out on a voyage meant to take him to Calcutta. Stops at Reunion and Mauritius, then refuses to go any further. He returns to France, arriving February 15, 1842.

1842 Inherits 100,000 francs from his father's estate.

1844 CB's extravagant spending leads his family to create a *conseil de famille* which appoints Narcisse Ancelle trustee of his fortune.

1845 Publication of his review of the Salon, and of a poem, "A une dame créôle." First translations of the works of Poe begin to appear in the French press. 30 June: CB attempts suicide by stabbing himself.

1846 Publication of his *Salon of 1846.*

1847 Publication of his short story "La Fanfarlo."

1848 February Revolution and uprisings of June. CB collaborates on a newspaper, *Le Salut public,* of which only two numbers appear. 15 July: publication of CB's first translation of Poe, *Magnetic Revelation.*

1851 Publication of his first study of wine and hashish, which contains prose versions of verse poems on wine to appear in *Les Fleurs du mal.* 2 December: coup d'état in which Louis-Napoléon declares himself emperor.

1852 March and April: publication in *La Revue de Paris* of CB's first study of Poe.

1855 June: *La Revue des deux mondes* publishes eighteen poems under the title *Les Fleurs du mal*. June: publication of the first of CB's prose poems, "Crépuscule" and "La Solitude."

1856 March: publication of CB's translations of Poe called *Histoires extraordinaires*.

1857 January–February: trial of Flaubert's novel *Madame Bovary*. 8 March: publication of CB's second volume of translations of Poe's short stories. 27 April: death of General Aupick. 25 June: publication of *Les Fleurs du mal*. 7 July: *Les Fleurs du mal* accused of being an outrage to public decency. 20 August: CB condemned to pay fine of 300 francs and suppress six of the poems.

1858 13 May: Publication of CB's translation of Poe's novel *Arthur Gordon Pym*.

1859 First notes for *Mon Cœur mis à nu* (*My Heart Laid Bare*).

1860 January: CB sells Poulet-Malassis and de Broise the second edition of *Les Fleurs du mal,* his study of the artificial paradises, and his articles of literary and art criticism. 13 January: suffers first attack of illness. May: publication of *Les Paradis artificiels* (*The Artifical Paradises*).

1861 February: second edition of *Les Fleurs du mal*. 15 June–15 August: *La Revue fantaisiste* publishes nine of the ten prose articles that make up the *Réflexions sur quelques uns de mes contemporains* (*Reflections on some of my contemporaries*). 11 December: CB presents his candidacy for the Academy.

1863 13 January: Baudelaire gives Hetzel for the sum of 1,200 francs the exclusive rights to publish his *Petits Poèmes en prose* and *Les Fleurs du mal* previously sold to Poulet-Malassis.

1864 24 April: CB arrives in Brussels. 2 May: lecture on Delacroix. 11 May: lecture on Gautier. 12, 23 May and 3 June: lectures on artificial stimulants. 13 June: CB reads from his works. 25 December: under the title "Le Spleen de Paris" *La Revue de Paris* publishes 6 prose poems.

1865 16 March: publication of CB's translation of Poe, *Histoires grotesques et sérieuses* (*Tales, grotesque and serious*).

1866 Around 15 March, CB visits Namur and falls on to the ground in the church. 22–23 March: his condition worsens. 30 March: paralysis of the right side. 31 March: *Le Parnasse contemporain* publishes *Nouvelles Fleurs du mal* (*New Flowers of Evil*). 2 July: CB brought back to Paris.

1867 31 August: death of CB. 2 September: burial in the Montparnasse cemetery.

1868 December: Michel Lévy begins publishing CB's complete works.

Note and Abbreviations

Except where otherwise indicated, all translations are my own. For details of translations by others quoted in the text see the bibliography of translations, pp. 237–239. In the text, poems from *Les Fleurs du mal* are referred to by FM followed by the Roman numeral Baudelaire assigned to the particular poem. Verse poems not included in *Les Fleurs du mal* are located by volume and page number of Baudelaire's complete works. The prose poems are referred to as PPP followed by the Roman numeral Baudelaire assigned.

I, II = Baudelaire, *Œuvres complètes*. Ed. Claude Pichois. 2 vols. Paris: Gallimard, 1975–1976.

CI, CII = Baudelaire, *Correspondance*. Ed. Claude Pichois and Jean Ziegler. 2 vols. Paris: Gallimard, 1973.

LAB = *Lettres à Baudelaire*. Ed. Claude Pichois. Neuchâtel: A la Baconnière, 1973.

L = *Selected Letters of Charles Baudelaire*. Trans. and ed. Rosemary Lloyd. Chicago: University of Chicago Press, 1986. (Some translations revised for this study.)

MO = *Un Mangeur d'Opium*. Ed. Michèle Stäuble. Neuchâtel: A la Baconnière, 1976. (Parallel texts of Thomas De Quincey's *Confessions of an English Opium-Eater*, his *Suspiria de profundis*, and Baudelaire's adaptation.)

NL = Baudelaire, *Nouvelles Lettres*. Ed. Claude Pichois. Paris: Fayard, 2000.

Pichois = Claude Pichois, *Baudelaire*. Trans. Graham Robb. London: Hamish Hamilton, 1989.

Baudelaire's World

CHAPTER ONE

To the Reader

A book about poetry ought to be a book about life.
—Richard Jenkyns, *Virgil's Experience*

Trim dualistic Baudelaire,
Poet of cities, harbours, whores,
Acedia, gaslight and remorse.
—W. H. Auden, "New Year Letter"

A temperament half nervous, half bilious. A cultivated mind, sharpened by the study of shape and color; a tender heart, wearied by sorrow, but still ready for rejuvenation. We could even, if you like, go so far as to admit former faults, and, as the inevitable result of a nature that is easily excited, if not real remorse, at least a sense of regret for time profaned and ill-spent. A taste for metaphysics, a knowledge of the various hypotheses philosophy has made about human destiny—these are certainly not useless additions. Neither is that love of virtue, an abstract, stoic or mystical virtue that can be found in all those books in which the modern child seeks nourishment, virtue seen as the highest summit to which a distinguished soul can climb. If we add to all that a great delicacy of feeling, which I omitted as something superfluous, I think I've assembled the most common elements generally to be found in the sensitive modern man, in what might be called the banal form of originality.

(I 429–30)

This is Baudelaire giving a portrait of what the eighteenth century might have called the sensitive individual or of what Romanticism might have dubbed the misunderstood, but that his own bourgeois age burdened with the epithet "original." It is also of course, and above all, a self-portrait of the writer who is for many not just the greatest of France's nineteenth-century poets, but one of modernism's founding voices. Remarkable for the variety and intensity of his vision, the breadth of his linguistic register, and the relationship he establishes between his themes and his poetic forms, Baudelaire remains both profoundly challenging and deeply satisfying.

Reading him demands an intellectual and imaginative endeavor that is different from the effort needed to respond, say, to Victor Hugo or William Wordsworth, Rainer Maria Rilke or Eugenio Montale, Les Murray or Elizabeth Bishop. Attempting to enter through imagination the poet's physical and affective world is one way of preparing a more satisfactory reading of his poetry. But how do we enter anyone's world, and especially the world of writers who not only lived in very different circumstances from our own, but also spoke a language that is not ours? How do we pick our way through the palimpsest of their memories and the spider's web of their reading? And if our task is not only to read but also to translate their writing, how best do we respond to that very considerable challenge?

In the opening paragraphs of his biography of Baudelaire, the poet's close friend Charles Asselineau justifies his task by saying that Baudelaire's "work, as has often been said, is the man himself; but the work is not all the man. Behind the written and published work there is another complete work which was spoken and acted and lived, and that needs to be known, because it explains the other and contains, as he himself would have said, its genesis."[1] My book is in part about the relationship between those two works—the public and the private—in his verse poetry, in the poems in prose, and in his criticism. By building an image of Baudelaire's world around major themes of his writing (childhood, women, reading, the city, dream, art, nature, death), I set the poems themselves in a richer context, made up of Baudelaire's other writings, the writers and artists who preceded him or were his contemporaries, and some of the historical and physical realities of life in mid-nineteenth-century Paris.

Baudelaire's collection of verse, *Les Fleurs du mal* (*The Flowers of Evil*), explores the development of a poet from childhood to death and thereby reveals the shaping of his character through a range of different experiences—love, art, city life, dreams, intoxication, revolt, perversion. The work opens with an unnumbered poem, "Au lecteur (To the Reader)," which precedes six books: *Spleen et Idéal* (*Spleen and Ideal*), *Tableaux parisiens* (*Parisian Paintings*), *Le Vin* (*Wine*), *Fleurs du mal*, *Révolte* (*Revolt*) *La Mort* (*Death*).

As Baudelaire remarked in a letter to the poet Alfred de Vigny, *Les Fleurs du mal* is not a mere album of randomly grouped poems, but one built according to what he termed a "secret architecture."[2] Each poem gains further resonance by its position in the work, by poems that precede and follow it. In some cases, poems of joy have counterparts of pain or rage, inviting us to read the collection not just as a progression but also as a series of cycles. The protagonist whose life *Les Fleurs du mal* charts in this manner is not identical with the Baudelaire who fought on the barricades in

---

[1] Jacques Crépet and Claude Pichois, *Baudelaire et Asselineau* (Paris: Nizet, 1953), 61.

[2] For an outstanding recent exploration as well as historical survey of this concept see James R. Lawler, *Poetry and Moral Dialectic: Baudelaire's "Secret Architecture"* (Madison, N.J.: Fairleigh Dickinson University Press, 1997).

1848 or walked across the New Carrousel in the 1850s, but the two figures exist in a close symbiotic relationship.

That relationship is even closer in Baudelaire's criticism, as he suggests in the opening paragraph of his study of Wagner. Justifying the use of "I" he affirms:

> This *I,* justly accused of impertinence in many cases, nevertheless implies a great modesty. It locks the writer into the strictest limits of sincerity. By reducing the task, the use of *I* facilitates it. Finally, there is no need to be a truly consummate probabilist to feel certain that this sincerity will find friends among impartial readers. Obviously there is the odd chance that the ingenuous critic, merely by recounting his own impressions, also recounts those of some unknown enthusiasts.
>
> (II 779)

Which did not, of course, prevent him from skating around the truth when it was expedient to do so. In a letter to his mother, for instance, he refers to Victor Hugo's *Les Misérables* which he had reviewed quite favorably, while still revealing the fundamental conflict between Hugo's belief in progress and his own conviction that evil is ineradicable. To his mother, however, he confesses: "The book is disgusting and clumsy. On this score I've shown that I possess the art of lying" (L 190: CII 254). For the reader, charting a course through the sincerity and the lies of the critical writing demands an awareness both of the rhetorical and of the biographical elements at play.

A more complex relationship between narrative "I" and author is at work in the prose poems, *Petits poèmes en Prose (Short Prose Poems)*, which appeared in volume form only after the poet's death. This is poetry inspired above all, Baudelaire insists, by the city and its crowds. As a result, the narrative persona changes from poem to poem, and the poetic voice is sometimes split between two characters, as it is in "Le Vieux Saltimbanque (The Old Mountebank)" or in "Le Mauvais Vitrier (The Bad Glazier)." And for the prose poems, Baudelaire no longer claimed a pre-established architecture, but instead insisted that they could be read in any order. He uses the image of a kaleidoscope: the poet has provided the fragments that the reader then assembles and reassembles to form multiple and ever-changing patterns.

Baudelaire's poems and criticism reveal a sharply observant eye and an analytical mind that drew its sustenance from everyday events but transformed them into something more powerful and more universal. This book is not a traditional biography, but it does draw on biographical funds and techniques, and like biographies it has been forced to schematize the haphazard nature of life. We live sequentially—what other choice do we have? But when we remember and particularly when we attempt to make some kind of sense and narrative of those memories, we work in a different time-frame, one that groups together disparate events, doubles back, and leaps forward. We experience time in terms of thickness rather than linear progression. That thickness I have attempted to represent here. Readers who would like to follow Baudelaire's development chronologically will find a concise chronology on pages xi-xii. Thinking about those events, however, we need to remember that, as Baudelaire himself argues in his study of the poet Théophile Gautier, this is the life of a man whose most dramatic adventures take place in silence under the dome of his brain (II 104).

In Baudelaire's case, moreover, the biographical record is often fragmentary or distorted. Letters are missing. He kept no diaries (the collection of jottings known as the *journaux intimes,* the intimate diaries, are disparate notes on his thinking and reading, preparations for possible future works, rather than any regularly kept exploration of his activities). He rarely comments in either letters or notebooks on his own works, or on their reception, except in the most general of terms. Gustave Courbet, who painted his portrait and knew him as a friend, is reported as lamenting, "I don't know how to bring off a portrait of Baudelaire. His face changes every day."[3] Contemporary memoirs depict him as shifting allegiances almost as often. The philosopher Emmanuel Swedenborg would be his idol one day, the next it would be the mathematician Hoëné Wronski. Bronzino, the Italian mannerist, would arouse his ardent enthusiasm for a brief period, then he would be abandoned in favor of the Flemish painter Jan Van Eyck. Baudelaire's notebooks include the cavalier aphorism, "I understand how someone could desert one cause in order to find out what it would be like to serve another" (I 676). Part of this is a mask, an aspect of his determination to forge his own personality. But masks have a habit of changing the features of those who wear them.

Yet, however much Baudelaire may have changed his allegiances and his masks, certain questions, preoccupations, and convictions run through all his writings. It is not that the answers are fixed, or that his esthetic positions remain constant. It is more that he did not erect barriers between the genres he used. You can follow debates and see him working out solutions across a range of different kinds of writing, from letters and criticism to poetry. My study of Baudelaire's writings sets out to investigate different aspects of the experience of reading him in order to trace a personal path toward a sympathetic response. Above all, I want to set the poems in the context of Baudelaire's other writings—his art and literary criticism, his translations of Edgar Allan Poe (see figure 5) and Thomas De Quincey, the studies of wine, hashish and opium, and his letters.

But I want also to explore translations of certain verse and prose poems, and to offer some of my own, in an attempt to indicate what elements (textual, thematic, rhetorical, rhythmic, and stylistic) demand particularly close attention, elements not always easily seized by non-French readers and frequently weakened or lost in translation.

Many people have tried their hand at translating or adapting Baudelaire. Nicholas Moore, in his thirty-one versions of one of the poems entitled "Spleen," the

---

[3] Quoted in Champfleury, *Souvenirs et portraits de jeunesse* (Paris: Dentu, 1872), 135.

one beginning "Je suis comme le roi (I am like the king)," gives an indication of how much variation there can be in a translation. One of his versions boils the essence of the sonnet down into four lines:

> Not riches, power, advisers, pets, sport, gold
> Nor even naked women cheer the old
> In heart. Bones will be bones. All that remains
> Instead of blood, green water, clotted veins.[4]

Is the best translation one that aims for accuracy or for imagination? Robert Fitzgerald includes a poem called "Baudelaire's Music" in his 1971 collection, *Spring Shade*. Here is Baudelaire's sonnet "La Musique":

> La musique souvent me prend comme une mer!
> Vers ma pâle étoile,
> Sous un plafond de brume ou dans un vaste éther,
> Je mets à la voile;
>
> La poitrine en avant et les poumons gonflés
> Comme de la toile,
> J'escalade le dos des flots amoncelés
> Que la nuit me voile;
>
> Je sens vibrer en moi toutes les passions
> D'un vaisseau qui souffre;
> Le bon vent, la tempête et ses convulsions
>
> Sur l'immense gouffre
> Me bercent. D'autres fois, calme plat, grand miroir
> De mon désespoir!
>
> (FM LXIX)

A straightforward translation might read something like this: "Music often seizes me like a sea! Towards my pale star, under a ceiling of mist or beneath the vast ether, I set sail. Chest out and lungs filled, like canvas, I climb on the back of the mountains of waves that night hides from me. I feel vibrating within me all the passions of a storm-tossed vessel. Favoring winds, storms and their convulsions rock me. At other times, dead calm, great mirror of my despair!" Fitzgerald's poem uses Baudelaire's as a springboard to give:

---

[4] For details of translations, consult the bibliography of translations, pp. 237–39.

On music drawn away, a sea-borne mariner,
Star over bowsprit pale,
Beneath a roof of mist or depths of lucid air
I put out under sail:

Breastbone my steady bow and lungs full, running free
Before a following gale,
I ride the rolling back and mass of every sea
By Night wrapt in her veil;

All passions and all joys that vessels undergo
Tremble alike in me;
Fair winds or waves in havoc when the tempests blow

On the enormous sea
Rock me, and level calms come silvering sea and air,
A glass for my despair.

Which both is, and is not, Baudelaire.

Should a translator seek to write for a particular Anglophone group (Scottish or Welsh, Irish or Cornish, English or American, South African or Australian, New Zealand or Indian)? Keep the rhymes at all cost? Favor rhythm over rhyme? Choose a particular idiom over another—prefer the archaic or the colloquial? Let's say I translate the tercets of the sonnet "Brumes et pluies (Mists and Rain)" in the following way:

Rien n'est plus doux au cœur plein de choses funèbres,
Et sur qui dès longtemps descendent les frimas,
Ô blafardes saisons, reines de nos climats,

Que l'aspect permanent de vos pâles ténèbres,
—Si ce n'est, par un soir sans lune, deux à deux,
D'endormir la douleur sur un lit hasardeux.

(FM CI)

as:

To a heart that's full of grief nothing's so sweet,
A heart long covered with the winter's sleet,
O pallid seasons, you who rule our airs,

Than knowing we'll always see your pale shade,
—Unless it is on a moonless night, in pairs,
To send our grief to sleep by getting laid.

With this translation, I convey part of the meaning, but the vulgarity of the final expression distorts the original, adds a veneer to what Baudelaire had made neutral,
and through the clash between its vulgarity and the tone of the rest of the poem,
suggests a sudden outburst of anger that is not only not present in the French, but
that also indicates a move away from the lethargy that dominates the narrative voice
throughout the sonnet.

Of course, translators can also impose a personal reading. Ciaran Carson, for instance, translates the title "Duellum" as "Warriors," which changes the emphasis
from the struggle to the protagonists and uses a highly individual idiom that also
gives it an unequivocally homoerotic focus. Here is the original:

Deux guerriers ont couru l'un sur l'autre; leurs armes
Ont éclaboussé l'air de lueurs et de sang.
Ces jeux, ces cliquetis du fer sont les vacarmes
D'une jeunesse en proie à l'amour vagissant.

(XXXV)

A literal translation would go something like this: "Two fighters rushed against each
other. Their weapons spattered the air with sparks and blood. These games, this
clattering of iron, are the uproar created by a youth preyed on by wailing love." In
Carson's version this becomes:

Two boys got stuck into each other, pushed and shoved
Their flick and shiv in bloody glimmers, fists on hafts
In blue-veined steel-struck sparks of adolescent love,
Like knights riding to joust with tumultuous shafts.

Baudelaire's sonnet makes that reading possible, but it does not force us to interpret
the *guerriers* as both male, as Carson's does, or confront us with that brash phallic
image of the shafts. Neither does the slang of "flick and shiv" represent the register of
Baudelaire's language, which remains mainstream even when his subject matter is
not.

Translators determined to preserve the rhyme can also distort meaning. Of
course, it is true that Baudelaire delighted in rhyme and used it, as we'll see, to convey truths or suggestions not stated in other ways within the poem; for this reason
he claimed that he had decided against translating the poetry of Edgar Allan Poe be-

cause to do so meant abandoning the pleasure of rhyme. But it is also the case that English has a long tradition of blank verse, as French does not, and that rhyme is less essential to our pleasure of English poetry than it is to traditional French poetry. Forcing a rhyme at the cost of restricting, distorting or changing the meaning throws a veil between us and the poem. Take for instance the poem "Spleen" beginning "J'ai plus de souvenirs que si j'avais mille ans (I have more memories than if I were a thousand years old)." Four lines here summon up boredom through analogies with slow, snowy winter days:

> Rien n'égale en longueur les boiteuses journées,
> Quand sous les lourds flocons des neigeuses années
> L'ennui, fruit de la morne incuriosité
> Prend les proportions de l'immortalité.

> (FM LXXVI)

Dorothy Martin translates this as:

> Naught could there be longer than these maimed days
> When, 'neath the snowy years' thick-falling maze,
> Spleen, of indifference the mournful flower,
> Grows more immortal through each lingering hour

which not only inflicts on Baudelaire an archaic idiom (naught, 'neath) that runs counter to his modernism, but in the search for a rhyme, turns into a flower the fruit of indifference, an image Baudelaire mentions to his publisher as being of particular importance to him (L 94, CI 395). Walter Martin, writing some 70 years later, gives us a fairly free version:

> Limping days as far as the eye can see,
> And snowblind years for all eternity;
> Indifference expands into ennui,
> With overtones of Immortality.

Martin has caught the intentional boredom of the repeated rhymes here (the rhyme of *journées* and *années* recurring phonetically in *incuriosité* and *immortalité*) and his idiom is much more analogous to Baudelaire's than that of Dorothy Martin. Yet to squeeze out those last two rhymes, he has sacrificed the image that links indifference to ennui, and reduced "the proportions of immortality" to the weaker "overtones of immortality."

Norman Shapiro's version is markedly different again:

Nothing can match those endless, crippled days
When, blizzard-blown, chill winter overlays
Ennui with heavy snows: drear apathy,
Taking the shape of immortality.

However much you might admire "the shape of immortality," the sense of snow
falling over long years is lost in Shapiro's second line, and that "drear apathy"
demonstrates the triumph of rhyme over the image connecting apathy and the lack
of curiosity. You win and you lose in reading a translation. The solution, it would
seem, is to read stereoscopically, drawing on several different versions, and keeping
the original to hand.[5]

Whether we read him in French or in translation, Baudelaire's writing is often
unnerving, as likely to get under our skin like a form of poison ivy as it is to delight
us. How does a modern reader, particularly a modern female reader, deal with
Baudelaire? How does one put up with his misogyny, his bouts of self-destructive
selfishness, and his flashes of acidic bad temper? One cannot simply separate out
the man and his work in this case, somehow distilling a calm quintessence in verse.
It does not happen, or if it does, something vital is lost. Personal experience is of
course transformed, metamorphosed into something quite different, but it is still
something that retains the strongest features of his personality. I think you have to
recognize that the destructive streak is what enabled him to be so wonderfully creative and so original at a time when a throng of powerful figures dominated poetry.
By tearing apart the comfortable universe that could have been his, by consistently
gazing at rather than glossing over the sources of evil not just in society but also in
himself, he did succeed in hacking out a domain that was his alone. No other writer
of his time saw so keenly the conflicts that make up modern life. His destruction is
also a creation, his misogyny and his misanthropy are as much hatred of himself as
of others; his mud, as he would put it, is also gold. But reading him has to be as
much a question of resisting him as of allowing him to take over. And unlike the
image of the world that Baudelaire gives us in "Le Voyage," experience does not
shrink his achievement: as a reader of the maps and prints that his writing offers,
I'm still the child who finds a universe as vast as my appetites.

[5] Clive Scott's *Translating Baudelaire* (Exeter: Exeter University Press, 2000) reached my library only after
I had sent my manuscript to Cornell. As with all Professor Scott's books, it is an erudite and eloquent exploration of poetry, drawing on his vast knowledge of French prosody. Its exploration of translation theory, its clarification of methodologies and possibilities, and its contributions to translating Baudelaire all
make it a striking addition to studies of both the discipline and the poet. My own purposes have been
rather different, driven above all by the desire to see "Baudelaire" as more than just the poet of *Les Fleurs
du mal*.

CHAPTER TWO

The Palimpsest of Memory

A man in his thirties, dressed with an attention to detail that cannot quite hide the straitened circumstances in which he is living, wanders through a Parisian landscape that is undergoing politically motivated structural changes imposed by Baron Haussmann, Napoleon III's minister. As he passes the western end of the Louvre and crosses toward the Tuileries Palace, there leaps into his mind the tragic figure of Andromache, driven into exile after the fall of Troy. Pondering this sudden memory, he recalls an earlier incident when in the same area he noticed a swan picking its way across the dry dust in search of the lakes it had lost. Obviously, this swan had escaped from a menagerie, one of those inexpensive sources of amusement for an increasingly urban population. He realizes now that what links the swan and Andromache is the theme of exile. The chance memory of the swan bewildered by the hostile urban environment sets the man to musing more generally on banishment, and at once the cityscape around him opens itself up to be read as a series of allegories on loss, nostalgia, and memory. Returning home, he writes the great poem that still for many stands as one of the founding texts of modernism, "Le Cygne (The Swan)." Later he is to send this poem to the exiled Victor Hugo, accompanied by a letter in which he clarifies that "the important thing for [him] was to express quickly all the suggestions sparked off by a chance incident, an image, and to show how the sight of a suffering animal drives our thoughts toward all those whom we love, who are absent and who suffer, toward all those who have lost something they will never find again" (L 137, CI 623).

Could it have happened like that? Well, yes. But it could also have been like this: a man sits at home, in his cheap lodgings with their worn out furniture, the sheets and towels grubby and torn, and the walls stained with candle smoke. Staring at his window grimed with dirt, the man sees his own distorted reflection, a pale outline that he transforms into a bird searching for the familiar landmarks in a city that has undergone rapid and extraordinary change. His personal sense of exile in a familiar world that has rejected him leads to meditation on the theme of change, rootlessness, and dispossession. Thinking back to a newspaper article he read years ago, he remembers the story of four wild swans flying into the large pond in the Tuileries;

they remained there until the fountain was turned on.[1] He picks up a pen and starts to write.

It is relatively rare that we know exactly how a poem came into being. Keats, on seeing the Elgin Marbles in the British Museum, found himself asking: "Who are these coming to the sacrifice? / To what green alter, O mysterious priest, / Leadest thou that heifer lowing to the skies?" Rilke, striding along the path that lead to the Duino castle, heard the opening line in his mind, "Wer, wenn ich schriee höre mich unter der Angel Ordnungen?" ("Who, if I cried, would hear me among the angel orders?") And Mallarmé, walking down the street, discovered himself standing in front of a shop selling musical instruments with the sentence "La Pénultième est morte" ringing in his ears. These are counter-examples which in any case we are forced to take on trust. The relationship between lived experience and poem is, of course, endlessly complex. Trying to understand the physical and emotional context in which the poems were written can help us read them in a more satisfying way, but the question remains: how do we enter the mind of another person, especially when that person not only lived in circumstances far removed from our own, but also thought and wrote in a language that is not our mother tongue? How can we perceive the nuances and images released by memories and readings we do not share? And if we also seek to translate that person's poetry, how can we meet so substantial a challenge?

First, I think there are elements that can be left aside as either too nebulous or too alien from the universe created by a poet's work seen as a whole. A case in point here, I would argue, is the newspaper article about the four wild swans. While it is true that Baudelaire was closely involved with this newspaper at the time the anecdote was reported, it is not only a good twelve years between that article and the writing of the poem, but the putative link between the two is irredeemably flawed. The swans that landed briefly on the pond in the Tuileries gardens were wild swans able to fly at will. Moreover, there were four of them. Baudelaire's swan is alone, isolated from its peers. Besides, since it has been in a menagerie, we can assume its wings have been clipped to prevent it from flying and that this is why it remains earthbound, despite its longing to seek out "the beautiful lake of its birth." Both elements, the earthbound condition of a creature whose nature involves flight, and its isolation among alien creatures in an alien landscape are essential to the poem. In other words, while the historical background, which explains the nature and purpose of the alterations that Paris was undergoing, offers a vital clue not just to this poem but to all Baudelaire's city poems (see chapter 8), associations with the idea of the swan are illuminating in this context only if they also link up to the central ideas conveyed by the bird: exile, isolation, and, by way of these two ideas, the condition of the poet. In other words, remaining sensitive to the ways in which ideas crystal-

[1] See Charles Baudelaire, *Les Fleurs du mal,* ed. Jacques Crépet and Georges Blin (Paris: Corti, 1942), 449.

lize around a certain image or set of images does not need to stop us from ruling out accretions that hang on only with the help of some artificial glue.

There is, of course, a degree of make-believe in talking about and attempting to enter into a poem in a different language, an artifice that immediately demands choices, imposes exclusions, and both lets in and rules out possibilities that the original language may not have offered. In my story about the poet and the swan, I have given as the poem's title "The Swan" which correctly limits the genus but still leaves open (as does the original) the possibility of a reader imagining a black bird with a red bill, a black and white bird, a white bird with a yellow bill, a silent bird, a bird whose honking call is the very essence of winter, one whose call is a high plaintive mew, or one whose "wild song [resembles] the tones of a violin, though somewhat higher and remarkably pleasant."[2] But my translation of the title removes the homophony immediately obvious to anyone who is familiar with French, where the phoneme "cygne" evokes both the bird and a sign. And how time-sensitive is this apparently innocuous title? Could a contemporary reader have responded with a precise image of the bird from the menagerie nearest to the Tuileries gardens? How common were such menageries? Is this really a swan from some stretch of the Seine, closely observed by the poet who carefully depicts its palmed feet, but linked to a menagerie for purely rhetorical or thematic reasons? Or has the poet never actually observed a swan at all closely, but merely bookishly based his description on the dictionary definition, "an aquatic web-footed bird"?

That dictionary definition suggests yet another scenario for the inspiration behind "Le Cygne": a man familiar with classical literature sits in a book-lined room pondering on two classical stories. He thinks of Andromache, exiled from Troy after her husband's defeat in battle. As one of the spoils of war she was handed over to her brother-in-law, Helenus, "two house-slaves together" according to the poet Virgil, who himself is sometimes known as the Swan of Mantua (*Aeneid* 3: 84). But our poet also thinks about the myth of the swan, that representative of poets, held to sing only at the approach of its death, and exiled to the constellation named for it, Cygnus. He sets out to adapt this symbol for modern conditions . . . but no. Here at least we can be relatively certain that so bloodless and etiolated a version of the poem's origins has little validity. When the poet claims that his thinking about Andromache has "fertilized his fruitful memory" we realize that he is talking about the interplay of imaginative reading and lived experience, of an enriching interflow between learning and living. We are surrounded here by the rubble, the dust, and the din of a building site. The tearing down of the old to make room for something new that is not yet perceived as anything but brash, the sense of things falling apart, and the despair of ever again finding harmony and continuity—that sharp awareness of contingency, in other words, that defines modernism—is built into the sounds and

---

[2] Quoted in Ebenezer Cobham Brewer, *Dictionary of Phrase and Fable* (London: Cassell, 1968), 870.

the order of the words. The line: "Ce tas de chapiteaux ébauchés et de fûts" (That pile of half-finished capitals and shafts) stumbles over its long central syllables (chapiteaux ébauchés) clumsily introduced by the deliberately banal "ce tas de" and falls flat on the bathos of "et de fûts." Weeds and puddles abound, as if this is the only form of nature that a city can produce, and confusion reigns. These images of change and of chaos recall yet another memory, the swan wandering through the dust and the steely cold air of a city waking to another day of work. This is clearly not merely a literary allusion, although it is of course also that. First and foremost, this is a swan observed and captured in sounds and images: the palmate feet scraping on the dry pavement, the beast's beak gaping as it searches for water, the whiteness of the wings trailing in the city's muck and grime. Before allegory can begin to work fully, it needs to be solidly anchored in physical experience. When the poet claims that his "dear memories are heavier than rocks" we need to have a strong sense of the weight of those rocks, their sharp edges, their uncompromising physical presence. This is what the structure of the poem signals to us, with the word rock coming at the end of a stanza, carrying all the weight of a long, undulating sentence. It is also suggested by the sounds, and particularly the contrast between the soft sounds of "chers souvenirs" and the harshness of "rocs."

Uncompromising physical presence is very much the hallmark of Baudelaire's writing, one of those elements that make him such a master of language in general and verse in particular. But readers who really want to respond to that mastery are, of course, like anyone wanting to understand any kind of mastery, faced with a series of challenges. In the most general terms, those challenges consist in a questioning of reading practices. What does it mean to read Baudelaire?

A useful starting place might well be the question: what does Baudelaire himself expect or even demand of his readers? How is reading represented in his writing? What reflections do we have of his own reading? At this point I am less interested in what he himself read, although it is useful—indeed vital—to know that he read widely among works of contemporary literature, that he was well versed in the classics, and that he professed a rather shamefaced affection for the French baroque writers. What I want to explore for the moment is less what he read than how he read, and how he responded to that reading, as a means of better understanding how he "read" the Parisian scene that lies at the center of "Le Cygne."

The realist painter Gustave Courbet twice depicts him lost in a book, one in a portrait, and once as part of his large work, *The Artist's Studio*. In the portrait we find him alone in his room, seated, it appears, on the arm of a sofa, cushions at his back, and his book propped against a desk on which surges up from a squat inkwell a splendid white quill. The book he reads, as he puffs away at his pipe, is large, somewhat dog-eared, its covers battered with use. On the desk lies a portfolio, perhaps containing engravings or perhaps drafts of his own writing. Later on, when times were particularly hard, when money was even shorter than usual, and when he was trying to interest his friend, the painter Manet, in buying it, he would describe this painting as being entirely red: "The figure, dressed in a *red* robe, seated on a *red* sofa, is working on a *red* table. The effect is fairly astonishing" (NL, 109). This is an affective reading of the portrait, more suggestive of emotion than of a precise memory. It is as though this moment of contentment—for whatever else it is, it is surely that—had stamped itself on his mind in shades of intense colors and unadulterated harmonies. His prominently displayed left hand shows the finely tapered fingers of which he was so proud. Courbet stresses this hand again in his large painting, *The Artist's Studio,* in which Baudelaire is at the extreme right, again lost in a book, despite the crowds of people—friends and strangers alike—who jostle around him. This time the left hand lies on a book while the poet pores over another volume held so it faces the viewer, as if challenging us to recognize it from the indecipherable marks meant to indicate writing. This is not Louis David, revealing Jean-Paul Marat's last thoughts in a chit requesting help for a widow, or showing us the letter Charlotte Corday used to ensure that she would be granted an audience. Courbet's squiggles here are merely conventional symbols, as conventional as the gesture that, all around the world, indicates a diner is asking for the bill. There is, indeed, little to suggest that Courbet read much of what Baudelaire had written at all, or that it was the creative writer rather than, say, the art critic, that he was attempting to capture in these portraits. The exultant pen in the little portrait, however, certainly suggests that Courbet wanted to indicate that once the reading was complete, the poet would transform that reading into a written record. In this, the portrait is certainly an accurate depiction of the challenge Baudelaire often records, directly or indirectly, of trying out the themes or the techniques of a passage he had just read. The poetry of Marceline Desbordes-Valmore, drenched in emotion and made supple with suffering, is a case in point. Baudelaire the man may fuss and fume at women writers, but Baudelaire the reader is swept away by what she can achieve in spite of being a woman. When he comes to write the final paragraph of the article he devoted to her poetry, it is clear that he was trying above all to show what could be done with her themes, her images, her vocabulary.

Victor Hugo's delight in metaphysical speculation and in concatenations of terms are both reflected in Baudelaire's review of Hugo's writing, the critic here taking pleasure in transforming into his own form of expression what reading has revealed. He thinks of Hugo's seascapes, and while expressing his enthusiasm for them, also indicates that he believes himself more than capable of outstripping the model: "If [Hugo] paints the sea, no *seascape* can rival his. The ships that furrow the sea's surface or who plow through its bubbling foam will possess, more than those of any other painter, that physiognomy of passionate strugglers, that character of will-power and animality that arises so mysteriously from a geometrical and mechanical structure made of wood, of iron, or rope and of canvas; this monstrous man-made animal to which wind and wave add the beauty of movement" (II 135). He may have in mind any one of a number of passages here, but typical of Hugo's depiction of the sea and of ships is his poem "A M. de Lamartine" which appeared in *Feuilles d'automne (Autumn Leaves)* (1831):

> L'autan criait dans nos antennes,
> Le flot lavait nos ponts mouvants,
> Nos banderoles incertaines
> Frissonnaient au souffle des vents.
> Nous voyions les vagues humides,
> Comme des cavales numides
> Se dresser, hennir, écumer;
> L'éclair, rougissant chaque lame,
> Mettait des crinières de flamme
> A tous ces coursiers de la mer! [3]

> (The south wind screaming in our masts,
> Our moving bridges washed by waves,
> Our banners flap uncertainly
> And tremble in the gale's blasts.
> We see the wet waves leap on high
> Like chargers from Numidia,
> Whinnying and foaming far and nigh;
> The lightening turns the waves to red,
> The lightening sets wild manes of flame
> On all those horses of the sea!)

Active reading is what dominates Baudelaire's literary criticism. Reading with what George Steiner would term the tact of the heart is central to what Baudelaire demands of us. "All those who have felt the need to create an esthetics for their own purposes will understand me" (II 23), Baudelaire asserts in an early literary review, prompting us to assume a more active response to reading and to beauty. An intelligent reader, he remarks elsewhere—and who does not want to be counted among Baudelaire's intelligent?— will find that this analysis is all that is needed to appreciate the spirit of research that animates a certain writer's work (II 91). Active intelligent reading is also a matter of memorizing: "I know," he remarks in a study of Théophile Gautier, the poet to whom he dedicated *Les Fleurs du mal* (see figure 7), "that there is not a writer, not an artist, provided he or she has a tendency to dream, whose memory is not equipped and adorned with these marvels," meaning the highpoints of Gautier's writing (II 106). Reading demands a further step, too, be-

[3] Victor Hugo, *Œuvres poétiques,* ed. Pierre Albouy (Paris: Gallimard, 1964), 1:738.

yond pastiche and memorization: that of an active analysis of what has been read and the effect created. "I've attempted (have I really succeeded?) to express the admiration that Théophile Gautier's works inspire in me and to deduce the reasons validating that admiration" (II 127). The pact between text and reader is both powerful and reciprocal. He affirms, "We report the facts; reader, the reflections are up to you" (II 409). Because reader and poet are part of a team, Baudelaire can strip the layer of obvious and personal emotion from his poems, knowing that readers will understand that their role consists precisely in providing that emotional response. Thus, in responding to the writing of the young novelist Léon Cladel, Baudelaire chides: "The highest form of art would have consisted in remaining glacial and self-contained, and in leaving to the reader all the merit of indignation. This would have intensified the effect of horror" (II 186).

It is hardly surprising, then, given this view of the reader in Baudelaire's critical passages, that he should set us a particular challenge right at the outset of *Les Fleurs du mal*. "The reader," Alison Fairlie pointed out in her excellent little study of the poems, "is to share the poet's experience not through admiration for a superior figure, not through pity for an inferior, not in any comforting complicity: he is the 'Hypocrite lecteur, mon semblable, mon frère!' "[4] Sharing an experience is what is asked of us first and foremost in the opening poem, which is specifically addressed to us as readers. But between our willingness to share, to read with the tact of the heart, and our ability to do so, there falls nevertheless a chasm made of countless elements: language, whether we share Baudelaire's mother tongue or not, alters from generation to generation, from social group to social group. The implications of a phrase once familiar as a pair of old shoes may be lost with time and distance. Think of advertising slogans: I know the phrase "refreshes the parts others don't reach" will summon up for some of my readers a slew of different advertising posters in which these apparently banal words took flight. Whatever tact of the heart they may have, other readers will not experience that response. What you may call a check mark, I may call a tick, while a tick for you may summon up only images of an unpleasant insect. Readers from a certain English-speaking country and a certain age group will remember with particular clarity the implications of "life wasn't meant to be easy"; those from another such country will have similar memories of the tag "on your bike" or "it depends on what you mean by sex." Recapturing those allusions decades later is always going to be, in part, artificial. We can read about the government figures who made those statements, but entering into the climate that produced and reacted to them is as difficult as returning from the underworld of antiquity to the light of day.

In similar ways, clichés were once flexible and meaningful images. Now language users can, if they're careless or in a hurry, so forget their initial meaning as to push

---

[4] Alison Fairlie, *Baudelaire: Les Fleurs du mal* (London: Edward Arnold, 1960), 34.

them cheek by jowl with other clichés that suddenly force that earlier meaning out in to the open, like a rash. "It was the kind of illness that cost you an arm and a leg" may not necessarily refer to leprosy, just as the speaker of the following lines was not necessarily a contortionist: "We're not just going to lie down and walk away from this!" Reading Baudelaire often brings with it a sense of clichés deliberately set free from their molds, catchwords liberated from their patina of familiarity and restored to life in troubling ways.

While this is disconcerting, we should realize that it is also intentional. Our sense of reading a slightly unfamiliar and therefore singularly revealing language is part of a much broader Baudelairean strategy, a strategy centered on surprising and astonishing, or provoking an explosion of anger, or disgust, or joy—the emotion itself is probably less important than the fact of feeling, and feeling intensely, in response to what has been written. Part of this is in direct response to Edgar Allan Poe whom Baudelaire not only greatly admired but saw as an alter ego: "It is a happiness to wonder," Poe claims, and Baudelaire translates the word wonder and its cognates with a series of words associated with astonishment and surprise: "I want to crush minds, astonish them like Byron, Balzac, or Chateaubriand" (L 108, CI 451); "my first impression was one of astonishment—which is always, moreover, an agreeable sensation" (CII 353); "the irregular, by which I mean the unexpected, the surprising, the astonishing are an essential part of the characteristics of beauty" (I 656).

There is, I think, yet another element of reading that is brought into focus by "Le Cygne." Part of the effect of surprise was meant to stem from the collision of two worlds— that of literature and that of everyday banal reality. When Baudelaire tells Hugo that, in writing his poem, he wanted to seize "quickly" the impression the lost swan made on him, he is touching on an esthetic argument he was developing at the time in his essay *Le Peintre de la vie moderne* (*The Painter of Modern Life*). There he argues that Constantin Guys's technique reveals two things: "First, a stretching of the memory, with its qualities of resurrection, of evocation, a memory that says to everything: 'Lazarus, arise!'; and secondly, a fire, an intoxication of the pen and the brush that is almost like fury. This," Baudelaire adds, "is the fear of not moving quickly enough, or letting the phantom escape before the synthesis is extracted from it and captured" (II 699). In this essay, the central premise is that beauty requires both the permanent and the fleeting, that it is "always, inevitably, double in composition, although the impression it provides is unified" (II 685), and that modernity consists in knowing how to "extract the eternal from the transitory" (II 694). Baudelaire begins this wonderfully complex essay by questioning what we today might think of as the canon, rejecting the idea that the consecrated writers and painters alone are worth visiting. "Fortunately," he maintains, "there arise from time to time righters of wrongs, critics, art-lovers, minds driven by curiosity, who affirm that not everything is in Raphaël, not everything is in Racine, that the *poetae minores* do have aspects that are good, solid, and delectable" (II 683). Baudelaire is thinking here, I would argue, less of Guys than of himself, and of his own great poem of modernity, "Le Cygne," that opens with a memory of Andromache's story and that moves on to evoke echoes of numerous other texts. What is more, the poem brings into potent collision the eternal—archetypal images of exile, for instance—and the transitory or momentary view of the swan.

"Andromache! I think of you!" the poet exclaims in his arresting opening line.[5] Andromache surges up here from Baudelaire's reading, but also from his thinking in the context of the essay on the painter of modern life about the function of memory, its lapses and its sudden miraculous, apparently inexplicable, resurgences. Andromache's function in the poem is partly to represent the suffering of the widow, exiled from the happiness of a marriage abruptly terminated, but she also functions to symbolize the human desire to hold on to memories, and the devices that enable this. Aeneas, visiting the hill city of Buthrotum, comes across her "in a wood near her city by a river named after the Simois" and discovers that not just the altar built to Hector's ashes but the city itself is a mnemonic for Troy. "As I walked onwards," Aeneas relates, "I recognized this little 'Troy', with its citadel built to resemble the old citadel, and a dry water-course called the 'Xanthus'; and I even saluted the threshold of the 'Scaean Gate'" (*Aeneid* 3). Exiles everywhere do much the same, carrying the names of their hometowns to countries on the other side of the earth, in the hope of harnessing memory though this random labeling.

Baudelaire's own mnemonics are embedded not just in elements of the city, but also in his reading. Virgil's story brings to mind, as we say in a formula I would like to restore to at least some of its original potency, that of Ovid, himself driven into exile among the Scythians where he was forced to recognize that to these barbarians he was the one who appeared barbarous. The great painter Eugène Delacroix, whom Baudelaire deeply admired and frequently cited, had devoted a painting to the exiled poet which may have been in Baudelaire's mind when he mentioned his name in "Le Cygne." But the principal link here is with Ovid's *Metamorphoses* whose very title evokes irreversible change and whose opening section depicts humanity born into Chaos: "Os homini sublime dedit, cœlumque tueri / Jussit, et erectos ad sidera tollere vultus," lines Baudelaire translates in a journal entry as "the human face, which Ovid believed had been formed to reflect the stars" (I 651). Humanity in exile reflecting the cold and unchanging perfection of the stars, the exiled swan thrusting its head toward the heavens, join with other figures from Baudelaire's reading and from his personal experience. Robinson Crusoe, the "sailor forgotten on an island," is there, remembered from the edition Baudelaire owned as a boy and that in 1841 he had somewhat histrionically bequeathed to his nephew as he set sail, rather against his will, for the tropics (CI 88). Suckling on grief as on a good

---

[5] A translation of the complete poem can be found at the end of the chapter, p. 30.

she-wolf, Romulus and Remus make a brief appearance, exiled from their home as infants and left to perish in the wild. Roland and Olivier, dying at Roncesvals in the last great stand of Charlemagne's army against the Moors, but blowing the horn even beyond death, are remembered in the line, "An old Memory wildly winds its horn."

There are contemporary and personal memories, too. Hugo, to whom the poem is dedicated, had gone into exile as a sign of disgust at Louis Napoleon's betrayal of the second republic and his usurpation of the throne. Shortly before this poem was written, Napoleon III (as Louis Napoleon now styled himself) had offered amnesty to his exiled adversaries, an offer Hugo grandiloquently refused: "No one will expect that I for my part, would grant a moment's attention to this thing called an amnesty . . ." (quoted I 1005). That Baudelaire followed this story is evident from a letter he wrote to Hugo in September of 1859 in which he offers his own judgment: "Your note [refusing amnesty] came and set our minds at rest. I knew perfectly well that poets were *worth* all the Napoleons, and that Victor Hugo could never be less great than Chateaubriand" (L 136, CI 598). Even if some of this is somewhat tongue in cheek, written mainly with a view to the advantages that might accrue from getting Hugo on side, what is indisputable and particularly pertinent for "The Swan" is that here figures are being folded together, or if you prefer, concepts are being allowed to crystallize around an idea (that of the poet, that of the tyrant) in ways that suggest the principal rhetorical gesture of Baudelaire's great poem in which Andromache, the swan, the orphans, the abandoned sailors are conflated into the single figure of the exile. Chateaubriand, that supremely eloquent emblem of the dawning of France's Romanticism, is called on in the letter to Hugo not just to recall the latter's youthful ambition—as a boy he wanted to be "Chateaubriand or nothing"—but also because his unbending opposition to the man he called Buonaparte parallels Hugo's unrelenting rejection of the man he termed Napoleon the Small.

Hugo was not the only contemporary to wander onto the stage of "Le Cygne." Baudelaire himself, whose father died when the future poet was only seven years old, joins the ranks of the "thin orphans withering like flowers," while the "négresse" shivering in the fogs of Paris recalls Baudelaire's very early poem "A Une Malabaraise," which asks why a servant girl from Malabar would dream of going to France, where she would be forced to toil for her food in the mud and muck of the city, and where her exiled spirit would seek out "in our foul fogs / the wandering ghost of your absent coconut trees," a line itself restored from the exile of poems not chosen for the specific framework of *Les Fleurs du mal* to make a triumphant appearance in "The Swan" as "seeking with wild eye / The absent coconuts of Africa the superb / Behind the immense barricade of the fog."

"Le Cygne," therefore, is in part a palimpsest of other texts, read and remembered, actively reassembled here to forge something new and unique, as someone might assemble bric-a-brac to transform those random elements into a specific piece of furniture. But the reading of texts and of memories is echoed and intensified by the determination to read the city itself as a series of symbols and suggestions. The word Baudelaire uses is "allegory," but this is not the one-for-one substitution that we find, say, in Spenser's use of allegory in *The Fairie Queen,* but a supple and broad category that the various passages of his critical writing help elucidate. In a magnificent passage devoted to the works of Poe, for instance, he confronts critics who reject contemporary literature because they consider it merely reflects the decadence of the age. Literature's sun may indeed be setting, he agrees, but "in the games of that dying sun certain poetic spirits will find new delights: they will discover dazzling colonnades, cascades of molten metal, paradises of fire, a poignant splendor, the bliss of regret, all the magic of dream, all the memories of opium. And the sunset will appear to them indeed like the marvelous allegory of a soul laden with life, sinking behind the horizon with a magnificent provision of thoughts and dreams" (II 320). An article on caricature allows him to recall "that marvelous allegory of the spider that has spun her web between the rod and the arm of this fisherman whom impatience could never drive to trembling" (II 565). Allegory for Baudelaire is much closer to what symbol was to be for Stéphane Mallarmé, the token or mark that indicated something more than itself, that asked to be joined to another token to reach its full potential. A swan, one might say, attains its full image as swan when it joins with its reflection on lake or river: Baudelaire's swan wandering through dust and paving stones acts as an allegory of exile, because its current situation is so clear a figure of an imperfect condition. In similar ways, Mallarmé's swan in "Le vierge le vivace et le bel aujourd'hui (The virgin, perennial and beautiful today)," caught in the frozen lake, symbolizes the failure to take flight and thus offers its own allegory of exile from a potential state of perfection.

Musing on the nature of modernism, on its need to seize the transitory in a world where contingency seems predominant, on the nostalgic longing to hold fast to memories, and on the theme of exile (both physical and spiritual), Baudelaire uses allegory as a means of reading the world in order to enable an understanding of the emotional and spiritual through the physical. The old suburbs and the new palaces, the building scaffolds, the blocks of stone, the unfinished columns and capitals are not so much evoked in order that each can stand for something else but rather to indicate that a process of powerful transformation is at work. This transformation, as the poet and critic Pierre-Jean Jouve suggested in his *Tombeau de Baudelaire,*[6] is what is really meant by Baudelaire's reference to the working day yawning itself into wakefulness. The physical swan wanders through a world where street cleaners are dourly preparing for the onslaught of workers into the city, where the silent air is about to be rent by the uproar of a great city going about its multifarious business. But in order to discover why the memory of this swan has suddenly leapt into the

---

[6] Pierre-Jean Jouve, *Tombeau de Baudelaire* (Paris: Editions du Seuil, 1958), 63–64.

forefront of his mind, the poet himself needs to get down to work, to discover coherent shapes in the jumble of bric-a-brac that clutters his thinking.

What makes the poem at once so powerful and so modern is that those shapes
are not made neat and tidy for us. They may lie as heavy as rocks, but they can shift
into countless patterns, like the fragments in a kaleidoscope. The wonderful dying
fall of the final line, where the voice fades away on the "many others still" that crowd
the poet's thoughts, is a handing over of the baton to us as readers to contribute our
own allegories of exile. Of course, I do not mean that I imagine Baudelaire sitting
back at this point and saying that "the task of filling in the blanks I'd rather leave to
you." Rather, I mean that he is able to resist the desire for containment and closure
that marks poets more associated with Romanticism than Modernism, for instance,
Alphonse de Lamartine or Victor Hugo. In particular Hugo—and this is what gives
his poems their wonderful sense of boundless energy—wants to pursue all the av-
enues his thinking has opened up, whereas Baudelaire reflects a different mentality,
one for which the fleeting beauty that marks the modern cannot be written in
bronze.

As an invitation to reading, "Le Cygne" will be dependent on the willingness of
readers to participate, to take up their role as the poet's double and sibling. Understanding how to do that is in turn dependent on an awareness of how the writing of
the poem invites certain interpretations, determines certain images, suggests certain
possibilities. Looking at some of the translations of this poem projects a sudden if
tricky light on those techniques. The translators here are attempting a vast and
thankless task, trying to capture the original in all its complexity of denotation and
connotation, sound and syntax, rhythm and rhyme. They need to find equivalents
for words where sound and sense echo each other, or where an abrupt change of
register forces new meaning, or where a well-worn cliché needs to be suggested in
the reader's mind, or where the interpretation of a word toggles between etymological meaning and modern meaning. Translators are forced to make choices, often
limited by rhythm or rhyme or linguistic register. Sometimes the French word does
not have a precise English equivalent. Sometimes many possibilities seem equally
valid. Nicholas Moore, in a virtuoso burst of creativity, in part inspired by a competition sponsored by the United Kingdom's *Sunday Times* to translate Baudelaire's
"Spleen" poem, beginning "Je suis comme le roi (I am like the king)," produced
thirty-one different entries. It is a wonderful demonstration not just of Moore's
skills, but also of the impossibility of producing a definitive translation. In exploring
certain versions in competition, my purpose is not to make little of these problems—they are often insuperable—but to try both to find an optimal reading of the
text and to reach some sort of accommodation between original and translation,
and not in such a way as to justify Jorge Luis Borges's characteristically wry comment that "the original failed to live up to the translation."

Andromache surges up from the void in the opening line of this poem, splitting the twelve syllables of the alexandrine into three clusters: the name itself, pronounced as four syllables because the mute "e" on which it ends is followed by a consonant; "je pense à vous," the action of thinking perfectly balanced with its cause; and the hook, the little stream which became for her a mnemonic for Troy, acting here as the floodgates that open to release the outpourings of memory. Indeed, a first reading of the verse might suggest that Andromache herself is the little stream, and while we correct for this on subsequent readings, that initial response is never entirely thrust aside. Nor need it be: Andromache is by metonymic replacement the stream she stands beside when Aeneas first meets her, the stream she has renamed in honor of a lost past. Somehow, a translation has to reflect that sudden opening, find a parallel for the balances of the line, and begin building up the momentum that will take us across the first stanza into the second, where the little stream meets up with its verb. It is no doubt this sense of momentum, together with the word "soudain" from the second stanza, that leads to Felix Leakey's translation: "Andromache! my thoughts all of a sudden are of you." But it takes too long to reach that important pronoun "you," and "all of a sudden" is too banally colloquial for the intensity of the moment. Roy Campbell waits until the fourth line to tell us that the poetic persona suddenly thought of Andromache, and then labors to convey that idea:

> Andromache!—This shallow stream, the brief
> Mirror you once so grandly overcharged
> With your vast majesty of widowed grief,
> This lying Simoïs your tears enlarged,
> Evoked your name, and made me think of you.

A brief mirror is odd, too, and its being grandly overcharged is murky, to say the least. Beresford Egan and C. Bower Alcock, who are more concerned with the poem's physical appearance on the page and who seem to conflate Baudelaire and the English fin-de-siècle illustrator Aubrey Beardsley, suggest the archaic "Andromache, my thoughts are to thee drawn," revealing yet again that in this case the weight of the line needs to fall not on the verb but on its object. Walter Martin tries: "I think about you now, Andromache!" But that shifts the balance from her to him—she is the one who surges up into the poem before we have any indication of an "I", and I think there is a difference, small perhaps but crucial, between thinking of and thinking about. The first implies memory, the second judgment. There is a similar problem with Norman Shapiro's "I turn my thoughts to you, Andromache." It is not just that this switches the opening emphasis from Andromache to the speaker, but that it implies that the speaker chose to think of her. I'm not arguing that such a reading is necessarily unjustified, but it seems to me that the rest of the poem is about images that suddenly make their presence felt, not about those that the poet selects at leisure and at will.

Richard Howard, whose translation seeks above all to capture what he terms "a certain *private register,* which Gide compares to Chopin's,"[7] gives us "Andromache, I think of you! that stream." The problem is not just that the rhythm is too abrupt here, or that the three elements lose their equilibrium, but with the choice of leaving the word "stream" on its own. Clearly "stream" is deemed sufficient to replace "petit fleuve," as logically it can, yet one might regret the absence of a word stressing smallness, since stream might have many connotations—of swiftness, or clarity, or a certain poetic register—that do not necessarily push to the surface its diminutive size. But that smallness is important to the image: the real Simois, Baudelaire is suggesting, like the real Troy, was huge in comparison to these foreign simulacra. James McGowan, who urges those unable to read French to explore Baudelaire through several different translations, and who sets out to create "a poem that will produce the kind of satisfaction to be gained from reading poetry originally created in English,"[8] suggests: "Andromache, I think of you—this meager stream." Meager is a nice touch, avoiding the pleonasm of "little stream" but still providing that sense of a poverty that goes beyond the physical and that Baudelaire's poem seems to demand.

But of course the little river that offered itself as a humble mirror for the former queen's mourning is not just the geographical entity Aeneas came across in his wanderings: it is also Baudelaire's imagination, which offers itself as a means to reflect her and to reflect on her.

[. . .] Ce petit fleuve
Pauvre et triste miroir où jadis resplendit
L'immense majesté de vos douleurs de veuve,
Ce Simoïs menteur qui par vos pleurs grandit,

A fécondé soudain ma mémoire fertile
Comme je traversais le nouveau Carrousel.

A chance event has suddenly triggered a memory here, or more precisely has fertilized an already fecund memory, leading to a swarm of specific recollections. Leakey struggles here to convey the overlapping levels of memory and myth, of original and namesake:

[. . .]
Majestic in your widowhood beside that stream,
That mere stream in Epirus, flowing full
With your sad tears as, grieving, you recall

---

[7] See R. Howard, *Les Fleurs du mal* (Boston: David R. Godine, 1982), xxi.
[8] J. McGowan, *The Flowers of Evil* (Oxford: Oxford University Press, 1993), liv.

The true river Simois in your own native Troy—
This image from your story, in my fertile mind
A further intimate memory stirs as I traverse
The new, wide Carrousel.

The description of the Carrousel as wide, not justified in the original poem as it appears in *Les Fleurs du mal*, seems to come from the version of the poem published in *La Causerie* in January 1860, where the line reads, "comme je traversais ce vaste Carrousel (as I was crossing the vast Carrousel)." Leakey's introduction asserts that "a translator may, on occasion, play a discreetly and usefully interpretative role, by clarifying points that in the original may seem obscure."[9] He is far from being unique in this view: Charles Chadwick, to choose a recent example, holds to it in his translation of Mallarmé. Nevertheless, I suspect Baudelaire might have been indignant at this claim, priding himself as he did on saying exactly what he meant to say. Had Hugo written this poem, I suspect he would have included an expansive retelling of Andromache's myth and the importance of the Simois in the *Aeneid*, where it returns on several occasions. Baudelaire's poetry is more one of concision and allusion. My own sense from seeing Leakey's assertion carried into practice in the lines above is that it rapidly becomes awkward and clumsy. And I cannot help feeling that while "stirs" may suggest an embryo stirring into life, the juxtaposition of *fécondé* and *fertile*, the apparently pleonastic nature of the juxtaposition of those two words, the way the alliteration draws attention to their proximity both spatially and in meaning, that all this means that reading to the full at this point demands a consideration of just what is taking place that Leakey seems to have overlooked in his anxiety about Simois. Howard, having found a brilliant solution to the *Simoïs menteur* in *mimic Simois*, skates away from further difficulties and simply pulls back the floodgates:

[. . .] That stream,
the sometime witness to your widowhood's
enormous majesty of mourning—that
mimic Simois salted by your tears

suddenly inundates my memory.

It is at this point, too, in Howard's poem that the choice of rhythm suddenly appears inadequate, the line presenting something a trifle meager and not quite heavy enough in comparison to the stately alexandrines Baudelaire uses. McGowan's lines are more ample, more suggestive of the weight of meaning and memory in these images:

[9] F. Leakey, *Selected Poems from "Les Fleurs du mal"* (Greenwich: Greenwich Exchange, 1997), 4.

[. . .] this meager stream
This melancholy mirror where had once shone forth
The giant majesty of all your widowhood,
This fraudulent Simois, fed by bitter tears,

Has quickened suddenly my fertile memory.

But there are some awkwardnesses here, some moments when the rhythm seems to be dictating the choice of words: "where had once shone forth"? Why not simply and more idiomatically "where once shone forth?" And isn't there in any case a problem with "once," which lends itself to a misreading undermining our certainty that Andromache wept often and not just once into this meager stream? "All your widowhood" is also otiose—and why not at least attempt to convey the element of grief? But "quickened" is an interesting choice, and one that also works well—in addition to the idea of fecundation—with that sense of swiftly seizing the moment.

As we follow the development of the idea at this point, it becomes clear that the first three stanzas provide an introduction to the central themes, preparing the way for the anecdote about the swan. It is typical of Baudelaire's sense of architecture—that of the collection as a whole, as well as that of the sections within it and of individual poems—that these three stanzas are balanced by the three at the end that provide the coda. Like Andromache, recreating Troy in imagination, the poet sees only "en esprit"—in his mind—the Paris he knew earlier, since cities change more rapidly than mortals. Making this as clear as it is in the original seems essential to any translation. But there are also elements in the rhythm and in the sounds of the poem, as well as in the images, that add to the meaning. Baudelaire expresses his affirmation about change in a rhetorical form that recalls the maxims of a Pascal or a La Bruyère: "Le vieux Paris n'est plus (la forme d'une ville / Change plus vite, hélas! que le cœur d'un mortel)." The constricted form, together with the echoes of the specific genre (that of the maxim), plays a role in how we read it, what kind of moral or intellectual weight it carries or at least promises to carry. Seizing something of those suggestions as well as the surface meaning seems essential here. The following selection is in chronological order:

Howard: *Old* Paris is gone (no human heart / changes half so fast as a city's face.)

McGowan: The old Paris is gone (the form a city takes / More quickly shifts, alas, than does the mortal heart.)

Paul: (—Old Paris is vanishing, alas; a city's shape / Changes faster nowadays than a human heart)

Leakey: Forever gone / Is the old Paris, the old Carrousel. / (A city's outward shape transforms, alas! / More swiftly than a human heart, locked in the past.)

Shapiro: Old Paris is no more. (Ah, truth to tell, / Cities change faster than the human heart.)

All of these have seized the essence without necessarily providing the kernel. Paul's rhythms (as in many of his translations) are flat, and he omits the essential stress on *mortel*. The "nowadays," moreover, is both uncalled for and banal—Baudelaire does not suggest in his poem that this phenomenon is new. McGowan's has a snappy first line, but the unidiomatic sentence order in the second line introduces a register that is not in the original and that detracts from the sense of urgency and the commonplace nature of the experience. Moreover, not only is the balance between the city's shape and a mortal's heart lost here, but there is the resultant possibility of a misreading in which both the form and the heart might be seen as belonging to the city. Howard's lines move at an appropriately spanking pace here, but the emphasis shifts from the human onlooker to the city, whereas the order in Baudelaire's poem, like the themes of the poem, show that what is at issue is the individual, whose mortal condition is thrust into prominence by the word's position at the end of the stanza. Shapiro's rhythms are good, but "truth to tell" is a banal makeweight, and the translation of *mortel* as *human* fails to emphasize that paradox that shows what seems eternal (a city) changing quickly, and what seems fleeting (the mortal poet) changing more slowly. Leakey gets the register wrong—forever gone is no doubt as melancholy as one could wish (one thinks of Poe's "never more" or Aida's "mai pui, mai pui"), but Baudelaire has not chosen to tap into the resources of high lyricism here. He uses a phrase any one might produce in the most banal of circumstances. One could imagine hearing it in the metro or in the market place. Not so "forever gone," which in Leakey's translation is thrust, moreover, into melodramatic prominence by being placed at the end of a line. And Leakey's desire to explain that there was a former Carrousel before this one slows things down, whereas Baudelaire's text had been moving rapidly from the specific statement about Paris to a more general maxim about the nature of the world that surrounds us and our own condition within it. The explanation that the human heart fails to change because it is locked in the past misses the point. Baudelaire is drawing on an apparent contradiction here: cities seem to offer permanence, where mortals are by definition transitory, and yet the poet faced with the rapid change of Paris recognizes this as endemic to modern life: change happens too fast for an individual to keep in step. "If only the mortal could stay locked in the past!" Baudelaire might well respond to this translation.

Of course, there is something intrinsically unfair about making these comparisons between text and translation, but they clarify what it is that the original is doing to create its network of meanings. Those meanings reach a particular intensity in the final verse, especially perhaps in this poem, with its dying fall and its refusal of closure. I want, therefore, to look briefly at how translators have dealt with the problems it poses.

> Ainsi dans la forêt où mon esprit s'exile
> Un vieux Souvenir sonne à plein souffle du cor!
> Je pense aux matelots oubliés dans une île,
> Aux captifs, aux vaincus! . . . à bien d'autres encor!

There is a moment here, at the end of the second line, when things do seem to be moving to a conclusion, but the poet pulls back from that and returns to the verb that has run through the previous two stanzas, "I think of." In doing so he invites us both to see him continuing this series forever and to add to it ourselves. Both aspects—the temptation to conclude and the refusal to do so—need to be retained in a translation. And the words here are freighted with memories of other poets and other poems: Alfred de Vigny's declaration that he loved to hear the horn at evening in the depths of the woods, Daniel Defoe's evocation of Robinson's island, made to the measure of the man, Torquato Tasso, remembered both for his song of the liberation of Jerusalem and for his own imprisonment, and specifically evoked by Baudelaire in the poem "Tasso in Prison." And no doubt many others still. . . .

The final stanza has also attracted a variety of different translations:

Sturm: And one old Memory like a crying horn / Sounds through the forest where my soul is lost . . . / I think of sailors on some isle forgotten; / Of captives; vanquished . . . and of many more.

Howard: and in the forest of my mind's exile / a merciless memory winds its horn: / I hear it and I think of prisoners, of the shipwrecked, the beaten . . . and so many more!

McGowan: And likewise in the forest of my exiled soul / Old Memory sings out a full note of the horn! / I think of sailors left forgotten on an isle, / Of captives, the defeated . . . many others more!

Leakey: [. . .] and for one reprieved / In his own forest of exile by the distant sound / The winding horn of an old memory, / The images of sailors castaway / On islands, victims, captives, endless images more!

Walter Martin: In the black forest of my mind's exile / The hunting horns of Memory begin—/ For the shipwrecked, forgotten on an isle, / And other derelict, defeated men . . .

McGowan's evocation of the horn is awkward and transforms into a single blast what Baudelaire's repeated *s* (Un vieux Souvenir sonne à plein souffle du cor!) indicates is a long series of notes. Howard and Leakey have both found in "wind" the exact word for the horn and one that helps carry memories of other poems for English speakers—perhaps Tennyson's "The splendour falls on castle walls / And snowy summits old in story," or Wordsworth's "the resounding horn / The pack loud bellowing, and the hunted hare." But I don't think the horn is sounding reprieve here as Leakey suggests: this is not the fanfare announcing the governor's arrival at the prison where Floristan lies in chains, or the cavalry arriving in the nick of time in "Stagecoach," but the hunter summoning the pack for the kill or Roland winding his horn in a desperate and fruitless bid to call back the main army at the pass of Roncesvals. Most importantly, the horn is a symbol for memory itself, as Walter Martin's version nicely indicates. In an interpolated comment in his roughly contemporaneous adaptation of De Quincey's *Confessions,* Baudelaire notes: "All the echoes of memory, if they could be awakened all at the same time, would form a concert, agreeable or painful, but logical and with no discordant note" (I 506).

Leakey's "castaway" is I think more accurate than the "shipwrecked" offered by Howard and Martin. Neither Leakey nor Howard capture the expansive rhythm of the stanza's first line, but McGowan comes closer even if "likewise" is somewhat clumsy. "Many others more" is clearly the best solution here, mumbling into silence rather than rising up in triumph as in Howard or in plenitude as in Leakey, or worse still, restricting us in Martin's case, to thinking only of men, after that triumphant rise of Andromache at the beginning.

Exploring why certain solutions are better than others and why some leave us unsatisfied is useful, because it highlights those elements on which readers need to place pressure. Here, in particular, the word "Souvenir," already signaled by Baudelaire through that capital letter, demands close attention. The long echoes of the horn wound with all the power the poet can command but eventually fading away in the forest are the poem itself, ringing with echoes of individuals, stories, and incidents revealing different aspects of exile. It is the poet's own false Simois, a heroic and doomed attempt to stem the flood of time and to hold fast to memory in a world of flux.

Le Cygne

A Victor Hugo

Andromaque, je pense à vous! Ce petit fleuve,
Pauvre et triste miroir où jadis resplendit
L'immense majesté de vos douleurs de veuve,
Ce Simoïs menteur qui par vos pleurs grandit,

A fécondé soudain ma mémoire fertile,
Comme je traversais le nouveau Carrousel.
Le vieux Paris n'est plus (la forme d'une ville
Change plus vite, hélas! que le cœur d'un mortel);

Je ne vois qu'en esprit, tout ce camp de baraques,
Ces tas de chapiteaux ébauchés et de fûts,
Les herbes, les gros blocs verdis par l'eau des flaques,
Et, brillant aux carreaux, le bric-à-brac confus.

Là s'étalait jadis une ménagerie;
Là je vis, un matin, à l'heure où sous les cieux
Froids et clairs le Travail s'éveille, où la voirie
Pousse un sombre ouragan dans l'air silencieux,

Un cygne qui s'était évadé de sa cage,
Et, de ses pieds palmés frottant le pavé sec,
Sur le sol raboteux traînait son blanc plumage.
Près d'un ruisseau sans eau la bête ouvrant le bec

Baignait nerveusement ses ailes dans la poudre,
Et disait, le cœur plein de son beau lac natal:
"Eau, quand donc pleuvras-tu? quand tonneras-tu, foudre?"
Je vois ce malheureux, mythe étrange et fatal,

Vers le ciel quelquefois, comme l'homme d'Ovide,
Vers le ciel ironique et cruellement bleu,
Sur son cou convulsif tendant sa tête avide,
Comme s'il adressait des reproches à Dieu!

II

Paris change! mais rien dans ma mélancolie
N'a bougé! palais neufs, échafaudages, blocs,
Vieux faubourgs, tout pour moi devient allégorie,
Et mes chers souvenirs sont plus lourds que des rocs.

Aussi devant ce Louvre une image m'opprime:
Je pense à mon grand cygne, avec ses gestes fous,
Comme les exilés, ridicule et sublime,
Et rongé d'un désir sans trêve! et puis à vous,

Andromaque, des bras d'un grand époux tombée,
Vil bétail, sous la main du superbe Pyrrhus,
Auprès d'un tombeau vide en extase courbée;
Veuve d'Hector, hélas! et femme d'Hélénus!

Je pense à la négresse, amaigrie et phtisique,
Piétinant dans la boue, et cherchant, l'œil hagard,
Les cocotiers absents de la superbe Afrique
Derrière la muraille immense du brouillard;

A quiconque a perdu ce qui ne se retrouve
Jamais, jamais! à ceux qui s'abreuvent de pleurs
Et tètent la Douleur comme une bonne louve!
Aux maigres orphelins séchant comme des fleurs!

Ainsi dans la forêt où mon esprit s'exile
Un vieux Souvenir sonne à plein souffle du cor!
Je pense aux matelots oubliés dans une île,
Aux captifs, aux vaincus! . . . à bien d'autres encor!

"THE SWAN"

For Victor Hugo

Andromache, I think of you! This meager stream,
This poor despondent glass where lately shone
The mighty majesty of a widow's grief,
Deceitful Simois swollen by your tears,

Suddenly made my fruitful memory bloom
As I was crossing the new Carrousel.
The old Paris is dead and gone (a city's shape
Changes faster, alas, than does a mortal's heart.)

It's only in my mind I see the huddled huts,
Piles of half-finished capitals and shafts,
The grass, the broad blocks puddles had stained green,
And, glinting in the windows, the jumbled bric-a-brac.

There long ago sprawled out a menagerie,
There one morning, under the sky's bright cold,
When Work yawned awake, when road crews
Sent a dark storm into the silent air, I saw

A swan broken out of its cage,
Palmate feet rasping the dry pavement,
On the ruts of the road dragging its white feathers.
Near a waterless watercourse the beast, beak agape,

Nervously bathed its wings in the dust,
And said, heart full of its lovely mother-lake:
"Rain, when will you fall? When will the thunder roar?"
I watched this poor creature, this strange fatal myth,

To the heavens occasionally, like Ovid's humanity,
To the heavens, ironic and cruelly blue,
On its shuddering neck stretching its thirsty head
As if it were sending reproaches to God!

II

Paris changes! But nothing in my misery
Has altered! New palaces, scaffolding, blocks,
Old suburbs, everything serves me as allegory,
Old memories in me lie weightier than rocks.

In front of the Louvre an image oppresses me.
I think of my great swan, with its gestures of madness,
Like exiles equally ridiculous and sublime,
And gnawed by unceasing desire! and then of you,

Andromache, from the arms of a great husband fallen,
Lowly beast, under the hand of the arrogant Pyrrhus,
Over an empty tomb bowed down in ecstasy;
Hector's widow alas! and wife to Helenus.

I think of the Negress, scrawny and consumptive,
Scrabbling in the mud and seeking with wild eye
The absent coconuts of Africa the superb
Behind the immense barricade of the fog.

Of whoever has lost what is never restored,
Never, never again!! Those whose thirst is slaked with tears
Suckling on Grief as if on a good she-wolf!
Of emaciated orphans who wither like flowers!

Thus in the forest where my spirit seeks exile
An old Memory rings out likely a wildly wound horn!
I think of sailors abandoned on islands,
The captives, the vanquished! . . . and many more still. . . .

CHAPTER THREE

Genius Is Childhood
Recovered at Will

If Andromache surges into the poet's mind when he thinks of exile, it is not just be-cause she represents the victims of war sold into slavery in foreign lands. At the end of the third line in "Le Cygne (The Swan)" we find all the power and weight of the classical alexandrine harnessed in order to thrust into prominence the word "veuve" (widow). Widows, especially widows with a child in tow, play a prominent role in Baudelaire's re-creation of contemporary Paris. The intensity he brings to bear on this figure, the compassion with which he depicts these lonely women, the sense of profound melancholy with which he paints them, all point to something much more than recognition of a sociological fact. As Baudelaire, dictionary-lover and good Latin scholar, would have known, the word "veuve" (like our word "widow") derives from *vidua,* which means deprived of or without a lover or companion. Widows in his writing are archetypal symbols of loss and loneliness.

More specifically still, the figure of the widow is intimately connected with the poet's personal memories, with the long months when, as a boy aged between six and seven, he watched his mother's response to his father's death. How profound was her grieving? Caroline Dufaÿs was born in 1793. When she married François Baudelaire, in September 1819, he was sixty years old and she was within weeks of her twenty-sixth birthday. Caroline herself had been orphaned when she was seven. Her father disappears from the records when she is an infant; her mother dies in poverty on November 23, 1800 (Pichois, 10–12). She had the great good fortune to be taken in charge by M. and Mme Pérignon, whom she describes as rich, living in a luxurious house, and having a large family of their own. (Why they took on an extra child is a mystery.) François Baudelaire and his first wife, Rosalie, were frequent guests at the Pérignon house. Rosalie Baudelaire died in late Decem-ber 1814 and soon after François, on the heels of the whirlwind set in motion by Napoleon's return from Elba, the Hundred Days, and Waterloo, retired from his position as a civil servant. The portrait that the artist Jean-Baptiste Regnault made of him a few years before his retirement shows him, according to Claude Pichois, as having a "strong nose, penetrating eyes, dark, bushy eyebrows, pursed lips and determined expression." Pichois concludes, "the portrait seems to reveal a rugged and irascible personality" (Pichois, 9). One of his former schoolmates described him as "dominating lofty circles with his gruffness, his caustic wit and the intransigence of his republicanism" (Pichois, 9). He hardly sounds a likely lover for a woman thirty-four years his junior. Caroline Baudelaire has left no account of her courtship, given no reason for marrying a man whom she had known since she was eleven. Perhaps it was mere convenience, a sense that her opportunities were limited and that here at least she had a chance to gain the status of a married woman. The fact that she did not wait long to remarry after his death is not necessarily an indication that she had not loved her first husband or was not grieved by his death. Like most widows at that time, she found herself in considerably straitened circumstances. The pension François Baudelaire had received from his former employers ceased on his death. Her stepson Alphonse, François's son by Rosalie, had already attained his majority and was making his own way as a lawyer, but she still found herself obliged to sell some of her furniture, and she left the apartment in central Paris to move with Charles to a small house in Neuilly on the outskirts of the city. Charles and his widowed mother lived there alone with a servant. It was a time that would be of considerable importance to the poet, at least when he came to look back at it years later when his mother was once more a widow.

Two passages reflect Baudelaire's memories of this period, no doubt massaged and repainted by time and experience. The beautiful little untitled ten-liner he inserted in *Tableaux Parisiens,* the second book of *Les Fleurs du mal,* sums up the sense of peace, genteel poverty, and companionship that he came to associate with this period:

Je n'ai pas oublié, voisine de la ville,
Notre blanche maison, petite mais tranquille;
Sa Pomone de plâtre et sa vieille Vénus
Dans un bosquet chétif cachant leurs membres nus,
Et le soleil, le soir, ruisselant et superbe,
Qui, derrière la vitre où se brisait sa gerbe,
Semblait, grand œil ouvert dans le ciel curieux,
Contempler nos dîners longs et silencieux,
Répandant largement ses beaux reflets de cierge
Sur la nappe frugale et les rideaux de serge.

(FM XCIX)

I have not forgotten, lying near to the city,
Our little house, so white and so calm,
Its plaster Pomona and its old Aphrodite
Whose naked limbs hid in the grove's scraggy trees,
How superbly the sun streamed in each evening,
Through the pane where its sheaf of rays scattered apart,
This huge open eye in the curious heavens
Would gaze on our dinners in their length and their silence,
Spreading the largesse of its candle-like glow
On the table's frugality, the cheap drapes in the windows.

And on May 6, 1861, in the midst of a flurry of publications and the anxiety of mounting debt, Baudelaire wrote one of his most moving letters to his mother. I am on the edge of suicide, he tells her. I need to be with you, I loved you passionately as a child, and now you are the only person on whom my life depends. And he returns to this theme later in this moving and emotional letter:

> In my childhood I went through a stage when I loved you passionately; listen, and read without being afraid. I've never told you this much about it. I remember a ride in a hackney cab. You'd just come out of a nursing home you'd been sent to,[1] and, to prove to me that you had been thinking about me, you showed me some pen and ink drawings you'd made for me. Don't you agree I have a terrific memory! Later, at the square Saint-André-des-Arts and Neuilly. Long walks, constant acts of tenderness! I remember the quays, which were so melancholy in the evening. Oh! for me those were the good old days of maternal tenderness. I apologize for describing as good old days a period that was rough for you. But I lived constantly in you at that time and you were mine alone. You were simultaneously my idol and my comrade. You may well be surprised that I can speak with passion of a time so far in the past. I'm astonished myself. Perhaps it's because I've yet again conceived the longing to die that pictures of these old things come so vividly to my mind.
>
> (L 169–70, CII 153)

It hardly matters for our purposes how much of this is special pleading, re-creation well after the event, imaginative reconstruction of what should have happened, a tugging on the heartstrings calculated to loosen the purse strings. Two things at least seem evident: Baudelaire expected his mother to recognize at least something of the

---

[1] This probably refers to the period when Baudelaire's mother had just given birth to a stillborn daughter (Pichois 22–23).

specificity of these anecdotes (the reminiscence about the drawings is placed as a guarantee of the emotional memories that follow) and she is also being called on to acknowledge a certain image of childhood. Whether as a child he felt this period of his mother's widowhood to be a kind of paradise where she was both idol and comrade, or whether he consciously or subconsciously built this image into his personal myth at a later stage, it is clear that the arrival of her second husband, Jacques Aupick, marked an abrupt end to a long period of intimacy between mother and child, long at least in the context of a seven-year-old's experience. And Baudelaire, the poet, certainly weaves these threads from his personal memories into the picture of children and childhood that he gives us in his writing.

The poem about the house in Neuilly, simple and anodyne as it may seem, carries a curious charge. It is tempting to skip over it, or at least to read it too quickly, in its context of the Parisian poems. It comes immediately after "L'Amour du mensonge (Love of Lying)" where the poet contemplates the impossibility of knowing whether the attraction he feels for a particular woman stems from her profound sense of melancholy or whether that melancholy is a mere surface, hiding no precious secrets:

Mais ne suffit-il pas que tu sois l'apparence,
Pour réjouir un cœur qui fuit la vérité?
Qu'importe ta bêtise ou ton indifférence?
Masque ou décor, salut! J'adore ta beauté.

(FM XCVIII)

But isn't it enough that you offer an appearance
To bring joy to a heart that flees from all verity?
So what if you're stupid, who cares about your indifference.
Mask or façade, I greet you! What I love is your beauty.

The poem immediately following "Je n'ai pas oublié" (I have not forgotten)" is another reminiscence of childhood that leads rapidly into a meditation on the dead, and that builds up to "Brumes et pluies (Mists and Rain)" with its praise for the sleepy seasons, late autumn, winter, springs soaked in mud, that prevent the "heart full of funereal things" from feeling anything with any intensity. The question the apparently simple little reminiscence poem seems to be asking is teleological: how did enjoyment of this fruitful quiet become, over time, the destructive longing for the quiet of the grave? But it is also pragmatic: what do I do when suicide tempts me? Whatever interpretation a reader might put on Baudelaire's claims about the secret architecture of *Les Fleurs du mal,* it is clear that there is a network of references and allusions set up between the wildly blowing horn of memory in "Le Cygne," childhood recollections never forgotten, and the poet's dawning awareness that the only valid response to the vertiginous sense of contingency brought on by the city's rapid change, the yearning to escape the self through sensuality or suicide, the bitter awareness of the contract between the beauty of dreams and the grim reality of quotidian existence is, as "Le Crépuscule du matin (Dawn Twilight)" concludes, to knuckle down to the work of living:

> L'aurore grelottante en robe rose et verte
> S'avançait lentement sur la Seine déserte,
> Et le sombre Paris, en se frottant les yeux,
> Empoignait ses outils, vieillard laborieux.

(FM CIII)

> Dawn, shivering in robes of pink and green,
> Moved slowly down the deserted Seine,
> And somber old Paris, rubbing his eyes,
> Picked up his tools for another day's work.

Work, Baudelaire would tell himself in his private notebooks, is "a progressive and accumulative force, bearing interest like capital, in terms both of your faculties and the results" (I 659). The ability to tap back into childhood, into the memories and associations of childhood, is one of the tools that Baudelaire, in his guise as hardworking old man, picks up here. Indeed, it is one of the most important items of his toolbox.

Around the same time as he was working on "Le Cygne," Baudelaire had been meditating deeply on the function of childhood within the formation of the adult, and particularly that of the creative artist. He did this not only in the study of "The Painter of Modern Life" but also in his translation and adaptation of Thomas De Quincey's labyrinthine *Confessions of an English Opium Eater.* Biography, De Quincey affirms, serves to explain and verify the mysterious adventures of the brain under the influence of opium. And Baudelaire adds, in a long and significant interpolation of his own, that childhood recollections serve to indicate the seeds not only of the adult's strange reveries, but better yet of his genius:

> All biographers have understood more or less fully the importance of anecdotes connected to the childhood of a writer or an artist. But it seems to me that this importance has never been stressed strongly enough. Often, in contemplating works of art, not in their easily comprehensible *materiality*, in the overly clear hieroglyphs of their contours or in the obvious meaning of their subjects, but in the soul bestowed on them, in the atmospheric impression they contain, in the spiritual light or dark they shed on our souls, I have found my mind visited by a kind of vision of their author's childhood. Small

disappointments, small joys experienced by the child, swollen beyond measure by an exquisite sensitivity, later become in the adult, knowingly or not, the principle of a work of art. Finally, to express myself more concisely, would it not be simple to prove through a philosophical comparison of the works of a mature artist and the state of his soul when he was a child, that genius is only childhood clearly formulated, now possessing virile and powerful organs of expression?

(I 497–98)

The sensuality Baudelaire attributes to the child, and childhood's importance for the adult artist, recur in the study of Guys on which he was working around the time he produced his adaptation of De Quincey.

The child sees everything as *novelty;* and is always *intoxicated.* Nothing comes closer to what is called inspiration than the joy with which a child absorbs shape and color. I'll dare to go further: I'll affirm that inspiration has some connection with *a brainstorm* and every sublime thought is accompanied by a nervous shudder, more or less strong, that reverberates right to the cerebellum. The man of genius has solid nerves; the child's nerves are weak. In the former, reason has assumed a considerable role; in the latter, sensitivity occupies almost the entire being. But genius is merely *childhood recalled* at will, childhood that now possesses virile organs and the analytical mind that allows him to order the sum of materials involuntarily collected, so that he can now give them expression.

(II 690)

The intoxicated child is a familiar figure to readers of *Les Fleurs du mal.* He is there in the opening poem of the first book, *Spleen et Idéal,* drunk with sunlight:

Et dans tout ce qu'il voit et dans tout ce qu'il mange
Retrouve l'ambroisie et le nectar vermeil.

Il joue avec le vent, cause avec le nuage,
Et s'enivre en chantant du chemin de la croix;
Et l'Esprit que le suit dans son pèlerinage
Pleure de le voir gai comme un oiseau des bois.

(FM I)

And in all that he sees and in all that he eats
Rediscovers ambrosia and incarnadine nectar.

He plays with the wind, chats with the cloud,
And grows drunk with the song of the stations of the cross.
And the Spirit that follows this miniature pilgrim
Weeps to see him gay as a bird of the woods.

Intoxication for Baudelaire is always, at least in part, a metaphor for inspiration and imagination. We all, he argues in his study of artificial intoxicants, carry within us our own dose of natural opium, which is imagination. The child's intensity of perception, Baudelaire contends in transforming a Romantic principle, is what the artist has to recover and convert into art. Where Baudelaire's image is at sharp variance with French Romanticism is in the sensuality, rather than the purity, he associates with childhood.

Shortly after this revealing passage in the De Quincey, Baudelaire inserts another that illuminates the intensity of his remembered relationship with his mother in her widowhood:

> Indeed, men raised by women and among women are not quite the same as other men, not even those who are like them in temperament and spiritual faculties. The way a nurse rocks a baby's cradle, a mother caresses her child, a sister cuddles her brother, especially when it's an older sister, a kind of diminutive mother, all this transforms so to speak, kneads you might say, the masculine dough. The man who in his early years has long been bathed in the soft atmosphere of woman, in the odor of her hands, her breast, her knees, her hair, her pliable, floating clothes,
>
> Dulce balneum suavibus
> Unguentatum odoribus,
>
> (the sweet bath perfumed with pleasant scents) has contracted a delicacy of the epidermis and a distinction of accent, a kind of androgyny without which the harshest and most virile genius remains, where perfection in art is concerned, an incomplete being. In a word, I mean that the precocious taste for the world of women, *mundi muliebris,* for all that undulating, sparkling and perfumed apparatus, creates the greater genius; and I'm convinced that the highly intelligent woman reading me will forgive the almost sensual form of my expressions as she approves and understands the purity of my thought. (I 499)

In a letter written in April 1869, Baudelaire responded to his publisher's criticism of this passage in a paragraph that takes his central idea even further:

> As for the rest of your criticism, my answer is provided by the work of the imagination I performed and the *intelligent* reader has to perform, too. What is

it that the child loves so passionately in his mother, in his nurse, in his older sister? Is it simply the being who feeds him, combs his hair, washes him, and rocks him to sleep? It's also the caresses and the sensual pleasure she gives him. For the child, this caress expresses itself, unknown to the woman, through all the grace she possesses. He loves his mother, his sister and his nurse, then, for the agreeable tickling of satin and fur, the scent of her breast and her hair, the jingling of her jewelry, the play of her ribbons etc., for all the *mundus muliebris* beginning with the shift and expressing itself even through the furniture wherever the woman leaves the imprint of her femininity.

(L 153–54, CII 30)

The sensuality of the child is not just a theoretical stance. Baudelaire explores it in one of the poems he places near the beginning of *Les Fleurs du mal* at an early point in his persona's progression through life. The irregular sonnet "La Géante (The Giantess)" follows the poem "L'Idéal (The Ideal)" in which the lyric "I" affirms—as though we could ever have been in doubt—that the ideal woman for him would never be the sort we find in contemporary fashion magazines, illustrated by such artists as Paul Gavarni who is dismissively classified as the "poet of anemia." What the lyric "I" wants is someone like Lady Macbeth or Michelangelo's Night, figures of great physical and mental strength. As though to give a further demonstration of the theme, the poem "La Géante" gives free rein to a fantasy of a past age when giants walked the earth:

Du temps que la Nature en sa verve puissante
Concevait chaque jour des enfants monstrueux,
J'eusse aimé vivre auprès d'une jeune géante,
Comme aux pieds d'une reine un chat voluptueux.

J'eusse aimé voir son corps fleurir avec son âme
Et grandir librement dans ses terribles jeux;
Deviner si son cœur couve une sombre flamme
Aux humides brouillards qui nagent dans ses yeux;

Parcourir à loisir ses magnifiques formes;
Ramper sur le versant de ses genoux énormes,
Et parfois en été, quand les soleils malsains,

Lasse, la font s'étendre à travers la campagne,
Dormir nonchalamment à l'ombre de ses seins,
Comme un hameau paisible au pied d'une montagne.

(FM XIX)

In the days when Nature in her powerful verve
Every single day conceived monstrous children,
I would love to have lived with a young giantess
Like a voluptuous cat at the feet of a queen.

I would love to have watched while her body and soul,
Flowered and grew freely in her terrible games;
To guess if her heart bred a melancholy flame
In the damp mists and fogs that swam in her eyes;

To explore at my leisure her magnificent form;
Clamber up the slope of her massive great knees,
And sometimes in summer when the unhealthy sun

Stretched her sleepily out across the terrain,
Lethargically doze in the shadow of her breasts,
Like a hamlet at peace at the foot of a mountain.

In this wonderfully exuberant poem, where the creativity of nature is linked to the poet's own creativity through the choice of the word "verve" (derived from Latin *verbum*, word), commentators have frequently seen memories of the child playing with the mother, the child's-eye perspective transforming her into a giantess of massive proportions. But there is more to see here. For one thing, this giantess is not a fully-grown adult, and that fact is essential to the poem. However powerful the infrastructure of personal memory in this poem, the poetic persona is not really the child here at all, but someone with an adult's understanding watching the physical and emotional development of a young female. The poem makes it quite clear that the watcher is eager to discover the moment at which an awareness of sexuality comes to life in that apparent innocence, its dark flame contrasting with the mists and fogs of childish perceptions. In his account of the art salon of 1859, Baudelaire makes the following avowal. If he couches it in the form of a confession, it is only as a rhetorical gesture where an appearance of embarrassment allows a confident affirmation of a personal taste that the critic is perfectly happy to make public. Addressing his judgments to the director of the periodical who had requested them, he announces: "I'm obliged to confess something that may well make you smile: in nature as in art,—all else being equal— I prefer *large* things to all others, large animals, large landscapes, large ships, large men, large women, large churches, and when, like many others, I transform my tastes into principles, I believe that dimensions play a not inconsiderable role in the eyes of the Muse" (II 646).

Transforming taste into principles, or, as he puts it elsewhere, pleasure into understanding, is a central tenet in Baudelaire's thinking. More precisely, to go back to the imagery of "Le Cygne," it is fundamental to the process that transforms the bric-a-brac into allegory. "La Géante," which, according to contemporary reminiscences, dates from well before the 1859 *Salon,* shows an early phase in that development of principles, where the vast proportions are crucial to the impression of beauty and happiness. What we have above all in this poem is a sense of largesse, of amplitude, but also of the kind of repose that teeters on the brink of action. The adult poet recaptures memories of childhood, harnesses the perceptions of childhood, but endows them with the adult capacity of response, figured here by the adult onlooker. And as an adult, he finds himself fascinated with the sensuality of childhood, represented here both by the poet's own delight in the giantess's abundant proportions and in the giantess's own dawning awareness of desire.

The sensuality of the child recurs in one of the prose poems where it is imbued with an ample sense of the child's intense emotion, an intensity barred from the sparser language of the art criticism and merely touched on in the controlled form of the sonnet. "Les Vocations" (PPP XXXI) sets four young boys against an opulent background, clearly meant, like that of "La Géante," to be read as bearing a particular emotional charge and as facilitating the kind of confession that is to follow: "In a beautiful garden where the rays of an autumnal sun seemed to linger impulsively, under a sky already tinged with green where golden clouds floated like traveling continents, four fine children, four boys, apparently tired of playing, were talking together." This is very familiar Baudelairean territory: a sun near setting, suggesting a period reaching an end (love, childhood, Romanticism . . .), the moving architecture of the wonderful clouds, the pleasure of conversation—Baudelaire once described Delacroix's conversation for instance as "brilliant, subtle, but full of facts, memories and anecdotes, in brief, words you could get your teeth into" (II 764). The first child to speak reminisces about a visit to the theater, a potent space in Baudelairean esthetics. One of the aspects that most seizes the boy's attention is the appearance of the actresses: "The women are far more beautiful and far larger than those who come and see us at home and although their huge, deep eyes and their enflamed cheeks make them seem terrible, you can't help loving them. You're scared, you want to cry, and yet you're happy . . ." (PPP XXXI). Baudelaire, who tells us elsewhere that when as a child he was taken to the theater he thought that the most beautiful element there was the chandelier (I 682), has thrust into the limelight the very essence of stardom, that sense of individuals being larger than life and of the curious nature of vicarious emotions. The complexity of desire—the fear and the pleasure, the tears and the sense of happiness—is beautifully encapsulated in this little passage, and if the language itself is not particularly that of childhood, Baudelaire clearly intends his readers to link that sensuality and that understanding to children.

When this confession is followed by a child's vision of God, a third boy scornfully dismisses the attraction of both theatres and religion. Taken on a journey by his parents, this child, whom Baudelaire describes as marked by an exceptional vivacity and vitality, has had to share a bed with the maid. Unable to sleep, the boy amused himself by running his hand over his maid's arms, neck, and shoulder: "Her arms and neck are much larger than those of all other women," he says, tapping into the preference for large things that Baudelaire acknowledges in the 1859 Salon, "and her skin there is so soft, so soft that you'd say it was letter paper or silk paper." This is well within the child's range of comparisons, although it suggests a child whose love of reading is intensified by the physical nature of the book. Intense pleasure, however, comes with fear—fear that the maid might wake, but also fear of something unknown, which the child neither can nor need specify, but that the reader knows to be the nature and consequences of desire. Baudelaire being Baudelaire, the child turns from the softness of the skin to the texture and scent of the woman's hair, and to an invitation to an active response: "Then I nestled my head in her hair as it hung down her back, as thick as a horse's mane, and, you know, it smelt as good as the flowers in the garden just now. When you get a chance, try it out for yourselves, and you'll see!" (PPP XXXI). The sulfurous halo of passion the narrator detects around this boy's head merely intensifies the extent to which Baudelaire's concept of the child diverges from that of the innocence most Romantic poets attributed to children.

The awakening of desire and sensuality, the awareness of loss and bereavement, the sense of being molded in a way that is different from the experience of children raised in predominately masculine households, these are the elements Baudelaire associates with children brought up by their mothers. It is not particularly important for us to know, even if we could, what relationship this might bear to some externally verifiable biographical truth: the image elaborated in Baudelaire's writing, his criticism as well as his creative work, is what is at issue here, and it is one that marks a significant change in the perception of the child. Moreover, the specificity of the images—the details of skin and hair and jingling jewelry—together with the complexity of the emotions—terror and tears and happiness all folded in together—indicate that much of this figure of the child fashioned by women arises from deep personal wellsprings.

However important the figure of the mother may be, however brief Baudelaire's acquaintance with his father, François Baudelaire also left his imprint on the imaginary world of *Les Fleurs du mal* and the *Petits Poèmes en prose*. Although he was later to describe his father as a "detestable artist" (CI 439), Baudelaire was fully aware of how much his father's love of the fine arts had influenced him. His bio-bibliographical notes include the following concise evocation of his childhood: "Old furniture from the period of Louis XVI, antiques, the Consulate, pastels, the society of the eighteenth century" (I 784). And he would attribute also to this time the birth of his love of paintings—my sole, my unique passion, as he terms it. Despite the frequent changes of apartment that made his adult existence so nomadic, he somehow managed to keep a collection of his father's drawings. In a letter of late March 1861, he told his mother how worried he was about the boxes he had left in his study in her house in Honfleur, fearing that his father's drawings might suffer from the dampness there (CII 170).

It was long thought that Baudelaire's description of his father as a defrocked priest stemmed merely from a desire to shock, and no doubt he relished the somewhat scandalous nature of that admission. But research has shown that this was indeed the case. The fact that his father had been trained for the priesthood has a bearing, although an indirect one, on a modern reading of Baudelaire. It meant François Baudelaire had a very good grounding in Latin, and it was that grounding that enabled him to find employment in 1785 as a teacher for the two young sons of the Choiseul-Praslin family. He was to stay with them for ten years and impressed them by the fine pedagogical qualities he displayed. Those qualities are reflected in a Latin vocabulary he created for the use of the two boys, who were only five and seven years old when he started teaching them. The vocabulary, which he called *The Latin Language Demonstrated by Drawings,* is a manuscript of some one hundred and fifty pages, most of them covered with delicate pen and watercolor drawings (see figure 2). This is a remarkable compendium, now held by the Lilly Library at Indiana University, and while there is no proof that Baudelaire ever set eyes on it, it does reflect on both his father's talent and his attitude towards children, his concept of what they could comprehend and what they could assimilate. Moreover, it is not too great a leap of the imagination to think of François Baudelaire making similar drawings to amuse or instruct his younger son.

The Latin vocabulary does make an effort to appeal to the children for whom it was written. Words for street and house, for instance, are illustrated with pictures of the street and house in which the Choiseul-Praslin family were living. The boy's names can be found in some of the drawings. Several pictures show monkeys playing with named objects or performing on the instruments whose Latin names the boys were meant to acquire. The importance of context is recognized and exploited in a series of pictures depicting specific rooms or scenes that allow for a natural grouping of objects whose Latin names are attached to them. But what is most likely to strike a modern reader is the violence of some of the scenes. A crucifixion may have been familiar enough to a church-going family, although this one is particularly grim and not associated with images of resurrection. There is a scene of a man whose leg has been amputated, and whose body is covered with ulcers. A figure labeled "miseratio" wringing its hands in the background does little to detract from the brutal directness of the picture. Perhaps this was meant to appeal to the bloodthirsty nature of little boys, but in the years leading up to the Terror it seems in hindsight both unusually pitiless and symptomatic. More striking yet are the groupings of concepts such as envy, wrath, contempt, jealousy and so forth where the child is clearly assumed to be familiar with quite complex and subtly differentiated emotions and to recognize them in the faces depicted in the vocabulary. And for anyone looking to find reflections of Baudelaire père there are indications that he enjoyed good food and wine, that he had a certain suspicion of soldiers, and that his attitude to women was somewhat ambivalent. Above all, however, there is a sense of wit, sometimes caustic but often good humored, that may have been diminished through ill health by the time of his second marriage but that it is hard to imagine disappearing altogether.[2]

One thing seems certain: the opening stanza of Baudelaire's magnificent closing poem for *Les Fleurs du mal* contains an echo of his father's legacy in its evocation of the child inspired by maps and drawings:

> Pour l'enfant, amoureux de cartes et d'estampes,
> L'univers est égal à son vaste appétit.
> Ah! que le monde est grand à la clarté des lampes!
> Aux yeux du souvenir que le monde est petit!

(FM, CXXVI)

> For the child, enamored of prints and of maps
> The universe is as vast as his own boundless dreams.
> How mighty the world in the light of the lamps!
> To memory's gaze how modest it seems!

The catalog of objects Madame Baudelaire sold after her husband's death includes several drawings, framed or unframed, gouaches, engravings, and "prints, among which are *Charles Ier, Suzanne in her bath, The Bathers, Madame de la Vallière, Télémaque* etc. and several paintings and pastels, some plaster statues and so forth" (Pichois 66). Among the prints were several by Piranesi, whose depictions of prisons and ruins so shaped the architectural imagination of Baudelaire's friend, the poet and art critic Théophile Gautier. The boy poring over engravings and maps of the world is more his father's than his mother's son. Indeed, he is there in one of the drawings of the Latin vocabulary, surrounded by prints, books, and globes, and whipping a top, like the "cruel Angel whipping suns" in "Le Voyage" (see figure 2).

The idyll Baudelaire recalls, the time of passionate love for his mother when she and he seemed absorbed in each other was, of course, in part an illusion. Worse still, it was about to come to an abrupt end. From the spring of 1828, barely a year after her first husband's death, Caroline Baudelaire was being courted by an army officer, Jacques Aupick. She was thirty-five, and in the early nineteenth century, that was an age well beyond youth. She did not waste her opportunities: on November 8, 1828, she and Aupick were married. This somewhat unseemly haste is explained

[2] For a detailed study of the Latin vocabulary, see my article "Le Latin sans pleurs: le vocabulaire illustré de François Baudelaire," *Essays in French Literature* 32–33 (November 1995–1996): 22–40.

by an archival record showing that on December 4, 1828, Caroline Aupick was delivered of a stillborn daughter. Almost certainly Baudelaire never knew about this pregnancy. But the apparent betrayal of his mother, who had turned from him to this stranger who was henceforth to play such an important role in his life, leaves its mark in his writing, in speaking images of knowing, melancholy, or destructive children.

That betrayal was made worse through coming at the point in his life when "the horror of school" (I 295) was beginning to loom on the horizon, with its attendant cortege, to use a Baudelairean image, of boredom, restrictions, and "horrid pugilistic" school mates (I 499). And, beginning in January 1832, he would be placed in pensions and boarding schools, giving rise to a long series of painful letters promising better behavior and improved grades, begging for permission to spend the weekend at home, pleading for intervention to reduce or remove some imposition or punishment. There is no document of civilization, as Walter Benjamin remarks in a different context, that is not also a document of barbarism.

It is in these depictions that we see most clearly, perhaps, what Baudelaire elsewhere terms "the universe of childhood, but with the poetic riches added now by a subtle, cultivated mind, that has the habit of drawing its greatest pleasures from solitude and reminiscence" (I 505). The universe of childhood is powerfully summed up in his prose poem "Le Joujou du pauvre (The Poor Child's Toy)" (PPP XIX) with its deceptively saccharine opening: "I want to give an idea of an entertainment that's innocent. There are so few amusements that are not reprehensible!" Baudelaire's profound sense of the duality of life, of human beings constantly tugged between the desire for goodness and the seduction of evil, infuses the structure of many of his prose poems. The very form of the prose poem, as we now conceive it, is largely Baudelaire's creation. Without the formal divisions by stanzas, without the inherent repetitions and pivots provided by, say, the *rondeau* and the *triolet,* the sonnet and alexandrine, it may well be that the prose poem appears formless, its freedoms seductive, while its very open-endedness seems daunting and dangerous.

One of the solutions Baudelaire adopts, and that allows the form to correspond to his convictions about human nature, is a binary structure, often deceptive in its apparent simplicity. That is the case here. The poem opens with its statement of purpose, leading into the invitation to the reader to buy cheap little toys and distribute them to the children of the poor. Then there is an abrupt shift, an apparently unconnected description of an attractive park, a pretty chateau, and a beautiful little child. The link between the two at last appears: an expensive toy lies forgotten at the child's feet. What he is staring at, with envy and longing, is a dirty little urchin who has a far more attractive toy: a caged rat. And the shared pleasure both children feel in this toy is illustrated by their smiles, which are equally *white*. The italicization of *white* is ironic: this is the only point of physical equality, but they share another aspect as well, which is their enthusiasm for the caged rat. There are many ways we might read this poem: as indicative of how pleasure is best shared and discovered instead of being bestowed, since when the adult in the poem's first half scatters his largesse among children they seize the gifts and run away to enjoy them where there is no threat of their being snatched back again; as a political statement about the equality of classes; as an indication about the relationship between children and animals. However we read it, and however we interpret the word "fraternally," one thing remains unchanged, and that is the clear-sighted vision of childhood that comes across here. Of course, it is possible to argue that this is not about children at all but about far more general tendencies. Yet that is irrelevant to the fact that even if these children are symbols of their class, or of humans in general, they are obviously also children. And they are not the children who dominate French literature at this time, since they are more likely to recall the urchins and scamps of the Spanish artist Murillo's fierce paintings.

More ferocious still in its unraveling of myths of childhood innocence and joy is the prose poem "La Corde (The Rope)," which is dedicated to Baudelaire's friend, the painter Edouard Manet. How, in translating this, can equivalents be found for the urbane tones with which the poem opens and for the atmosphere of philosophical questioning that makes the horror of what happens all the more stark and telling? How can I best convey the slightly self-mocking note of the painter painting himself, or listing the subjects of paintings for which he employed the boy as model? How do I suggest the gap in comprehension between his expectations of maternal behavior and the material preoccupations that prompt the mother's request? And in a poem where the metaphorical umbilical cord linking mother and child has so brutally and callously been sundered, shouldn't I be translating "La Corde," with its whispered suggestion of the "cordon ombilical," by a term that has the same capacity for suggestion? Would "The Cord" be possible? Exploring this prose poem from *Petits Poèmes en prose* sheds considerable light on Baudelaire's image of childhood.

"THE CORD"

For Edouard Manet

"Illusions," my friend was saying, "may well be as legion as the relationships that link individual to individual, or individuals to objects. And when the illusion vanishes, I mean when we see the being or the fact as it exists outside ourselves, we experience a bizarre and complex sensation, half regret for the phantom now faded, half pleasant surprise in the face of something new, in the face of something real. If there exists a phenomenon that's obvious, banal, unchanging, whose nature can't possibly be mistaken, it's maternal love. It's as hard to imagine a mother without maternal love, as it is to imagine light without heat. So wouldn't you say it's perfectly legitimate to attribute to maternal love everything a mother does and says, where

her child is concerned? And yet, just listen to this bizarre little tale, which shows me singularly mystified by the most natural of illusions."

Of course, George Sand knew better when she showed her heroine Brulette, in the novel *The Master Pipers* (1853), struggling to learn to love her little foster son Charlot. One could of course argue that Charlot is not her natural child, but one she has been asked to take care of. Yet that is to miss the point. If the essentialism of Baudelaire's argument is jarring us into pulling a grimace at this point, that is surely the correct response. The endless pleas Baudelaire addresses to his mother in letters that are even now painful to read suggest that this poem is based on the conviction that mothers are not shaping all they do and say around the love of their children, that they have their own lives and their own concerns, beyond the control and often beyond the comprehension of those children, even when they grow up. The urbanity of the friend's voice in this opening passage is a rickety mask behind which we see Baudelaire sneeringly suggesting that maternal love is as rare as hen's teeth.

"My profession as a painter," the friend continues, "impels me to look attentively at faces and physiognomies that I come across on my route, and you know what pleasure we derive from that faculty that in our eyes makes life far more lively and more meaningful than for the mass of humanity."

"Hypocrite reader, my double, my brother": Baudelaire's invitation at the outset of *Les Fleurs du mal* to read with sympathy and tact finds different, more aggressive expressions in the prose poems. We are the readers who are goaded with the accusation that we are too lazy to read more than one or two poems at a sitting, or far less sensitive than the poets and artists whose profession lends such intensity to their experiences. I do not think for a moment that Baudelaire believes this rhetoric: the romantic image of the artist as seer and magus that Hugo or Lamartine had given us had already been replaced by Banville's image of the artist as tightrope walker (another kind of "cord"), just as Baudelaire himself would replace it with the image of the artist as rag picker. We're meant to snort our rejection—and to start looking more intensely at the faces in the street.

"In the outlying suburb where I live, where vast grassy spaces still separate buildings, I often observed a child whose ardent and mischievous physiognomy, more than those of the other children, first seduced me. He posed for me more than once, and I had transformed him sometimes into a little gypsy, sometimes into an angel, sometimes into the Cupid of mythology. I made him carry the strolling player's violin, the Crown of Thorns and the Nails of the Passion, and the Torch of Eros. It reached a point where I took such intense pleasure in the child's sense of humor that one day I asked his parents, who were poor, to be kind enough to hand him over to me, prom-

ising to dress him well, give him some money and not to inflict on him any other duty than that of cleaning my brushes and running my errands. Once the mud was washed off him, the child became charming and the life he led at my place must have seemed a paradise to him, in comparison with what he would have suffered from in his parents' hovel."

The argument is particularly familiar to anyone following Australia's stolen generation story or who has seen the American equivalent in such novels as Barbara Kingsolver's *Pigs in Heaven*. Is the child better off adopted by rich parents? How much personal and family history is lost in such a situation, and who makes the decision, the child or its parents? Does the child see the handing over as a wonderful opportunity or as a rejection by its parents? And if homesickness is compounded by the sense that those at home do not want you, what do you do, as a child? If I behave so badly at school that I'm expelled, will my mother and her lover want me back? The parallel is anachronistic, of course, but not the argument—Baudelaire indicates as much by moving smartly from the separation of child and biological parents, through the loaded word paradise, to the irruption of the snake. And the sudden influx of evil is made all the more powerful by the understated word that introduces the theme: "seulement," only.

"Only I have to say that this little kid astonished me sometimes by singular crises of precocious sadness, and that he soon revealed an uncontrolled taste for sugar and liqueurs, with the result that one day when I realized that, despite countless warnings, he had yet again committed another such theft, I threatened him with sending him back to his family. Then I went out, and business kept me away from home for some time.

Imagine my horror and my astonishment when, on returning home, the first object that struck my gaze was my little fellow, the mischievous companion of my life, hanging by the neck from the closet. His feet almost touched the floor, and a stool, no doubt kicked away with his feet, lay overturned beside him; his head leaned convulsively on one shoulder; his swollen face and his eyes which were open wide in a terrifying fixed stare initially gave the illusion of life. Detaching him was not so easy a task as you might think. He was already very stiff and I found inexplicably repugnant the thought of making him fall abruptly to the floor. I had to support his entire body with one arm, and with the hand of my other arm cut the rope. But once I'd done that it was still not over. The little monster had used a very thin string that had gone deep into the flesh and now I had to take a pair of narrow scissors and seek out the string between two rolls of swollen flesh in order to liberate his throat.

I should have told you that I had shouted vigorously for help, but all my neighbors had refused to lend me a hand, thus showing their fidelity to the habits of civilized human beings, who, for a reason that escapes me, never want to get involved in the affairs of a hanged man. At last a doctor arrived, and declared that the child had been dead for several hours. When, later on, we had to take his clothes off for the burial, the rigor mortis had reached such a stage that despairing of bending his limbs we had to rip and cut the clothes to take them off the body."

The language here is unflinching. The physical details of the swollen neck, the string buried in the flesh, the body too stiff to allow easy removal of the clothes, are all essential both to the psychological reality of the artist unable to forget every tiny detail of the horrible event and also to the moral point of the prose poem as it builds up to the encounter with the bereaved mother. In reading it, as in translating it, there is no looking away, no slipping over the physical terms to replace them with abstracts or euphemisms. This also is part of childhood—the deep depression and the fact of rigor mortis are not somehow lessened for a child.

"The police chief to whom I had, naturally, to declare the accident, gave me a side-ways glance and said: 'There's something a bit suspicious in all this!' driven no doubt by an inveterate desire and a professional habit of scaring innocent people just in case, in the same way you do those who are guilty.

There remained a final task that had to be carried out, and the very thought of it caused me terrible anguish; I had to let the parents know. My feet refused to carry me there. At last I found the necessary courage. But, to my great amazement, the mother was impassive, not a tear glinted in the corner of her eye. I attributed this strange reaction to the very horror she must be feeling, and I remembered the well-known maxim: 'The most terrible pain is that which is silent.' As for the father, all he did was say half moronically and half dreamingly: 'After all, it may be better like this; he was always going to end badly!'

Meanwhile the body was stretched out on the divan and with the aid of a servant I was getting it ready for burial when the mother came into my studio. She wanted, so she said, to see her son's corpse. I could not, I really could not, prevent her from immersing herself in her grief. How could I refuse her that supreme and somber con-solation? Then she begged me to show her the place where her baby had hanged him-self. 'Oh, no, Madame!' I replied, 'it would be too painful for you!' And as my eyes involuntarily turned to the funereal closet, I saw, with a sense of disgust mixed with horror and anger, that the nail was still stuck in the panel with a long piece of rope that still swung from it. I leapt swiftly to tear out these last traces of the accident, and as I was going to throw them outside through the open window, the poor woman seized my arm and said to me in irresistible tones: 'Oh, sir! Let me have that! Please do! I beg you!' Her despair had no doubt, or so it seemed to me, driven her so beside herself that she was now filled with tenderness for what had been the instrument of her son's death, and she wanted to keep it as a horrible and cherished relic. And she grabbed the nail and the string.

At last, at last! everything was done. All I had to do was return to my work even more intensely than usual to drive slowly from my mind this little corpse that haunted the recesses of my brain, and whose phantom wearied me with its great staring eyes. But the following day I received a packet of letters; some from fellow tenants in my apartment building, others from nearby houses; one from the first floor, another from the second, another from the third and so on, some in a half-joking style, as if trying to disguise under an apparently jesting tone the sincerity of their request; others, heavy in their effrontery and full of spelling errors, but all of them with the same goal, that of getting from me a piece of the tragic and beatific rope. Among the signatories there were, I have to say, more women than men but not all of them, you can truly believe me, belonged to the lower and common classes. I kept some of these letters.

And then, suddenly a light blazed in my brain, and I understood why the mother was so eager to seize the string from me and by what transactions she intended to seek consolation."

Robert Kopp, one of the finest editors of the *Petits Poèmes en prose,* affirms that the story related here is drawn from life. He quotes several of Manet's friends to substantiate this claim, among them the art lover, Antonin Proust, the critic, Moreau-Nélaton, and Manet's sister-in-law, the artist Berthe Morisot.[3] While it is equally possible, given that the earliest of these affirmations dates from some forty years after the event, that this is a memory not of a lived event but of a reading of Baudelaire's prose poem, which Moreau-Nélaton specifically mentions in his account, the essential issue here is that Baudelaire has transformed the stuff of newspapers into something far more arresting and resonant. The deep depression to which children can be subject, together with its terrible consequences, are a far cry from the elements that had gone into the standard depictions of childhood before Baudelaire. His is a new susceptibility, a new vision, one that draws on his own personal memories in the realization that such a vision lies much closer to the truth of contemporary existence.

[3] Charles Baudelaire, *Petits Poèmes en prose,* ed. Robert Kopp (Paris: Corti, 1969), 303–4.

CHAPTER FOUR

An Evocative Magic

When he came to write his memoirs, the realist writer Champfleury (see figure 8), a close friend of Baudelaire in the late 1840s, adds a footnote to his evocation of the poet: "I would have liked to see a biographer insist on the especially rhetorical side of Baudelaire. [. . .] He often speaks of a certain art of decadence, but an art that nevertheless has its laws, its Manuals, its Dictionaries and its rhetoric."[1] Baudelaire was a writer who enjoyed working within the constraints of traditional prosodic forms, but what he seems to have found most stimulating was extending the limits of those forms, testing and exploring their possibilities, as he does, for instance, with his imaginative use of irregular sonnets. After meditating on the value of particular methods of painting in his review of the Salon of 1859, he makes the following claim for literary method: "It is obvious that rhetoric and prosody are not tyrannies arbitrarily invented, but a collection of rules made necessary by the very way in which the intellect organizes thought. Prosody and rhetoric, moreover, have never prevented originality from making its own distinct appearance. The contrary, by which I mean, that they help originality to blossom, would be infinitely more accurate" (II 626–27). In this, Baudelaire's thinking is close to that of Stéphane Mallarmé, who would affirm with typical whimsy that prosodic rules simply prevent you from blundering, in the same way, say, that being able to keep upright depends on our not attempting to fly.[2]

Scattered through Baudelaire's letters and notebooks, as well as lying more abundantly in the more predictable places—his art and literary criticism, for instance—are esthetic convictions, invocations to powerful sources of inspiration, or angry denunciations of false or confused thinking about the role of beauty, truth, and morality in art. The determination to achieve fame as a poet, the sense that bourgeois philistinism debased the concepts of great art, the constant battle to earn money, above all the imperious longing to wrest approval from that most unresponsive source—his mother—all collide to produce a potent but unstable source of information about his thinking. Moreover, as he asserts in an angry assessment of the popularity given to the likes of a minor poet, Hégésippe Moreau, and denied to such innovative writers

---

[1] Champfleury, *Souvenirs et portraits* (Paris: Dentu, 1872), 133.
[2] Stéphane Mallarmé, *Œuvres complètes* (Paris: Gallimard, Pléiade, 1945), 361–62.

as Gérard de Nerval and Edgar Allan Poe, a great writer's method is almost inevitably mysterious to his or her readers (II 157). He himself finds that creating esthetic systems for his own critical or creative purposes is flawed and fruitless:

> I've attempted on several occasions, like all my friends, to lock myself into a system that would let me preach more comfortably, but a system is a kind of damnation that forces us into constantly renouncing it. You are persistently obliged to make a new one, and the weariness of doing so is a cruel punishment. And yet my system was always beautiful, vast, spacious, commodious, clean and above all sleek, or so it seemed to me. But some unexpected and spontaneous by-product of the vitality of existence was always giving the lie to my puerile and antiquated knowledge, that deplorable daughter of utopia. No matter how much I moved or widened the criterion, it was always lagging behind universal humanity, always trotting along behind beauty which, with all its multiplicity of form and color, moves in the infinite spirals of life.
>
> (II 577–78)

Always open to the flux of modern life, and deeply aware that beauty defies all attempts to pin it down or to make it fit into any system, Baudelaire's esthetics are as elastic and mobile as modern existence. What is more, he was convinced that the great poets of Romanticism had carved up the pie so thoroughly that there was nothing left for those who followed. It was this, he claimed, that led him to focus on the crumbs remaining, the underside of beauty, its unexpected and often unacceptable forms. Of course, in doing so he changed our perception of beauty. And there are certain constants, just as there are moments of blindness, that underpin his creative practice.

Publicly, Baudelaire frequently asserts that "the generating condition of art is the exclusive love of beauty" (II 111), though privately he acknowledges that something else is also needed, something that will transform that obsession with beauty from the contemplative to the active, and switch the central focus from the material to the intellectual. Otherwise writers would find themselves in the predicament revealed in his poem "La Beauté":

> Je suis belle, ô mortels! comme un rêve de pierre,
> Et mon sein, où chacun s'est meurtri tour à tour,
> Est fait pour inspirer au poète un amour
> Eternel et muet ainsi que la matière.
>
> (FM XVII)

> I am lovely, o mortals, as a dream of stone,
> My breast, where each soul in turn is battered,

Inspires in each poet a love as lone,
As eternal, as mute as matter.

Baudelaire is engaging here in a wider contemporary debate on the relationship between the spiritual and the material in art, a debate that he has carried on with particular enthusiasm with the witty and virtuoso poet Théodore de Banville (see figure 4), but the central point for our purposes here is that the one thing a poet's love cannot be is mute. As Mallarmé was to say later in the century with that puckish humor so characteristic of him, "meditating, without trace, becomes evanescent."[3]

Transforming contemplation into action can come about, Baudelaire suggests, through logic. Here the influence of Edgar Allan Poe is obvious. In his notebooks, Baudelaire persistently enjoins himself to "create something through the pure logic of opposites" (I 591), or to "find the conclusion by means of analysis" (I 594). We might think of the balances achieved in *Spleen et Idéal,* the first book of *Les Fleurs du mal,* where ideal turns to spleen in such contrasts as those provided by the way in which "Obsession" (FM LXXIX) takes up the themes of "Correspondances" (FM IV) only to overturn them in a gesture reflecting all the ambivalence of Baudelaire's nature. "Correspondances" offers us Nature as temple, formed of trees that gaze on us with familiar eyes and sometimes seem to speak to us through "confuses paroles" (jumbled words) (FM, IV). In "Obsession," however, the living pillars of the trees are no longer likely to cast familiar glances or to suggest the quiet contemplation of the temple:

Grands bois, vous m'effrayez comme des cathédrales;
Vous hurlez comme l'orgue; et dans nos cœurs maudits,
Chambres d'éternel deuil où vibrent de vieux râles,
Répondent les échos de vos *De profundis.*

(FM LXXIX)

Great woods, you terrify me just like cathedrals;
Your howls are like the organ; and in our accursèd hearts,
Rooms of eternal mourning where throb old death rattles,
Respond the echoes of your *De profondis.*

Within *Les Fleurs du mal* the entire book titled *Fleurs du mal,* with its depiction of perversity, debauchery, destruction, and suffering can be seen as driven by the logic of contrasts, deliberately and provocatively taking themes and images that seem the opposite of the domain of beauty reserved for poetry. Oppositional esthetics lie at the dark heart of the poem that opens that book, "Destruction":

[3] Ibid., 369.

Sans cesse à mes côtés s'agite le Démon;
Il nage autour de moi comme un air impalpable;
Je l'avale et le sens qui brûle mon poumon
Et l'emplit d'un désir éternel et coupable.

Parfois il prend, sachant mon grand amour de l'Art,
La forme de la plus séduisante des femmes,
Et, sous de spécieux prétextes de cafard,
Accoutume ma lèvre à des philtres infâmes.

Il me conduit ainsi loin du regard de Dieu,
Haletant et brisé de fatigue, au milieu
Des plaines de l'Ennui profondes et désertes,

Et jette dans mes yeux pleins de confusion
Des vêtements souillés, des blessures ouvertes,
Et l'appareil sanglant de la Destruction!

(FM CIX)

The Devil is constantly stirring beside me,
Swimming around me like impalpable air.
I swallow him and feel him burning my lungs
Filling my heart with the longing for evil.

Knowing of course my great love for the arts,
He sometimes appears as the loveliest woman,
And under fictitious pretences of boredom
Accustoms my lips to infamous potions,

Thus leading me far from the eyes of the Lord.
Gasping and broken with weariness I wander
The great plains of Boredom, extensive and empty,

And he hurls in my eyes that are full of confusion
Filth-stained apparel and wide-open wounds,
All of Destruction's foul bloodstained tool kit.

More obviously, perhaps, several of his prose poems draw their inspiration from this logic of opposites, which is driven by the desire for analysis. "Le Gâteau (The Cake)," with its clash between the beauty of the countryside and the violence of the children who live there; "Laquelle est la vraie? (Which is the real Benedicta?)" with its collision between the man's image of female perfection and the woman's determination to retain her own personality, however flawed; "Solitude" with its rejection of the way in which a "philanthropic journalist" castigates solitude as being bad for humanity, are all cases in point. The technique is perhaps deployed most imaginatively in "Le Mauvais Vitrier (The Bad Glazier)" with its partly comic, partly violent demonstration of the ways in which "certain individuals who are, by nature, given purely to contemplation and are utterly unsuited to action," nevertheless sometimes act, "under a mysterious and unknown impulse," "with a speed which they themselves would have thought beyond them" (PPP IX), and in the deceptively titled "Crépuscule du soir (Evening Twilight)" where the calm that descends on those wearied by the day's labor clashes with the "sinister ululation" of those who "like owls, take the coming of night for the signal of a witches' Sabbath" (PPP XXII).

Logic alone is not, of course, enough. The notebooks offer endless variations on the following: "Work, a progressive and accumulative force, bears interest just as capital does, in terms of ability and results" (I 659); "every time you get a letter from a creditor, write 50 lines on an extra-terrestrial subject and you'll be saved!" (I 656); "just get down to writing. I rationalize too much" (I 672). His critical writing, especially the literary criticism, is also eager to reveal or at least to hint at what he terms in a letter to Armand Fraisse "the work that turns reverie into art" (L 147, CI 675), even if he refuses to take the crowd backstage to see the strings and pulleys that make the illusion work (I 185).

What is needed above all is will-power, that vital element that Satan the alchemist in the opening poem of *Les Fleurs du mal* transforms from rich metal into insubstantial steam. Honoré de Balzac as theoretician of determination, as creator of a vast array of characters all filled to the brim with will-power, inspires Baudelaire with the image of one for whom any abdication of will was the greatest source both of shame and suffering (I 438). In his eyes, Eugène Delacroix, too, united immense passion with a formidable will-power (II 746), just as Victor Hugo, especially in his novel *Les Travailleurs de la mer* (*The Toilers of the Sea*), offered a "glorification of the Will" (II 244). It is something whose loss, perceived or real, Baudelaire frequently laments in his letters (see, for instance, CI 214, CII 139). It was demanded not just of creative writers and artists: readers and spectators were also expected to possess an abundant measure of will-power. "Critics and spectators must perform within themselves a transformation that bears the hallmarks of mystery, and that through a phenomenon of will-power acting on imagination allows them to learn how to enter into the context that has given rise to the unusual flowerings [of art]" (II 576). But of course will-power alone is not enough either, even in the most gifted. "In art, the portion allotted to human will is much less than is believed," Baudelaire argues in a passage acknowledging the role of a "kind of special and satanic grace" (II 573). Modern art, indeed, with its powerful melancholy, reveals, directly or indirectly, the "latent Lucifer installed in each human heart" (II 168). And to do so it needs something beyond what can be taught, instilled, or acquired; in other words, it needs inspiration.

Inspiration, he argues, can only flourish if the poet or artist is free to follow its lead. Baudelaire adheres to Victor Hugo's insistence that the choice of subject is entirely up to the individual writer or artist, a credo he asserts in the teeth of numerous contemporary critics determined to foist on their age the imperatives of morality—a particular view of morality, often politically motivated and always determined by class and gender preconceptions. What matters for Baudelaire is both artistic freedom and the modernity with which such subjects are treated. In a note on Poe, published in 1854, he does, however, offer a rapid sketch of those subjects that, at least at that early date, he considered the only ones that were truly important and worthy of the attention of the intelligent: "Probabilities, spiritual illnesses, conjectural sciences, hopes and calculations concerning the life hereafter, analysis of eccentrics and pariahs here on earth, farces that have a directly symbolic significance" (II 289). These are clearly subjects central to the prose poems, with their wonderful array of eccentrics and pariahs, their street entertainers and clowns whose farces offer an oblique and wryly witty reflection of modern life.

Freedom in the choice of subjects may be central to his esthetics, but it does not follow that freedom of form is equally desirable. On the contrary, in both prose and poetry, Baudelaire argues (and here the influence of Poe is paramount), there are two essential conditions, "unity of impression and totality of effect" (II 674). I am, he argues in a letter to the journalist Alphonse de Calonne, one of those who "believe that every literary composition, even a piece of criticism, should be written and manipulated with the conclusion constantly in mind. Everything, even a sonnet" (L 121, CI 538).

Poetry is marked and typified by its splendor and by its conciseness—for Baudelaire, deeply influenced here by Poe, a long poem is simply a contradiction in terms. But it is also marked by the strength it derives from prosodic rules. As we've seen, he insists that prosody and rhetoric have never prevented originality, but rather have helped originality to flower by providing the structures that leave the mind free to dream (II 627). Baudelaire's love of the sonnet derives in large measure from this belief. As he argues in a letter to Armand Fraisse, "because the form is restricting, the idea bursts forth all the more intensely" (L 148, CI 676). But here too the reader cannot simply play a passive role. We are expected to respond to those moments—and there are many—when Baudelaire breaks away from the strict sonnet form, with its two quatrains rhyming abba and its tercets following the scheme: ccd ede. The variations he weaves on this form carry their own immense pleasure and suggest the extent to which the flowering of originality that he mentions derives from the dual temptations to adapt form to meaning and to push the form to its furthest limits. Graham Robb argues that to many of Baudelaire's first readers the shock produced by *Les Fleurs du mal* resulted less from the subject matter, from the extent to which it offered a dictionary of melancholy and crime, than from the extraordinary liberty with which Baudelaire treated the sonnet.[4]

In a witty treatise on French poetry, Théodore de Banville sets out in tabular form the rules for the sonnet:

> The Sonnet always consists of two quatrains and two tercets. In the regular sonnet, the following rhyme with each other:
> 1° the first and fourth lines of the first quatrain and the first and fourth lines of the second quatrain;
> 2° the second, and third lines of the first quatrain; the second and third lines of the second quatrain;
> 3° the first and second lines of the first tercet;
> 4° the third line of the first tercet and the second line of the second tercet;
> 5° the first and third line of the second tercet.
> If you introduce into that arrangement any modification whatsoever,
> If you write two quatrains with different rhymes,
> If you begin with the two tercets and conclude with the two quatrains,
> If you use crossed rhymes in the quatrains,
> If you make the third line of the first tercet rhyme with the third line of the second tercet,—or indeed the first line of the first tercet with the first line of the second tercet,
> If, in a word, you deviate by however little from the classic type of which I have just given two examples,
> The Sonnet is irregular.[5]

To his credit, Banville, even if he always prefers the regular sonnet to the irregular, recognizes that "the irregular sonnet has produced master-pieces, a fact easily verified by reading the most romantic and the most modern of all the books of this time,—the wonderful book titled *Les Fleurs du mal.*"[6]

It seems to be the case that the vitality that animates Baudelaire's sonnets bursts asunder even the mechanism that is the most natural or at least the most inherent to the form. "So true it is that there is in the manifold productions of art something that is always new and that will for all eternity escape from academic rules and analyses!" (II 578), remarks the poet of the *Fleurs du mal,* the poet who has never ceased to vaunt "the value of the unexpected" (II 390).

---

[4] See Graham Robb, *La Poésie de Baudelaire et la poésie française 1838–1852* (Paris: Aubier, 1993), 237.
[5] Théodore de Banville, *Petit Traité de Poésie française* (Paris: Les Introuvables, 1978), 173–74.
[6] Banville, 174.

"De profundis clamavi," a poem first published in 1851, can be seen as a fourteen-line form that constantly questions the "rules" that Banville orders all writers of sonnets to obey. If the rhymes in the quatrains are indeed embraced (abba), as Banville insists they must be, each quatrain has different rhymes, and the tercets are composed of couplets, a procedure that, unlike the habitual formula, offers no formal closure: in this poem, the reader feels that the last six lines could very well form a quatrain followed by the first two lines of another quatrain, which, of course, serves to reinforce the message of the final line, with its evocation of a time that hardly passes at all: "Tant l'écheveau du temps lentement se dévide!" (So slowly does the skein of time unwind) (FM, XXX).

Part of the force behind this experimentation with the sonnet form comes from the simultaneous need Baudelaire detects in the human mind for both symmetry and surprise (I 663). Rhyme and rhythm respond to that need (I 182), each of them being essential to the development of beauty, which Baudelaire judges the highest and noblest aim of a poem (II 329). For him, these are sources of intense pleasure— he says that his refusal to translate Poe's poetry stems entirely from the fact that if he did translate it, he would be forced to sacrifice the "volupté" of rhythm and rhyme, where "volupté" has the force of ecstatic, indeed sexual, pleasure (II 347). I know a poet, he says at one point, in the formula consecrated to personal confessions couched in impersonal form, "a poet whose nature is always stormy and vibrant, and whom one line of Malherbe's verse with its symmetrical and straightforward melody, throws into long ecstasies" (II 754). Rhyme also inspires pleasure, a pleasure Baudelaire characteristically depicts as mathematical and musical (II 335–36), and its role is so central to his concept of poetry that we find him arguing pugnaciously at one point that any poet who does not know exactly how many rhymes each word possesses is incapable of expressing any idea whatsoever (I 183).

With its echoes and its ability to suggest words not included in the poem, rhyme acts not just as a source of musicality, but also as a means of memory, or a suggestion of the constant return of what a mind may be trying to suppress. Think of the moment in "The Pirates of Penzance" when the pirates seize the maidens and threaten them with instant marriage thanks to a doctor of divinity who resides in this vicinity. Here all the "nity" rhymes (opportu*nity*, impu*nity* etc.) help suggest the word that cannot be spoken but that is inextricable from the theme: "virginity." Baudelaire sometimes uses rhyme to suggest a word's history and thus extend its resonance. In "Le Voyage," for example, the pairing of "astres" (stars) with "désastres" (disasters) reminds us that disasters were held to come about through inauspicious combinations of constellations. Rhyme can also indicate human blindness by suggesting the falseness of expectations: "horizons" rhyming with "prisons" again in "Le Voyage" is an obvious case in point. It can add an unexpected and *sotto voce* commentary: when "chimériques" (chimerical) rhymes with "Amériques" (Americas) especially given that the stanza's two other rhymes are "à la mer" (to the sea) and "amer" (bitter), all the intrinsic bitterness of Americas that exist only in the imagination leaps into focus.

This wonderfully suggestive power of rhyme is partly what Baudelaire means when he talks about language and writing as magical operations, as an evocative enchantment (I 658). Even grammar can become a source of magic (I 431), he argues, drawing, as Mallarmé would also do, on the etymological relationship between the word for a book of spells, "grimoire," and the word "grammaire," so that the cunning manipulation of language enables the practitioner to create a suggestive sorcery (II 118). Poetry, after all, is "what is most real, what is completely true only in *another world*" (II 59), with the result that "in describing what exists, the poet is degraded and sinks to the role of teacher; by recounting the possible, poets remain true to their function, acting as a collective soul that questions, weeps, hopes, and sometimes guesses" (II 139). Pure art in the modern conception of the term is, therefore, "the creation of an evocative magic, containing both object and subject, the world outside the artist and the artist him or herself" (II 598).

Yet there are significant differences between prose and poetry in the ways in which each can summon up such magic. Baudelaire presents lyricism as largely synthetical, while the novel and short story are primarily analytical (II 165). The prose poem, that hybrid genre that Baudelaire did so much to fashion, fits awkwardly into this division. His "Notes nouvelles sur Edgar Poe," first published in 1857, include a kind of *cri de cœur* suggesting how fragile was his own sense of dominance over the medium, how limited his own belief in what he'd been able to achieve in that domain:

> I know that in all literatures there have been efforts, often auspicious, to create purely poetic tales. Edgar Poe himself has written some very beautiful tales of this sort. But these are struggles and efforts that serve only to reveal how strong the true means are, when they are adapted to the writer's particular aims, and I am not far from believing that in the case of certain writers, the greatest one might choose, these heroic attempts are the fruit of despair.
>
> (II 330)

It is clear that for Baudelaire poetry is the greatest of all genres, but he does allow the short story to be superior to it in one regard:

> Rhythm is necessary to the development of the idea of beauty, which is the highest and most noble aim of the poem. But the artifice of rhythm poses an insurmountable obstacle to the painstaking development of thoughts and expressions whose object is *truth*. For truth can often be the aim of a short story and reasoning is the best tool with which to construct a perfect short story.
>
> (II 329–30)

Poe's tale, "The Gold Bug," is a case in point, like "The Murders in the Rue Morgue" or "Descent in to the Maelstrom."

The interrelationship of truth, beauty, and good is part of a long drawn out and bitter argument in the mid-nineteenth century. In a time of frequent and dangerous uprisings and of an apparently unstoppable evolution in the class fabric of society, it is perhaps not surprising that many of those who held and wished to retain positions of power sought to bully, cajole, or shame art into repeating gestures of subservience and conservatism. The power of art to mold opinions was beyond dispute: what was questionable was the power of the state to control the artists. The government's failure to censor Gustave Flaubert's *Madame Bovary* in 1857 may well have played a significant role in putting Baudelaire on trial for "affronts to public morality" when the first edition of *Les Fleurs du mal* was published later that year. (The trial inspired the journalist Charles Monselet to pen the following bit of doggerel: "Ce succès / Ou procès / Populaire / A fait plus grand et plus beau / le nom de Charles Bau /delaire" (one might translate this as: "This popular success, this judicial affair, / has raised and embellished the name Baudelaire," although that does not capture the all-too-frequent pun on the first syllable of Baudelaire's name, and the word for beautiful) (Pichois 371–72)). That he lost the trial came as a surprise to no one but Baudelaire himself. Théophile Gautier, when he read the first version of the dedication to him, was horrified to find Baudelaire describing the collection as "this miserable dictionary of melancholy and crime." Gautier sensibly urged the poet not to draw unwanted attention to those aspects of his book, and for once Baudelaire was sensible enough to act on the advice. But the atmosphere of conservatism and philistinism was deeply entrenched, and Baudelaire's writing offers an angry and cogent testimonial to the pettiness and restrictions of such reactionary arguments. Aware that "the great folly of morality usurps the place of pure literature in all literary discussions" (I 495), he insists that his sole fault lay in counting on "universal intelligence." It was, he affirmed, because he trusted the intelligence of his readers that he had not written a preface revealing his literary principles and "that very important question of Morality" (I 194). This would have been all the more essential in that his collection of poems was "destined to represent THE AGITATION OF THE SOUL IN EVIL" (I 195). Philistine morality, he furiously retorts again in the notes prepared for his lawyer, would boil down to this: "HENCEFORTH, NO ONE WILL WRITE ANYTHING BUT CONSOLING BOOKS DEMONSTRATING THAT MAN IS BORN GOOD AND THAT ALL MEN ARE HAPPY," a conclusion he judges an "abominable hypocrisy" (I 196) and one, he might have added—although it would not have helped his case—that had already been thoroughly ridiculed by Voltaire's *Candide*.

The problem, of course, lay in his personal dislike, indeed hatred, of all "exclusively moral intentions" in a poem, as he argues in a letter to the English poet Algernon Swinburne (L 198, CII 325). In many letters he sums up his position in terms weaving variations on the following: "Anyone who looks for pure idealism in art is a heretic in the eyes of the Muse and of art . . . *Morality* seeks *good,* science seeks *truth,* poetry and sometimes the novel seek only *beauty"* (L 121, CI 537).

The difficulty of conveying any kind of moral standpoint in such a depiction of beauty, even if Baudelaire truly believed this rather than using it to defend his actions in hindsight, is increased by the objectivity of his approach. "The height of art would consist," he argues at one point, in "remaining glacial and unmoved and leaving to the reader all the merit of indignation" (II 186). According to Baudelaire, it is always up to the reader to draw the conclusions, but this does not mean, of course, that the poet does not point the way.

One of the means by which he most clearly points the way is in the form he gives his two books of poetry, *Les Fleurs du mal* and the *Petits Poèmes en prose.* It can be argued that the trial served a useful purpose, since the excision of the six poems held to contain obscene and immoral passages forced Baudelaire to reconsider the work as a whole when he came to write new material for it. In an often quoted letter to Alfred de Vigny (whose diary entry describing his meeting with Baudelaire identified him not as a poet but merely as Poe's translator), he asserted: "The only praise I ask for this book (the second edition of *Les Fleurs du mal*) is that people recognize it is not a pure album and that it has a beginning and an end. All the new poems were made to fit into the strange framework I had chosen" (L 175, CII 196). That strange framework, or secret architecture, assumes different forms, offers different perspectives and changing horizons according to the preoccupations of its readers. Numerous critics have sketched out the main outlines of such an architecture, drawing inspiration from literary precedents, especially Dante's *Divine Comedy,* from the numerology of the social reformer Charles Fourier, or from more mystic forms of numerology. The five poems at the beginning of *Spleen and Ideal* are seen as corresponding to that book's last five poems, standing to them as an inverse reflection, and finding a further reflection in the five poems of *Le Vin (Wine)*—the number five being suggested by the five senses. The central group of love poems consists of nine poems, just as there are nine muses and nine prayers to the Madonna. Even those who do not seek out such precise structural details tend to see in *Les Fleurs du mal* an organized reflection of the experiences of a poet passing from childhood through maturity to death, enriched and vitiated by the experiences the poems distill. It is because of this powerful organization that the poems offer what Alison Fairlie has termed "the intimate epic of the progress of human desire," adding, "desire of three kinds: to enjoy, to understand and to create."[7] Other critics have tended to stress the sense of failed endeavor, arguing that the collection's driving force comes from an increasingly desperate sense that each avenue followed ends in a cul-de-sac. Yet such a reading is clearly too schematic to deal with the very different sense of complexity and achievement in, say, *Tableaux parisiens (Parisian paintings),* as compared

---

[7] Fairlie, *Baudelaire* (London: Edward Arnold, 1960), 34.

with *Révolte* or *Le Vin* and *La Mort*. More convincing, perhaps, is a reading that separates out the narrator's experiences and the poet's success.

The structuring principle of the *Petits Poèmes en prose* is much looser than that of *Les Fleurs du mal,* giving readers responsibility for the order in which they read, in ways that parallel the chaos and mobility of modern life as Baudelaire depicts it within the prose poems. The image here is of the kaleidoscope in which the elements fall into constantly renewed patterns, or the mythical snake that can be cut in to numerous pieces and restored to wholeness at will. "Remove one vertebra," Baudelaire explains in the letter he sent to the editor Arsène Houssaye, "and the two halves of this tortuous fantasy will have no difficulty in reuniting. Cut it into a number of fragments and you will see that each can exist on its own" (PPP, 30). Of course the structure is more complex than this apparently artless description seems to suggest. Most strikingly, there are several pairings of poems that offer different aspects of the same subject: the poem called "L'Etranger (The Stranger)," for instance, gives a romantic gloss to a theme brought abruptly down to earth by "La Soupe et les nuages (The Soup and the Clouds)." The teleology of the verse poems has been replaced here by something much more modern in its apparently anarchic order, as well as in its demands on the reader not just to respond with fraternal comprehension but to take responsibility for the path to be followed through the text.

If the reader is responsible in large measure for the structure he or she confers on the *Petits Poèmes en prose,* so also is the reader actively present in Baudelaire's conception of commonplace and cliché, of sayings so familiar and so rooted in everyday language as apparently to have lost any spark of originality. This is not the Romantic conception of the poet as magus, speaking for the public, but rather an image in which popular speech provides the base materials the poet transmutes into art. However paradoxical it might seem, for Baudelaire commonplace and cliché, the worn leavings of popular speech, can be exploited as sources of inspiration. This is part of what he ironically terms his "diabolically passionate taste for stupidity" (I 185), illustrated for example in "La Fausse Monnaie (The Counterfeit Coin)" where the narrator ponders long and hard the causes and implications of his friend's motives for giving a beggar a false coin. He concludes, in terms just ponderous enough to leave us wondering about the depth and complexity of irony in this maxim: "There is never any excuse for being wicked, but there is some merit in knowing that you're being wicked. The most irreparable of vices consists in doing evil out of stupidity" (PPP XXVIII).

The stupidity that attracts him is also, indeed perhaps primarily, linguistic. "Does there exist anything more charming, more fertile and more positively *exciting* than the commonplace?" (II 609) he asks at the beginning of his account of the Salon of 1859, just as elsewhere he notes the "immense depths of thought in popular expressions, holes dug out by generations of ants" (I 650). Flaubert expressed the same fascination. He remarks in a letter of May 24, 1855, that "only commonplace expressions and countries we already know contain an inexhaustible beauty." The voice of the crowd edges its way into Baudelaire's voice in the prose poems, in slang expressions such as the "mirettes" used for eyes in "La Chambre double (The Double Bedroom)" or, as James Hiddleston and Barbara Johnson have shown, in the working out of such banal expressions as "killing time," "rose-colored glasses," "seller of clouds."[8] It also appears in utopian jargon such as "fraternitaire" (PPP XXIII) or the colloquialism of "good old devil" (PPP XXIX) or the pseudo-scientific "polyphagous monster" (PPP XLII), where omnivorous would do perfectly well. The voice of the scriptures or well-known tags of classical French literature can be heard particularly in the prose poems, situating them firmly at the crossroads, within the bustling city, transforming them into sounding boards reverberating back the polymorphous voice of the crowd.

Plagiarism is another way in which other voices can be brought into a text, and Baudelaire is far from unwilling to channel some of his reading into his writing. Lines of the English poet, Thomas Gray, join those of Henry Wadsworth Longfellow in Baudelaire's lightweight sonnet "Le Guignon (Bad Luck)," while his prose poem, "Le Thyrse (The Thyrsus)," takes up and refashions Thomas De Quincey's explanation of the structural principals in his *Confessions*: "The whole course of this narrative resembles, and was meant to resemble, a *caduceus* wreathed about with meandering ornaments, or the shaft of a tree's stem hung around and surmounted with some vagrant parasitical plant. [. . .] The true object in my *Opium Confessions* is not the naked physiological theme, [. . .] but those wandering musical variations upon the theme,—those parasitical thoughts, feelings, digressions, which climb up with bells and blossoms round the arid stock" (MO 96–97). In Baudelaire's version, however, the two elements, the central stick and the tendrils that surround it, are equally important: "What is a thyrsus? [. . .] Physically it is merely a stick, nothing but a stick, a stake for hops or vines, something dry, hard and straight. Around this stick, in capricious meanders, stems and flowers play and frolic, like sinuous runaways, leaning over like bells or upside down cups" (PPP XXXII). And now he's away, leaving De Quincey well behind him as he embroiders on this theme, delighting in playing with the concept, seeing how far he can take it. And it leads him to an affirmation that runs counter to De Quincey, as if here, too, we are listening to a conversation beginning in unison and then breaking apart into separate voices. Here he is addressing the composer and pianist Franz Liszt: "The stick is your willpower, straight, firm and unmovable; the flowers represent your fantasy wandering around your will; they are the feminine element executing around the masculine element its prestigious pirouettes. Straight line and arabesque, intention and expres-

---

[8] See Barbara Johnson, *Défigurations du langage poétique* (Paris: Flammarion, 1979), 160 and James Hiddleston, " 'Fusée,' Maxim and Commonplace in Baudelaire," *Modern Language Review* 80, no. 3 (1985): 563–70.

sion, firmness of the will, sinuosity of the word, unity of the aim, variety in the means, an all-powerful and indivisible amalgam of genius, what lover of analysis would have the odious courage to divide and separate you?" (PPP XXXII). Here, as in his expropriation of cliché, the voice of the other enters his text, allowing us to hear the voice of the crowd, but overlaid as if by a compelling descant with the poet's own dominant voice, that takes up the familiar to make it strange.

This exploitation of voices is also part of the technique of bric-a-brac that Baudelaire suggests in "Le Cygne." Parody and pastiche allow him to fold other voices and other viewpoints into his own creative and critical practice. The poet, he affirms in "Les Foules (The Crowds)," benefits from "an incomparable privilege which allows him to be, at will, himself and others. Like those wandering souls in search of a body, he enters, when he so desires, into the character of each individual" (PPP XII). His pastiche of the poet Marceline Desbordes-Valmore in the final paragraph of the article devoted to her is at the same time a wonderfully creative piece of criticism, summing up her themes, her major sources of imagery, and the atmosphere of her writing:

It is a simple English garden, romantic, quixotic. Flowerbeds represent the abundant expressions of sentiment. Ponds, limpid and motionless, that reflect everything clinging upside down to the overturned vault of the skies, are images of a profound resignation imbued with memories. There is nothing missing in this charming garden from a past age. There are gothic ruins hiding in a rural spot. There is an unknown mausoleum that, as you come round an avenue, surprises your soul and advises it to meditate on eternity. Sinuous, shady paths lead to sudden distant prospects. Thus the poet's thought, having followed capricious meanders, flows into vast perspectives of the past or the future, but these skies are too vast to be completely cloudless and the temperature of those climes are too warm for storms not to build up. The stroller, in contemplating these vast expanses veiled in mourning, feels his eyes fill with *hysterical tears.*

(II 149)

This is pastiche, a testing out of someone else's techniques, a playful rather than a mocking recreation.

Mockery, however, is clearly at issue, however gentle it might be, when Baudelaire parodies Gautier's already parodic questions in the famous preface to his novel *Mademoiselle de Maupin*—"No, imbeciles," Gautier explodes to the utilitarian critics of his day, "no, cretins and blockheads that you are, a book does not make a gelatin soup; a novel is not a seamless pair of boots; a sonnet is not a syringe that pumps continuously; a play is not a railway line, all things that are essentially civilizing, things that promote humanity's march on the road to progress."[9] Surprisingly,

Baudelaire, who might have been expected to share these sentiments, takes up arms against them in his short article that attacks the Pagan School, perhaps just to show he can: "Can you drink ambrosia soup? Can you eat Paros cutlets? How much do you get for a lyre at the pawn shop?" (II 47). Flaubert would remark along similar lines in a letter to Louise Colet of July 15, 1853: "It's not Grecian tunics we need in the North, but fur cloaks."

Here Baudelaire may be just leaving one camp to see what it would be like to fight for the other side, but in other examples it is clear that he finds inspiration in using someone else's position as a starting point and then showing how it should be done. This is obviously the case with both the letter he sends Houssaye accompanying a group of his prose poems, and one of those prose poems, "Le Mauvais Vitrier (The Bad Glazier)," to which he specifically draws attention in his letter. "You yourself," he asks in the letter, now generally included by way of an introduction to the prose poems, "isn't it true that you've attempted to translate in a *song* the strident cry of the *Glazier,* and to express in lyrical prose all the distressing suggestions that this cry sends to the very attics, through the highest fogs of the street?" (PPP 30–31). As Robert Kopp has revealed, Baudelaire not only shows Houssaye how to express that cry rather more powerfully but also reformulates Houssaye's reference to his own style as a "primitive rhythm without rhyme, without verse and without poetic prose."[10] Baudelaire's formula takes off from this, giving us: "Who among us has not, in moments of ambition, dreamt of the miracle of a form of poetic prose, musical but without rhythm and rhyme, both supple and staccato enough to adapt itself to the lyrical movements of our souls, the undulating movements of our reveries, and the convulsive movements of our consciences?" (I 275). But Baudelaire takes his appropriation and rewriting of Houssaye much further when he reformulates the song that attempts to convey the Glazier's "strident cry." Houssaye's narrator, seeing the windowpane seller so weak from hunger that he has to lean against a wall for support, describes him as being like a drunkard. This is the voice of the smug bourgeoisie, assuming that the suffering of the poor is self-inflicted. Houssaye's narrator responds by giving the glazier something to drink: "But the glazier's teeth clattered against the glass and he fainted;—yes, Madame, he fainted away;—which caused him a loss of three francs and ten sous, half his capital! For I couldn't prevent his panes from breaking."[11] Baudelaire, in a mood of bitter ironic parody, has his narrative figure deliberately break the panes, thus laying bare the complicity and guilt of those who merely give to the poor without attempting to change social conditions, but who do so stupidly thinking there is something meritorious in what they are doing.

Of course this prose poem is more than a political commentary: it is primarily a

[9] Théophile Gautier, *Mademoiselle de Maupin* (Paris: Garnier-Flammarion, 1966), 42.
[10] Charles Baudelaire, *Petits Poëmes en prose,* ed. Robert Kopp (Paris: Corti, 1969), 180–81; Arsène Houssaye, *Poésies complètes* (Paris: Charpentier, 1850), 168.
[11] Houssaye, 148–51.

commentary on art, playfully pivoting around the central pun in which the word for window pane (*verre*) sounds the same as the word for verse (*vers*). The crystal palace that the glazier carries with him allows for a view of the world only as it is. The narrative voice, at once social commentator and poetry critic, demands an embellishment of the world, and in shattering the panels into smithereens sets the medium free both of its rigid form and its representational limitations. But Baudelaire as writer is both the one who reveals the world as it is and the one who transforms and embellishes it. As he asks in his notes for a never-completed letter to the jovial critic and writer Jules Janin, "why should the poet not be a grinder of poisons just as well as a maker of candy? Why should he not raise serpents for miracles and spectacles? Why should he not be a snake charmer in love with his reptiles, enjoying the frozen caresses of their coils at the same time as he delights in the terrors of the crowd?" (II 238).

Allowing the voices of the crowd to speak through him in cliché and maxim, echoing the voices of other writers in parody, pastiche, and sometimes in plagiarism, transforming the familiar in to the unfamiliar, Baudelaire's esthetics fuse those of snake charmer and crowd, actor and observer, realist and idealist.

CHAPTER FIVE

Anywhere Out of the World

"Le Cygne (The Swan)" is full of characters longing to escape. That escape may be seen in terms of space, as it is for the swan and the "négresse," or in terms of time, as it is for Andromache, longing to return to a happier past, or for Victor Hugo, waiting until the political moment is ripe for him to return from exile. It may also be seen as a desire for something other than the human condition, represented by the narrator's poignant sense of his own longing for stability in a world of rapid flux. For Baudelaire himself, escape to other countries is rarely contemplated as either possible or desirable. Paris, after all, lying at the heart of his ambitions, defines and delimits the kind of existence he recognizes as the only possible one for a writer seeking renown. Moreover, while many of his contemporaries, both artists and writers, drew on their journeys, especially to Spain or North Africa, Baudelaire's own early experience of travel was inextricably linked with constraint and unhappiness, all the more so, perhaps, since it brought to so abrupt an end a period of relative happiness.

The most joyful period of his life was the two years or so between his expulsion for insolence from the *lycée* Louis-le-Grand in 1839 and May 1841. These were months of freedom and friendships when he roamed the Latin quarter, ostensibly studying law, but spending his time in cafés and bars, meeting other budding poets, lining up to see the procession bringing Napoleon's ashes to Paris, and—already—running up debts, mainly for clothes and boots. It was a time for experiments and adventures, a time, as he would claim twenty years later, that he always looked back on with delight (II 179). It was at this time, too, that he contracted the venereal disease that probably led to his premature death. In May 1841, Aupick, Baudelaire's step-father, decided something must be done with this rebellious and spend-thrift step-son who was determined to devote his life to poetry, rather than anything respectable like the law or the civil service. Aupick took the decisive but not destructive step of sending him on a sea journey, which, as he argued, would at least give the future poet something to write about. The intention was that Baudelaire would travel as far as India, and indeed he later affirmed in his bio-bibliographical notes that he had gone as far as Ceylon and Hindustan. The facts, however, are somewhat different, for he left the ship when it reached Reunion Island and returned to Bordeaux. He seems to have written neither to his mother nor to his step-father during this voyage, and our records of his time on board are second-hand, through other passengers or the captains of the two ships, who report his behavior as generally quiet but courageous in moments of danger. According to an anonymous report published in *La Chronique de Paris* in September 1867, when the ship came round the Cape of Good Hope, it was struck by a violent wind which drove it over on its side. It was only by a difficult and risky maneuver, in which Baudelaire played a part, that it was brought upright again.[1] He seems not to have mixed very much with other passengers, and the journey itself left few happy recollections in his creative or critical writing. Yet, however unpleasant he may have found the living quarters on board ship, and however much he may have missed Paris and his bohemian friends, he was certainly inspired by the beauty of the vegetation and the women he saw on Mauritius and Reunion. Sufficiently so, indeed, to write a sonnet for a young couple he met on Mauritius. It was to be the first poem he published under the name of Baudelaire:

A UNE DAME CRÉOLE

Au pays parfumé que le soleil caresse,
J'ai connu, sous un dais d'arbres tout empourprés
Et de palmiers d'où pleut sur les yeux la paresse,
Une dame créole aux charmes ignorés.

Son teint est pâle et chaud; la brune enchanteresse
A dans le cou des airs noblement maniérés;
Grande et svelte en marchant comme une chasseresse,
Son sourire est tranquille et ses yeux assurés.

Si vous alliez, Madame, au vrai pays de gloire,
Sur les bords de la Seine ou de la verte Loire,
Belle digne d'orner les antiques manoirs,

Vous feriez, à l'abri des ombreuses retraites,
Germer mille sonnets dans le cœur des poètes,
Que vos grands yeux rendraient plus soumis que vos noirs.

(FM, LXI)

---

[1] W. T. Bandy and Claude Pichois, *Baudelaire devant ses contemporains* (Paris: Editions du Rocher, 1967), 59.

In a perfumed land where the sun loves to blaze,
And tamarinds' shade invites us to laze,
I saw beneath a dome of over arching palms
A Creole lady of nameless charms.

Her skin was pale and warm, and the brown enchantress
Had a bearing that spoke of noble and studied charm.
Tall and slim she walked like Diana the huntress,
Her smile tranquil and her eyes sure and calm.

Madame, were you to go to Glory's true domain,
By the green river Loire or the banks of the Seine,
Lovely and worthy of adorning the old halls,

Sheltered in their mossy retreats you'd inspire
A thousand sonneteers whose hearts you'd set afire,
And more than your Blacks you'd hold them in thrall.

Baudelaire returned to France, experiencing, as he recalls in his bio-bibliographical notes and as the ship's captain reported, a violent storm in the Azores. By mid-February 1842 he was back in Paris. The voyage had left him with memories of the tedium of shipboard life, as well as recollections of an exotic and luxuriant landscape that would from time to time enrich his poetry. But it also left him with the conviction that travel merely brought spectacles already seen at home, presented differently perhaps but essentially carrying the same message of human baseness and cupidity, of the corruption of power, and of the inescapable dominance of desire. Henceforth, at least until the last few years of his life, when he sought to avoid the constrictions of an increasingly difficult financial predicament by living in Belgium, his escape would take quite different forms, all of them powered to some degree by the imagination, either alone or in conjunction with artificial stimulants.

Returning home in 1842, Baudelaire faced an experience potentially far more tedious and far less easy to terminate than the sea voyage: conscription into the army. On March 3, 1842, he learnt, no doubt to his immense relief, that his number, 265, was high enough for him to escape this particular fate. (The conscripts that time were those who had drawn the number 211 or lower.)

Just over a month later, he attained his majority and was thus able at last to draw on the inheritance left to him by his father. He moved out of the family house and rented a sumptuous apartment on the Ile Saint-Louis. Charles Asselineau describes him as being lodged in lordly fashion in a historic house, "consecrated to the visits of several literary and artistic notables, where Théophile Gautier set the scene for one of his short stories, the Club of Hashish eaters."[2] Over the next few months he spent money so extravagantly—on works of art, fine furniture, and clothes—that he was forced, or at least chose, to sell the property at Neuilly that had been part of the inheritance. Alarmed, his family took the judicial step of setting up a "conseil de famille," which, having proved that over the eighteen months since he had attained his majority, Baudelaire had spent almost half of the hundred thousand francs he had inherited, was able to place the remaining funds in the care of a lawyer, Narcisse Ancelle. Henceforth, Ancelle would pay Baudelaire an allowance and occasionally cover some of his debts. The problem, as has often been pointed out, was that the *conseil de famille* failed to take into account that Baudelaire had not only spent money but had also borrowed, often at high interest rates, so that for the rest of his life he would face the exponentially increasing problem of raising money to cover the interest on a series of ill-judged loans. He himself took no part in the legal proceedings leading up to this solution, ignoring the summons to appear at the court, and angrily refusing to discuss his affairs before a "group of strangers," as he put it. In a long, at times bitter, letter written to his mother in 1861, Baudelaire recalled that at the time of the legal proceedings he had been in a "horrible state," a "resignation worse than fury," and insisted that as a result of the decisions taken then, he now found himself, where his honor was concerned, in a "frightful" situation. "Never any rest," he insists. "Insults, outrages, affronts you can't imagine, which corrupt the imagination and paralyze it" (L 169, CII 152).

Why did he put up no fight against the decision? Why not present his own case? Promise reform, as he had already done on numerous occasions and was to do so often again? Jean-Paul Sartre has argued that to a large extent the abject state in which Baudelaire was to find himself, the relative poverty inflicted on him for much of his life, was of his own choosing, in the strongest meaning of the term. In other words, the dual postulation that he considered was dominant in humanity (one towards good, the other towards evil) finds a parallel in his dual longing, on the one hand, for luxury, beauty, and works of art, and, on the other, for the bohemian existence of few possessions, no responsibilities, a sense of living outside a society he despised for its materialism. Baudelaire captures something of this ambiguity metaphorically in the prose poem "Perte d'auréole (Loss of a Halo):"

> "For heaven's sake! You here? You, in a den of vice! You, the drinker of quintessences! You the eater of ambrosia! Truly, it's enough to amaze me."
>
> "You know how horses and vehicles terrify me. A moment ago, as I was crossing the boulevard, in great haste, and hopping over the mud, through that moving chaos where death arrives at the gallop from all directions at once, my halo, in a sudden movement, slipped from my head and fell into the

---

[2] Crépet and Pichois, *Baudelaire et Asselineau* (Paris: Nizet, 1953), 66–67.

mire of the street. I didn't have the heart to pick it up. I thought it would be less disagreeable to lose my insignia than to break my bones. And then, I said to myself, it's an ill wind that blows no one any good. Now, I can stroll about incognito, perform despicable acts, indulge in the pleasures of the scum, just like ordinary mortals."

(PPP XLVI)

Escape into the despicable, into the scum, is at least as appealing to a poet of Baudelaire's complexity as escape into the exotic and the beautiful. It isn't, of course, quite as easy as knocking a halo off a head, and Baudelaire's letters rarely find that wonderful tone of disabused urbanity that dominates the prose poem.

In the dedication he wrote for *Les Paradis artificiels (The Artificial Paradises)*, his study on wine, hashish, and opium, Baudelaire affirms how good sense tells us that the things of this earth have only a very limited existence and that true reality can be found only in dream (I 399). "Good sense" is a provocation. It is entirely predictable that in an article of literary criticism he should castigate the self-proclaimed school of good sense, a sundry assortment of minor writers eager to batten on to bourgeois demands for literature to be moral and uplifting. There was, after all, a prize—the "Prix Monthyon"—for those works "most calculated to raise the morals of the people," while no prize existed for those exploring the seamy side of modern existence. What Baudelaire conceived in his dedication has of course nothing to do with philistine demands for art to serve a moralistic purpose. He is thinking of the kind of good sense that illuminates an artist's or a creative writer's vision of the world. The longing to understand and interpret the world and the individual's place within that world, a longing that drives much of his writing, leads him to turn to the imagination and dream as a vital means of comprehension and interpretation.

Imagination is a notoriously slippery and personal concept. Baudelaire takes time in his remarkable review of the Salon of 1859 to explore this notion, both specifically, in terms of art, and more generally, as he pays tribute to that "mysterious faculty" (II 620). Imagination, he argues, is connected to all our other faculties, arousing them and sending them into combat. At once synthesis and analysis, imagination is what binds together and sets up correspondences among the real, the possible, and the infinite. Most importantly, this passage suggests, although it does not state, that imagination works spontaneously to recreate reality, whereas artistic minds have to reproduce this recreation through an act of will: "Imagination unravels creation, and, using the materials gathered together and arranged according to rules whose origin can be found only in the deepest corners of the soul, it produces something that seems new" (II 621). In a letter to the editor and journalist Alphonse de Calonne, Baudelaire drew on a similar image to suggest the way in which dream functions. It is significant, moreover, that the letter dates from early 1860, a time when Baudelaire was working on his *Paradis artificiels*. "Dream," he explains in this letter, "separates and unravels, making *something new*" (L 151, CII 15). The parallel worlds that Baudelaire creates in both *Les Fleurs du mal* and the *Petits Poèmes en prose* are formed in much the same way that the piles of rubble on the building site of "Le Cygne (The Swan)" are rearranged to offer the allegories the poet needs in order to make sense of his rapidly changing world.

Dream is for him an enigmatic revelation, as infrequent and as difficult to decipher as the leaves that Nature's temple occasionally drops in the poem, "Correspondences." Much of the poetry that he most admires has the quality of dream, a quality captured only by a determined intellectual effort, the kind of willed effort that dream itself at worst precludes and at best saps. In extending this thinking, Baudelaire evokes the essence of Edgar Allan Poe's poetry in a formula that links dream both with mystery and with clarity: "It is something as profound and as shining as dream, as mysterious and perfect as crystal" (II 336). The French word I've translated here as "shining" is *miroitant,* a word openly revealing its etymological link with mirror. The dream sparkles, refracting light, but it also reflects, like a mirror, perhaps a distorting mirror, but one that in any case returns to the viewer the images projected onto it. To put it slightly differently, the word Baudelaire chooses, and that defies adequate translation into English, reverberates with meanings that open up the complexity of the concept of dreaming.

In his notebooks Baudelaire jotted down this poignant call to arms: "You have to want to dream and know how to dream. Evocation of inspiration. Magical art" (I 671–2). Art is itself a stimulus to dream. "Ovid among the Scythians," Eugène Delacroix's great evocation of exile, a theme in any case likely to appeal to Baudelaire, inspires the following reaction: "The mind sinks into it with slow and greedy pleasure, as if into the sky, or the horizon of the sea, or eyes brimming with thought, in a fertile and pregnant tendency to dream" (II 636). Indeed there is an extent to which Baudelaire judges works of art primarily by their power to inspire reverie.

Yet dream is in itself a source of dire danger to the writer, dazzling in its beauty and mystery, but undermining the energy and will-power needed to transform the ephemeral nature of dream into the permanence of the work of art or literature:

> Dreams! Never anything but dreams! And the more ambitious and delicate the soul, the further those dreams remove it from the possible. Each of us carries within us our own dose of natural opium, ceaselessly secreted, unendingly renewed, and from the hour of our birth to the hour of our death, how many hours can we count that have been filled with positive pleasure, with actions planned in advance and executed with success?
>
> (PPP XVIII)

While, as he argues in this prose poem, we all carry within us our own dose of natural opium, the temptation to deploy artificial means to provoke such revealing dreams was considerable. Two of the guiding figures in his career, Edgar Allan Poe and Thomas de Quincey, whose works Baudelaire knew with the particularly intimate familiarity that comes from translating them, are shaped in his presentation by his sense of them both as deriving much of their creative power from artificial intoxicants—alcohol in the case of Poe, opium in that of De Quincey—and as being destroyed by that dependency. Armand Fraisse, a public servant from Lyon who published some of the most sensitive articles on Baudelaire that appeared during the poet's lifetime, wrote to him in 1860, asking if he recommended experimenting with hashish and opium. Baudelaire's reply was categorical: "I urge you not to make any experiments in this regard. The *worst* that can happen is that you'll take *pleasure* in it. [. . .] I consider hashish as the more dangerous of the two substances. The entire danger can be summed up from my point of view in these words, "*a dwindling of the will-power*" (NL 31). He goes on to clarify this statement in the following terms: "I hold all stimulants in horror because of the way they amplify time and make things seem so vast. It's impossible to be a mere businessman, let alone a writer, if you live in a continuous spiritual orgy" (NL 32).

The amplification of time and space that he associates with these intoxicants is very much part of the world of imagination that Baudelaire depicts both in his study of the artificial stimulants and in his poetry. In this, he seems very close to De Quincey, whose work he discovered in the late 1850s. "The sense of space," writes De Quincey, "and in the end, the sense of time, were both powerfully affected. Buildings, landscapes, etc. were exhibited in proportions so vast as the bodily eye is not fitted to receive. Space swelled, and was amplified to an extent of unutterable infinity. This, however, did not disturb me so much as the vast expansion of time" (MO 185). A poem Baudelaire wrote in 1857, enigmatically entitled "Le Poison (Poison)," both affirms a sensation of the infinite extensibility of time and space, and simultaneously, through its rhythms, throws this affirmation into doubt. The very title, playing on the etymological and the current meanings of "poison," suggests a love potion as well as something lethal:

> L'opium agrandit ce qui n'a pas de bornes,
>> Allonge l'illimité,
> Approfondit le temps, creuse la volupté,
>> Et de plaisirs noirs et mornes
> Remplit l'âme au-delà de sa capacité.
>
> (FM XLIX)

> Opium extends what cannot be contained,
>> Expands what has no limits,
> Deepens time, intensifies rapture
>> And with dark, dismal pleasures
> Fills the soul beyond its capacity.

It is not just that the alexandrines, with their traditional caesura after the sixth syllable, carry with them a consciousness of limits; more telling is the way in which the claim that even the limitless can be expanded is ironically placed not in an alexandrine but in a six-syllable line. Typically, Baudelaire, as if wanting to have his cake and eat it too, then contradicts himself through the penultimate line's enjambment, allowing his thought to expand, thus offering a rhythmical parallel to the sense of rapture pouring into the soul until it can take no more.

Baudelaire knew only too well the addictive powers of these substances, not only from personal experience but also because of De Quincey's powerful evocation of the way in which opium both transforms space and time and destroys the addict's desire to do anything but dream. Yet part of the attraction and beauty of De Quincey's text is that it is driven by the desire to "reveal something of the grandeur which belongs *potentially* to human dreams" (MO 221). In the Confessions the desire to harness that potentiality becomes the dangerous intellectual justification for continuing to take the drug.

It is also the case that the articles Baudelaire devoted to the artificial stimulants allowed him ample opportunity to explore the nature of dreams. While no one reading these articles is likely to miss the intensity that comes of personal experience, there is a degree to which depicting the actual source of inspiration, or the precise cause of the dream, is less important than the analysis of differences in the types of dream and the study of the mechanisms of dream.

Like the Greeks, Virgil distinguished between dreams by suggesting the dreamer entered them either through doors of ivory or through doors of horn, according to whether they were dreams of truth or falsehood, a distinction Baudelaire's friend Nerval took up in his *Aurélia ou la vie et le rêve (Aurelia or Life and Dream)*. Dream, Nerval insists, is a second life, and his novella explores moments when dream overflows into real life. After a long series of dreams and dream-like experiences, his protagonist is left with the melancholy conviction that all that had happened to him had been done with the aim of teaching him "the secret of life," but he had misinterpreted the signs, had failed to decipher the dreams, and now it is too late.[3] The Romantic fascination with interpreting dreams as a series of symbols to be deciphered was no doubt familiar to Baudelaire, whose explorations recall those of several theorists of the time, notably the German writer Gotthilf Heinrich von Schubert. Schubert's *Symbolism of Dreams* offers a concept of the hieroglyphical nature of dream which is close to Baudelaire's, but since Baudelaire did not read German and Schubert's work was only partially translated, and even then in scattered publications, it is more likely that his images are imbued with current thinking without drawing on a specific source.

In his study of marijuana, written in prose but titled *Le Poème du hachisch (The*

---

[3] Gérard de Nerval, *Œuvres*, ed. Albert Béguin and Jean Richer (Paris: Gallimard, 1974), 392.

Poem of Hashish), Baudelaire divides dreams into two classes, those that merely combine in varying ways the dreamer's nature with his or her experiences, and those that appear to have no connection with the character, life, or passions of the sleeper. This dream world offers, in ways very similar to Nature, a dictionary to be studied, a language whose key must be sought. Baudelaire insists, however, that in dreams induced by hashish there is no such escape into a potentially significant experience. Hashish can act on the dreamer's nature and impressions only like a mirror that returns an enlarged or distorted image: it cannot transform that image. Wine, too, in Baudelaire's enthusiastic praise for this stimulant merely intensifies normal characteristics: "The bad man becomes execrable as the good man becomes excellent" (I 387).

His octosyllabic sonnet, "Le Vin des amants (The Wine of Lovers)," illustrates this egotistical tendency with particular eloquence:

Aujourd'hui l'espace est splendide!
Sans mors, sans éperons, sans bride,
Partons à cheval sur le vin
Pour un ciel féerique et divin!

Comme deux anges que torture
Une implacable calenture,
Dans le bleu cristal du matin
Suivons le mirage lointain!

Mollement balancés sur l'aile
Du tourbillon intelligent,
Dans un délire parallèle,

Ma sœur, côte à côte nageant,
Nous fuirons sans repos ni trêves
Vers le paradis de mes rêves!

(FM CVIII)

How wonderful the world today!
With nothing to stop nor drive nor stay
Let's gallop off, astride our wine,
For a sky fantastic and divine.

Like two angels tormented and tried
By a fever that cannot be pacified

Into dawn's blue crystal light
Pursue the mirage in our flight!

Loosely lulled by the steady beat
Of an intelligent whirlwind fleet
Each in our own hallucination

Sister, swimming in parallel streams,
We'll flee without respite or recreation
To the paradise of my dreams!

The sensation of speed and inevitability is created in part by the choice of eight rather than twelve syllables to the line, and is increased by the couplets of the quatrains which enhance the sense of forward progression, where crossed or embraced rhymes with their echoes, delays, and backward glances would have tended to slow down the movement of the thought. The speed and joy of the poem's opening, also signaled visually by exclamation marks, stop abruptly at the volta, the change of direction frequently encountered in a sonnet, which here as so often is situated between the quatrains and the tercets. The quatrains speak of the lovers' identity, since both are tortured by an unrelenting fever, and both are following the far-off mirage into the crystal blue of morning. But the winged horse on which they ride is that of wine, and if we know from reading Baudelaire that the spectacles of wine are great, illuminated by the inner sun, we also know their sequels: "How redoubtable, too, are its crushing pleasures and enervating enchantments" (I 379). The word "mollement" (feebly) which opens the tercets abruptly slows this movement down and inaugurates a series of words which are relatively difficult to pronounce and even more so if one is drunk, words that are further remarkable by a proliferation of the letter *l*. The lovers who had set out astride wine, riding the Pegasus of wine, now find themselves, having abdicated their own intelligence to accept delirium, "balancés sur l'aile / Du tourbillon intelligent" (literally: carried on the wing of the intelligent whirlwind—Norman R. Shapiro nicely suggests: "Lulled on the cunning whirlwind's wing"). They no longer form a couple, since their delirium is parallel, and as we all know, parallel lines meet only at infinity. Moreover, the *we* of the quatrains is replaced here by the *she* created by the alliteration and the rhyme (*aile parallèle* releasing the homophonous "elle") as it is replaced in the second tercet by the first person singular, "my sister" being invited to flee no longer towards the paradise of *our* dreams, but rather to the paradise of *my* dreams. And if the reader were tempted to see in the fact that the poem ends on the word *dream* any justification for an optimistic reading, the rhyme and the alliteration never allow us to forget that a dream that has to be pursued without rest or respite quickly becomes a nightmare.

Like wine, opium, at least in Thomas De Quincey's view, has a particular power to increase the natural faculty for dreaming, though it too is dependent on the nature of the dreamer. "He whose talk is of oxen," affirms De Quincey in a passage Baudelaire does not translate, "will probably dream of oxen." As we have seen, De Quincey's stated aim in writing the confessions was first "to reveal something of the grandeur which belongs *potentially* to human dreams" and secondly to show the power of opium in assisting the faculty of dreaming, its ability not merely for "exalting the colors of dream-scenery but for deepening its shadows" (MO 221). But to discover these colors and shadows we need not only a "constitutional determination to reverie" but also a meditative habit, an ability to withdraw from the dissipation of contemporary life. And he adds in a typically powerful formulation: "No man ever will unfold the capacities of his own intellect who does not at least checker his life with solitude" (MO 221). Baudelaire, only too keenly aware of the dangers posed by the vaporization of the self, expresses this need in such prose poems as "Solitude," the counterpart to "Les Foules (The Crowds)."

De Quincey offered Baudelaire a further image he clearly found stimulating: "What else," the English opium-eater asks, "than a natural and mighty palimpsest is the human brain?" (MO, 241). The palimpsest, the parchment written over many times and thus containing multiple texts, offers a particularly rich image for the imagination and for memory. Navigating through that palimpsest was in large part facilitated by the artificial intoxicants and in particular by dream. Baudelaire suggests that it was in order to experience again the kinds of chains of coincidence or simply of images that are encountered in dreams that Poe sought inspiration in intoxication. He asserts in his study *Edgar Poe, sa vie et ses ouvrages (Edgar Poe, his life and works)*:

> There exist in drunkenness not only chains of dreams, but whole series of reasoning which if they are to be reproduced demand the environment that gave them birth. Readers who have followed me without repugnance will have guessed my conclusion already: I believe that in many cases, though certainly not all, Poe's drunkenness was a mnemonic, a method of work, an energetic and deadly method, but one suited to his passionate nature. The poet had learned to drink as a careful writer fills notebooks with observations.
>
> (II 315)

Here, as in the writings on nature, Baudelaire uses the word *mnemonic,* yoking together inspiration and memory, and suggesting yet another way in which inspiration finds sustenance. Catching that memory and giving it permanent form demands in all cases a rapidity of execution and a determined act of will, neither of them possible if the poet is debilitated by the very means through which he has activated the mnemonic device. This is part of what gives an element of the tragic to Baudelaire's modernist vision, not just the sense of fragility and exile, of flux and contingency, but the conviction that the ability to confer permanence on the ephemeral is forever lost—not because of a fatal flaw within the poet him or herself, which would be closer to the thinking of Romanticism, but because of something done and often knowingly done in order precisely to find a means of overcoming contingency.

When Baudelaire explores this theme in relation to Poe and De Quincey, his mood is somber and the keynote of the articles is that of a dark personal tragedy, set against the splendors of the artistic creation. When he investigates the same theme through an anonymous figure, albeit one closely resembling Baudelaire himself, the tone is far less bleak. For example, Baudelaire's novella *La Fanfarlo* explores the tendency to dream and to replace action with reverie, but here, in a work of the poet's youth, the theme is treated very much in mocking vein. Depicting his hero, Samuel Cramer, Baudelaire snidely notes: "One of Samuel's most natural flaws was to consider himself the equal of those he had admired; after passionately reading a fine book, his involuntary conclusion was 'now there's something beautiful enough to be by me'—and from there to thinking: 'so it is by me!'—is only the space of a dash."[4] The same tendency to conflate intention and action can be found in several Baudelairean protagonists. The prose poem "Les Projets (Plans)," for instance, shows a lover dreaming up a series of settings for his beloved: in a luxurious palace, in a tropical landscape, in a tidy little inn. His conclusion is steeped in irony:

> And as he went home alone, at the hour when the voice of Wisdom is no longer silenced by the hum of external life, he said to himself: "Today I have had, in imagination, three homes, each of which has given me equal pleasure. Why force my body to move from place to place, since my soul can travel so nimbly? And why turn plan into reality, when the plan is in itself sufficient pleasure?"
>
> (PPP XXIV)

Of course, given Baudelaire's assertion that one of the unacknowledged rights of the individual was that of self-contradiction, he also insists elsewhere that "he would for his part be happy to leave a world in which action is not the sister of dream" (FM CXVIII).

Several of Baudelaire's poems and prose poems illustrate not only the faculty of dreaming splendidly but also the bizarre logic of dreams. Before exploring them, however, we should look briefly at a dream he claims to have had and that he described in considerable detail for his friend Charles Asselineau. It is not surprising that he should have sent it to Asselineau, for in an article reviewing a collection of short stories the latter had published under the significant title *La Double Vie* (*The Double Life*), Baudelaire praised him not only for his deep understanding but also

---

[4] Baudelaire, *The Prose Poems and La Fanfarlo,* trans. and ed. Rosemary Lloyd (Oxford: Oxford University Press, 1991), 2.

for his description of the absurd and the improbable. "He seizes and traces out, sometimes with rigorous fidelity, the strange reasoning of dream," Baudelaire noted in the review (II 89). The dream Baudelaire described for his friend has been analyzed in considerable detail by the novelist and essay writer Michel Butor, who, in homage to Baudelaire's translations of Poe, called the work in which he published his description *Histoire extraordinaire* (*Extraordinary Story*). The dream Baudelaire recounts suggests, in a somewhat pedestrian manner when compared with his creative representations of dream, the extent to which dream offers an escape or more precisely an outlet for fears, hopes, sources of dismay or embarrassment. In the dream, Baudelaire sees himself sharing a carriage with the journalist and novelist Hippolyte Castille. Leaving Castille, he visits a brothel, where he plans to give the Madam a copy of his book. He is embarrassed to find not only that his flies are open but also that his feet are bare. Climbing the stairs, he completely forgets about the book, as he notes in commenting on the dream, and wanders through the many galleries that make up this curious brothel. The walls are covered with paintings and prints, some of them representing strange monsters who are the aborted fetuses of the prostitutes. He realizes that of all the Parisian papers only *Le Siècle,* a newspaper that declared itself dedicated to progress, knowledge, and the diffusion of enlightenment, could imagine a brothel that would also be a museum of science. Typically, he draws the conclusion that "modern stupidity and folly have their mysterious usefulness and that often what has been created for purposes of evil, turns, through some spiritual mechanism, to good" (L 82, CI 340). The tendency to draw a moral from the situations encountered in a modern city is characteristic of Baudelaire, and is what gives his prose poems in particular their unique blend of observation and commentary, the sense that the most random of events offers itself to interpretation. Among all the strange embryos, there is, he tells us, one that did indeed survive, a monster standing on a pedestal. The creature is described in some detail, especially the long dark appendage that falls from his head and that he wraps around his limbs. The creature and the poet talk, and the monster describes how much he suffers at mealtimes, when he is obliged to eat with the prostitutes, keeping his appendage carefully wrapped around him.

It is not my purpose here to enter into an analysis of this dream, which Baudelaire attributes in part to the strangely twisted position in which he was sleeping, a position that suggested to him the image of the twisted monster. Baudelaire himself introduces the dream by saying that this is the kind of vision that "always encourages me to believe that dreams are an almost hieroglyphic language to which I do not hold the key" (Letter 81, CI 338). While it would no doubt be interesting to attempt to find the key, as Butor has set out to do, it is more important for my purposes to note the degree to which this dream, with its abrupt changes of scene and its blend of the illogical—the need to give the Madam a copy of the book, for instance, together with the act of forgetting it—and the apparently logical—the rationally-formed though sardonic conclusion that only *Le Siècle* could create such a blend of brothel and museum—is both much more familiar and much more humdrum than the dreams evoked in his poetry. Indeed, the dreams of Baudelaire's creative writing seem to belong to a quite different world from this one, a world that offers a more coherent inner logic and provides a more powerful means of escape. Art, for Baudelaire, is never just the raw materials drawn from personal experiences, but always the transmutation of that base matter into a finer metal. But such transmutation requires a liberation of the imagination.

Releasing the imagination from the shackles of the everyday demands a multiplicity of approaches. Sometimes the mind seems miraculously clear, capable of seeing into the heart of things, able to decipher that mighty palimpsest that De Quincey offers us as an image of the human brain (MO 241). "There are days," Baudelaire writes in his *Poème du hachisch,* "when you wake with a young and vigorous genius," days when the external world offers itself in powerful relief, its contours remarkably clear, its colors admirably bright, days when you feel more artistic and more unprejudiced, "more noble, in a word" (I 401). The question is how to provoke such exceptional experiences at will, how to ensure that clarity that allows you to read the moral dimensions of existence with such power. Wine, hashish, opium—all these are explored in many of Baudelaire's finest texts as means of enabling and stimulating dream and reverie, sharpened and expanded by what he describes as the queen of faculties, the imagination. But all of them, as he frequently insists, carry with them a destructive power that may ironically leave the writer incapable of giving permanent form to the fleeting visions and insights they have procured. As he puts it in his *Poème du hachisch,* "human vices, however full of horror one might suppose them to be, contain the proof (if only in their infinite expansion!) of the longing for the infinite; but it is a longing that often takes the wrong path" (I 402). Expansion and concentration are a further set of polar opposites in Baudelaire's dualistic vision of the world and of human nature, each presented in his poetry as capable of causing fierce raptures and profound despair. The problem is that the moments of profound insight arise apparently randomly—Baudelaire associates them with the Catholic concept of grace—and can be stimulated by debauchery just as much as by purity. He argues:

> It is certain that a constant elevation of longing, a tension of your spiritual forces toward the heavens, would appear to be the regime most likely to create that moral health, which is so dazzling and so glorious; but what is the absurd law that decrees that such health sometimes occurs after the culpable orgies of the imagination, after reason has been abused through sophistry, an abuse of its honest and reasonable employment that would be like dislocating the body instead of using healthy gymnastic exercises?
>
> (I 401–2)

Hence, of course, the attraction of indulging in those "culpable orgies." The reasoning of addiction is clearly legible here, counterbalanced by Baudelaire's insistence that one of the aims of his study of the artificial stimulants is precisely to reveal "the immorality implied in the very pursuit of a false ideal" (I 403). The intensity of the experience of intoxication—and here the source hardly matters, since what Baudelaire is evoking is a state of sharply heightened awareness—allows a deeper sense of color and shape, a conviction that the allegorical nature of the world offers itself with all its pleasures and with key in hand. But, as Baudelaire acknowledges, after the heights of intoxication, after the conviction not just that the thinker has attained complete understanding of the universe but that he or she is indeed a god, comes "the terrible day after" (I 437). And with the day after, the recognition that while imagination, especially, perhaps, heightened through such artificial aids, is the queen of faculties, the most precious of all faculties is undoubtedly will-power, and will-power is what is primarily attacked by such attempts to escape. You are left with "the imagination shorn of the ability to make use of it" (I 440).

It is part of Baudelaire's complex personality, part, too, of the intricate modes of his inspiration, that he should take such an apparently unpromising situation and transform it into poetry. The relationship between what might be seen as his critical and his creative writing is indeed as complex and intricate as the thyrsus he describes in one of his prose poems. The sharp contrasts between the world seen through the mirror of intoxication and the world of the day after reappear in his prose poem "La Chambre double (The Double Room)," whose very title carries that sense of two worlds superimposed on each other, each apparently commenting on the other, but in ways so steeped in allegory and even more in irony as to render any one-for-one equivalence impossible. The prose poem opens by depicting a world of heightened pleasures, a room that resembles a reverie, a room that resembles even more the transformations resulting from a reverie induced by one of the artificial intoxicants. The title, however, warns us that this room has another side to it, since reverie is only one part of existence and is constantly threatened by the irruption of everyday reality. In the room's ideal manifestation, everything speaks to the imagination, offering a kind of dictionary that seems easily understood, as though here at last inner and outer worlds have combined in perfect harmony. The very furniture in the room seems to dream, its shapes transformed by the power of reverie. The materials themselves speak a silent language like the language of flowers, the language the narrator of "Elévation" (one of the early poems of *Les Fleurs du mal*) believed he understood. Here we feel that transforming power of the inner eye, capable of bestowing on everything "the complement of beauty that it lacked, thus enabling it to become truly capable of causing delight" (I 431). The "Idol," the beloved, is also present, brought by some unknown and mysterious demon or magic power. But the fragility of this sense of rapture is suddenly made evident, for in the very act of asserting that he not only holds the key to this "supreme existence" but that he savors it minute by minute, second by second, the dreamer has allowed the concept of time and thus of limits to enter his double room. He may attempt to undo the damage with the affirmation that time has disappeared and that "Eternity reigns, an eternity of delights," but the strange alchemy of the artificial reverie is about to transform gold into iron, as Baudelaire puts it in his poem "Alchimie de la douleur (Grief's alchemy)." The eternal enemy, Time, depicted in "Le Voyage" as the fighter equipped with the net in the Roman gladiatorial contests, surges triumphantly back into the room, bringing with him the trivial demands and exigencies of the quotidian. Now the eternity that holds sway is one of boredom and ugliness, the perfume that seemed otherworldly is merely that of stale tobacco and nauseating damp, and whereas the dream room contained no artistic representations, leaving the imagination free to wander, now the traces of mundane reality are everywhere, in the tracks the rain has left on the filthy windows, on the calendar marked with its sinister dates, on the pile of incomplete and crossed-out manuscripts. The idol is revealed as a flask of laudanum, a derivative of opium, which the poet describes as being "an old and terrible female friend," and like all female friends, "abounding in caresses and betrayals" (PPP V). But if time has returned, bringing with it the harsh demands, limitations, and disappointments of reality, it is also time that enables the poet to write, for in the dream world he was held subjugated by the idol's subtle and terrifying gaze.

Baudelaire makes the same point in his study of hashish when he compares the drug to sorcery and magic, since all three attempt to "suppress the work of time" (I 439). Moreover, the moral opprobrium that attaches to these means of escape also applies to "all those modern inventions that attempt to diminish human freedom and the indispensable element of suffering" (I 439). It is too easy to depict Baudelaire as insouciantly amoral, dependent on drugs, and careless of the effect on his mind and faculties of his attempts to escape reality. On the contrary, he is, as he often claimed, a highly moral voice, but one whose morality is deeply rooted in personal experience and that is in no way constrained by accepted and conventional social or Christian values.

The exploration of the ways in which artificial stimulants shape the imagination also informs the poem entitled "Rêve parisien (Parisian Dream)," which again offers the kind of stark yet enabling contrast between dream and reality that we find in "The Double Room." Even more than the prose poem, however, this verse poem expands on the adage jotted down in the series of notes entitled "Hygiène:" "You have to want to dream and know how to dream" (I 671–2). The ways in which dream and the imagination unravel reality and thus create something radically new is admirably illustrated in this poem, which, as Claude Pichois contends in his notes to the Pléiade edition, is at once poem and poetics, meditation on how to write and what is written. Felix Leakey has suggested that the poem finds its initial inspiration in a painting that Baudelaire could have seen at the Paris World Fair of 1855.[5] Baudelaire describes this painting, by the British artist Henry Edward Kendall, in his study of Théophile Gautier, and then repeats the passage in his account of the Salon of 1859. The artist is evoked as a "pensive architect, building on paper, cities whose bridges, in lieu of pillars, have elephants that allow to pass between their legs gigantic three-masters under full sail" (II 123). Certainly architectural fantasies such as these and those of the Italian artist Piranesi may well have helped shape Baudelaire's thinking. Perhaps Baron Haussmann's construction of a new Paris may have goaded Baudelaire into meditating on better or at least more imaginative solutions. Literary influences have also been suggested, including Poe and De Quincey. And there are certainly strong parallels with the dreams of water he associates with the intoxication caused by hashish. Here he is referring specifically to an early phase in the unfolding of the kind of intoxication induced by hashish:

> It is also to this essentially pleasure-filled and sensual phase that belongs the love of limpid water, water that is flowing or standing, a love that has reached such astonishing dimensions in the cerebral intoxication of certain artists. Mirrors become a pretext for this reverie, which resembles a spiritual thirst, linked to that physical thirst that dries out the throat and that I have already mentioned. Swiftly flowing water, fountains, harmonious cascades, the immense blue expanse of the sea, roll, sing, and sleep with an inexpressible charm.
>
> (I 431)

Clearly Baudelaire has drawn on a variety of different experiences and sources of inspiration. The great man, as he says elsewhere, does not suddenly arrive on earth like a meteorite but is always announced by predecessors; yet what really counts here is how he has fused those sources together to create the luminous impression of a dream:

RÊVE PARISIEN

A Constantin Guys

De ce terrible paysage,
Tel que jamais mortel n'en vit,
Ce matin encore l'image,
Vague et lointaine, me ravit.

Le sommeil est plein de miracles!
Par un caprice singulier,

[5] Felix Leakey, "Baudelaire and Kendall," *Revue de littérature comparée* (1956): 53–63.

J'avais banni de ces spectacles
Le végétal irrégulier,

Et, peintre fier de mon génie,
Je savourais dans mon tableau
L'enivrante monotonie
Du métal, du marbre et de l'eau.

Babel d'escaliers et d'arcades,
C'était un palais infini,
Plein de bassins et de cascades
Tombant dans l'or mat ou bruni;

Et des cataractes pesantes,
Comme des rideaux de cristal,
Se suspendaient, éblouissantes,
A des murailles de métal.

Non d'arbres, mais de colonnades
Les étangs dormants s'entouraient,
Où de gigantesques naïades,
Comme des femmes, se miraient.

Des nappes d'eau s'épanchaient, bleues,
Entre des quais roses et verts,
Pendant des millions de lieues,
Vers les confins de l'univers;

C'étaient des pierres inouïes
Et des flots magiques; c'étaient
D'immenses glaces éblouies
Par tout ce qu'elles reflétaient!

Insouciants et taciturnes,
Des Ganges, dans le firmament,
Versaient le trésor de leurs urnes
Dans des gouffres de diamant.

Architecte de mes féeries,
Je faisais, à ma volonté,

Sous un tunnel de pierreries
Passer un océan dompté;

Et tout, même la couleur noire,
Semblait fourbi, clair, irisé;
Le liquide enchâssait sa gloire
Dans le rayon cristallisé.

Nul astre d'ailleurs, nuls vestiges
De soleil, même au bas du ciel,
Pour illuminer ces prodiges,
Qui brillaient d'un feu personnel!

Et sur ces mouvantes merveilles
Planait (terrible nouveauté!
Tout pour l'œil, rien pour les oreilles!)
Un silence d'éternité.

II

En rouvrant mes yeux pleins de flamme
J'ai vu l'horreur de mon taudis,
Et senti, rentrant dans mon âme,
La pointe des soucis maudits;

La pendule aux accents funèbres
Sonnait brutalement midi,
Et le ciel versait des ténèbres
Sur le triste monde engourdi.

PARISIAN DREAM

For Constantin Guys

I

A landscape terrible and strange—
No mortal ever saw such sight—
Though vague and distant still this morning
Remains in memory to delight.

How full of miracles is sleep!
Through my fantastic coquetry

I had banished from the view
Growing things' asymmetry,

Artist delighting in my gifts,
I savored as its sole creator,
Enthralling uniformity
Of metal, marble and of water.

Babel of stairways and arcades
This palace filled a space untold,
Rich in pools and waterfalls,
Tumbling in dull or burnished gold,

And there were heavy cataracts
Like hanging curtains all of crystal,
Whose dazzling drapes fell slowly down
Over sheer metallic walls.

Not trees but colonnades surrounded
Pools of water all quiescent,
Where naiads of gigantic size
Like women gazed on their reflection.

Sheets of water spread out, blue,
Between the quays of pink and green,
Flowing for miles on endless miles
Towards the universe's rim;

Stones that none before had seen,
And magic streams; and also present
Mighty mirrors all bedazzled
By everything that they reflected!

Insouciant and taciturn
These Ganges in the firmament
Poured the treasure of their urns
Into gulfs of diamond.

Architect of my fairylands
I sent, according to my will,

An ocean that moved at my command
Through a tunnel of gems and jewels.

Everything, even the color black,
Seemed polished, clear and rainbow bright.
Within the rays of crystal glow
The liquid set its haloed light.

No star, what's more, nor yet no trace
Of Sun, not even sinking in its pyre,
To send its light and rays upon
These marvels glowing with inner fire!

And over all these moving marvels
Hovered (a terrible novelty!
For all was seen and nothing heard!)
A silence of eternity.

II

Opening eyes still full of flame
I saw my hovel's horror there,
And felt, going deep into my soul,
The knife blade of accursèd cares;

The clock with its funereal voice
The brutal chimes of noonday tolled,
And the sky poured down its murky dark
Over the sad and weary world.

The structure of the escape seems pretty clear: setting out on the inspiration of wine or hashish, opium or art, the poet induces a dream of powerful splendor that abruptly ends, dropping him back into a bleak, grim world of limits and constraints. Those limits seem all the more constricting in comparison with the vast and unearthly beauties just conjured up, the play of light on liquid, the strangely tactile quality of the water the poem evokes for us, the eerie and yet profoundly appropriate absence of any sounds, the sense of infinite space and time against which the architecture imposes its meaning. But there is a gritty courage in Baudelaire's determined response and in his refusal to let himself be overwhelmed by the dull realities of the daily routine. He not only finds a means of giving permanent expression to the fleeting visions; he analyses their causes and seeks out the esthetic lessons that can be extracted from them.

All of which might sound extremely serious. Indeed comedy is not necessarily the first association one might have with Baudelaire. And yet, his prose poetry—a genre after all capable of including powerful beauty and rapture and melancholy but also ideal for outbursts of humor and the twists of irony—does include examples of dreams which are not only witty in themselves but which lead to humorous assessments on the part of the self-mocking narrator. "Le Joueur généreux (The Generous Gambler)," moreover, sheds light on yet another means of escape that holds out temptations for our poet, or at least for the individuals that inhabit his imaginary universe: gambling.

What is at issue here is not the vulgar expectation of making a rapid fortune, but far more powerfully, far more originally, the suggestion that gamblers concentrate so intently on the game, focus so sharply on the draw of the cards or the fall of the dice, that they are lost to the world around them, have escaped the quotidian. Baudelaire had already depicted them in one of the poems in *Tableaux parisiens*, "Le Jeu (Gambling)," which he designates as a "nocturnal dream":

[. . .]
Autour des verts tapis des visages sans lèvre,
Des lèvres sans couleur, des mâchoires sans dent,
Et des doigts convulsés d'une infernale fièvre,
Fouillant la poche vide ou le sein palpitant;

Sous de sales plafonds un rang de pâles lustres
Et d'énormes quinquets projetant leurs lueurs
Sur des fronts ténébreux de poètes illustres
Qui viennent gaspiller leurs sanglantes sueurs;

Voilà le noir tableau qu'en un rêve nocturne
Je vis se dérouler sous mon œil clairvoyant,
Moi-Même, dans un coin de l'antre taciturne,
Je me vis accoudé, froid, muet, enviant,

Enviant de ces gens la passion tenace [. . .]

(FM XCVI)

Around green cloths are lipless faces,
Colorless lips, and toothless jaws;
Fingers convulsed by an endless fever
Search empty pockets, clutch pounding hearts;

Under dirty ceilings a row of pale lights
Huge oil lamps casting their glow

On the shadowy brows of illustrious poets
Who come here to waste their blood and their sweat;

That's the black picture that in a nocturnal dream
My clear-sighted eyes could watch unfolding:
Myself, in a corner of the silent lair,
I saw myself leaning, cold, silent and envying

Envying those people and their tenacious passions.

The theme finds a lighter touch in "Le Joueur généreux (The Generous Gambler)," which provides its own whimsical take on the Faust legend. Goethe's Faust, in the play that Baudelaire's friend Nerval translated into French, makes a pact with the devil's henchman Mephistopheles that in exchange for his soul he will receive, for a necessarily limited period, whatever his heart desires. Christopher Marlowe's version of the legend shows even more clearly than Goethe's how difficult it is, in such a situation, to desire anything worth the loss of a soul, and how frivolous any such desire will inevitably seem. Baudelaire plays beautifully with this unglamorous truth in ways that cast light back on the emptiness of the artificial paradises, which may in De Quincey's terms offer an intensification of the power of dreaming splendidly, but which exact in payment a sapping of the will-power needed to transcribe those very dreams.

In this prose poem, Baudelaire's narrator, as ever a man of the crowds, is strolling along the boulevard when he suddenly finds himself in the presence of a "mysterious Being," one he had long wanted to meet. What is more, the narrator announces with a comic insouciance, the mysterious Being seems to have been just as eager to meet him. There is no fire and brimstone, and certainly nothing of the beautiful melancholy of Romanticism's Satan, but for all that there is a powerful sense here of who is master, since the Being sends our narrator a meaningful glance, which he hastily obeys. In the somber but splendid gambling den to which he is led, the narrator encounters the same exquisite scents and the same pleasurable lethargy as the lotus eaters described by Tennyson when "they came unto a land where it seemed always afternoon."[6] Looking at the gamblers, the narrator finds not the lipless and toothless caricatures of the verse poem, but faces marked with a fatal beauty and eyes gleaming energetically with the "horror of boredom and the immortal longing to feel they were alive" (PPP XXIX). Over the course of a lengthy meal, the narrator and his new friend, drinking steadily, although, so the narrator believes, unaffected by the alcohol, play several hands, during which the narrator "with heroic indiffer-

---

[6] Alfred Lord Tennyson, "The Lotus Eaters," *In Memoriam, Maud and Other Poems,* ed. John D. Jump (London: J. Dent and Sons, 1974), 22.

ence" pledges and loses his soul. But, he says, "the soul is so impalpable, so often of no use and sometimes such a nuisance, that, where this loss was concerned, he felt rather less emotion than if, on a stroll, he had lost his visiting card." They chat urbanely of this and that, including the absurdity of progress, and as the night wears on, the Devil, in order, so he says, to prove he can sometimes be a pleasant old devil, offers his gambling partner something to make up for the irremediable loss of his soul:

> Never will you formulate a desire without my helping you to achieve it; you will reign over your vulgar peers; you will have flattery and even adoration heaped upon you; silver, gold, diamonds, fairy-tale palaces, all these will come in search of you and beg you to accept them, without your making the slightest effort to earn them; you'll change home and country as often as the fantasy takes you; you will grow drunk on pleasures, unwearyingly, in charming lands where it's always warm and where the women smell as good as the flowers,—et cetera, et cetera. . . .

It gives it all away, doesn't it, that *et cetera?* And indeed, the narrator's high hopes and deep gratitude gradually evaporate, so that when he goes to bed, he forgets that he no longer has the right to pray, and sleepily begs the good Lord: "Dear God! Lord God! Make the devil keep his promise to me."

The fear that the devil might not keep his promise could well serve as a summary of the dilemma posed by the attempt to escape from the human condition, an escape made all the more desirable for a poet seeking to break into new realms of experience, emotion, and thought.

Baudelaire always recognizes that kind of escape, through dream or through art, as a lie, but it is this lie that gives the great creative works their power and their essential truth. As Baudelaire unforgettably argues in his review of landscape paintings exhibited in one of the annual art salons: "I want to be taken back to those dioramas whose brutal and enormous magic is able to impose upon me a useful illusion. I prefer to contemplate theater sets where I find my dearest dreams artistically expressed and tragically concentrated. These things, because they are false, are infinitely closer to truth: whereas the majority of our landscape painters are liars, precisely because they neglect to lie" (II 668).

CHAPTER SIX

Mundus Muliebris
The World of Women

Andromache surges into the poet's mind in "Le Cygne (The Swan)" as exile and as widow but also more straightforwardly as woman. Her grief for the loss of Hector would be less powerful if Baudelaire presented it merely in terms of loss of status and homeland. The second half of "Le Cygne," where the disparate bric-a-brac of memory is pulled together to form the allegory of loss, makes it abundantly clear that we are to see Andromache's grief as going beyond the despair caused by a loss of power or dignity. She is bowed down in ecstasy before Hector's empty tomb. Ecstasy here has its full weight: she has left the world of the senses through the powerful force of a mystical experience, in this case, the desire to find union once more with her great husband. The fusion of the beloved with the lover is for Baudelaire always a state to be remembered, to be longed for, or to be experienced only as a fleeting moment. His great love poems draw much of their poignancy from the urgent sense they convey that union is at worst delusion and at best ephemeral.

It is traditional to refer to the three love cycles in *Spleen et Idéal* (one is tempted to say embedded within this first book of *Les Fleurs du mal*) as being "dedicated" to three particular women in the poet's life. Of course, they are nothing of the sort. Between the women the poems evoke and the women Baudelaire knew in boarding rooms or salons, whom he had glimpsed in the street or gazed at on the stage, with whom he'd enjoyed unions of the mind or the body, the connections are tenuous in the extreme. "Woman," he remarks in the dedication to his study of artificial paradises, "is the being who projects the greatest shadow or the greatest light into our dreams. Woman is fatally suggestive; she leads another life in addition to her own; she lives spiritually in the imaginations she haunts and fertilizes" (I 399). Reading this line as a woman—remembering the study is dedicated to a woman—produces a provocative stumbling block, provocative in that it reveals that what Baudelaire is talking about is, of course, not woman so much as passion, seduction, and love. Call it what you will, but recognize that the term needs an imaginative translation. Similarly, it is not important for these purposes to be able to show that Baudelaire did actually experience any of the feelings or live through any of the emotions he conveys in his poetry. The essence here is in the power of conviction.

You gave me your mud, the poet says to Paris in an unfinished epilogue, and I turned it into gold. The flesh and blood women he encountered delighted or irritated, enchanted or goaded him into his long exploration of sexual passion, but the exploration itself is the alchemist's transubstantiation of metal into miracle. Three women, in particular, provided the raw material: Jeanne Duval, whom he first encountered in the early 1840s (when he was living on the Ile Saint Louis) and whose often exasperating presence threads its unpredictable way through his letters right to the bitter end; Aglaé-Apollonie Sabatier, whom he molded into a figure he could idolize, but who is better known to literary scholars as the recipient of an extraordinarily erotic letter written by the poet, Théophile Gautier; and the actress, Marie Daubrun, who was for some time Théodore de Banville's mistress. Relationships, such as they were, with the last two were brief. From the mid 1850s, he presents his relationship with Jeanne as one more of duty and charity than love or passion, but after all, he says this in a letter to his mother. There is little in the record as it stands, the letters, the diaries, the remarks and assessments of contemporaries, to suggest that Baudelaire was willing to work at either love or friendship. What we have is much more the image of an essentially lonely person, who savored in isolation the recollection of moments of passion or pleasure. In any case, whatever the reality of his love affairs, it is clear that the relationship that most mattered to him, most shaped and doubtless most stunted him, was that with his mother. And even then, the figure he created in his mind is hard to reconcile with the flesh and blood woman. Better here to focus on the verse and prose poems themselves, their place within the collections, the echoes and reverberations set in train by the poems around them, and to widen an understanding of Baudelaire's vision of women by remembering also all those other poems, where women are not lovers, but beggars or victims, bowed over with old age or sorrow, suffering in childbirth or wasting away with tuberculosis, emblems of human greed, or folly, or boundless ambition.

In his twenties he wrote a series of what he termed consoling maxims on love, following very much in the footsteps of such cynical and witty writers as Stendhal and his *De l'amour* (*On Love*), and Balzac, whose *Physiologie du marriage* (*Physiology of Marriage*) was inspired by Stendhal. Baudelaire's maxims are little more than an amusing pastiche of his predecessors, a clever pirouette written in part to embarrass his rather stuffy step-brother Claude-Alphonse Baudelaire, and particularly the latter's wife, with whom he pretended to be wildly in love. Only occasionally are there brief flashes of something like the later Baudelaire, as in the following suggestion:

"For certain more curious and more world-weary minds there is a delight to be found in ugliness, a delight stemming from a feeling more mysterious still which is the thirst for the unknown and the taste for the horrible" (I 548–49).

With the exception of this little finger exercise, what makes Baudelaire different from almost all his contemporaries is that the women in his poetry are so often distinctively individual, not mere outgrowths of the writer's own desire. The narrative voices in the prose poetry, like the lyric "I" in the verse poems, may seek to deny that individuality, may want to impose their own personalities and their own judgments, may enjoin them to be beautiful and hold their peace, but they cannot make these women fade into the stereotypes produced by so many of Baudelaire's contemporaries. Nerval's love poetry derives its beauty from the degree to which it is steeped in nostalgia and from the sense that, as he puts it in his short novel *Sylvie,* an idealized woman seen close up revolted the lover's naivety. As he asserts in his exploration of Constantin Guys, Baudelaire may well prefer woman adorned, made up and dressed in ways that create what he recognizes and prizes as the artificiality of beauty, the dandyism he also values in men, but the task of creating that image is one he, as artist, admires, whereas Nerval prefers to remain in studied ignorance of it. The lyrical beauty and charm of Nerval's "Fantaisie," for instance, stems from distancing the woman in space and time:

> Il est un air pour qui je donnerais
> Tout Rossini, tout Mozart et tout Weber,
> Un air très vieux, languissant et funèbre,
> Qui pour moi seul a des charmes secrets!
>
> Or, chaque fois que je viens à l'entendre,
> De deux cents ans mon âme rajeunit . . .
> C'est sous Louis treize; et je crois voir s'étendre
> Un coteau vert, que le couchant jaunit.
>
> Puis un château de briques à coins de pierre,
> Aux vitraux teints de rougeâtres couleurs.
> Ceint de grands parcs, avec une rivière
> Baignant ses pieds, qui coule entre des fleurs;
>
> Puis une dame, à sa haute fenêtre,
> Blonde aux yeux noirs, en ses habits anciens,
> Que, dans une autre existence peut-être,
> J'ai déjà vue . . . et dont je me souviens![1]

---

[1] Gérard de Nerval, *Œuvres* (Paris: Gallimard, 1974), 18–19.

There is a melody for which I'd give
All of Rossini, all Mozart and all Weber,
A melody of long ago, languid and gloomy,
That to me alone offers secret charms.

Every time I chance to hear it
My soul goes back two hundred years . . .
It's in the reign of Louis-Treize—and my mind's eye can see
A spreading green hill turned yellow at sunset.

Then a castle of bricks with corners of stone,
Its windows stained with a reddish glow,
Great parks all around it, and, at its feet,
A river flowing through flowers.

Then a lady, at her high window,
Blond with black eyes, in garments of long ago . . .
Whom in another existence perhaps
I've already seen—and whom I remember!

Baudelaire's poem "A une passante (To a woman passing by)," like the poem evoking a red-haired beggar girl or the prose poem describing an encounter with Miss Scalpel, suggests an entirely different relationship between man and woman. These are poems of contemporary city life where the woman is neither placed in some distant historical or personal past, nor relegated to the physical distance implied by her position high in the castle Nerval imagines. On the contrary, she is part of the roaring city street, emerging out of the crowd in a lightning flash to fade back into it almost as quickly as she is noticed. But noticed she certainly is, in what can be read as a transformation and modernization of the sixteenth-century poetic device of the "blazon," with its series of praises for disparate parts of the woman's body. We see her agile leg, and her hand delicately lifting her hem. The conventional dark eyes of Nerval's lady are replaced in Baudelaire's poem by a gaze in which the poet sees—or onto which he projects—the tempests of passion. Nerval's melody sends him back to the reign of Louis XIII: Baudelaire's passerby wrenches the poet's soul back to life in the present. Similarly, the red-haired beggar girl, with her ragged clothes and her freckled, sickly body, may encourage a brief fantasy in which the poet imagines her dressed in a superb formal robe and instantly garnering pearls and sonnets. Yet the poem ends with a robust affirmation that all she needs is her own beauty, a recognition of her as she is, dirt, rags and all. However beautiful and seductive riches might make you seem, the poet affirms, somewhat cavalierly, I prefer to face the grittiness of reality:

—Cependant tu vas gueusant
Quelque vieux débris gisant
Au seuil de quelque Véfour
    De carrefour;

Tu vas lorgnant en dessous
Des bijoux de vingt-neuf sous
Dont je ne puis, oh! pardon!
    Te faire don.

Va donc, sans autre ornement,
Parfum, perles, diamant,
Que ta maigre nudité,
    Ô ma beauté!

                    (FM LXXXVIII)

—And yet you go scrounging
Leftovers, peelings,
At the back of a Ritz
In the sticks;

You cast longing eyes
On gems for a dime
That I'd love to present
But I haven't a cent.

Go then without furs,
Scent or diamonds or pearls,
Your skinny nudity—
That's your true beauty!

The poet Théophile Gautier, to whom Baudelaire dedicated his collection of poems, also provides a useful point of comparison for seeing what it is that is so different in Baudelaire's vision of woman. A woman's resistance, in Gautier's love poetry, is presented as the result of the indifference, frivolity, or blindness of her sex: what else, the indignant poet seems to ask, would explain the fact that a woman has turned me down? Baudelaire's poetic voice may move beyond indignation into rage and fury, but his women are individuals who exercise their right to choose. And he recognizes that his own desire is in part dependent on that sharp sense of uncertainty:

Et je t'aime d'autant plus, belle, que tu me fuis,
Et que tu me parais, ornement de mes nuits,
Plus ironiquement accumuler les lieues
Qui séparent mes bras des immensités bleues.

(FM, XXIV)

I love you all the more, my beauty, when you flee
And when you seem, o dark gem of my nights,
To stretch out all the miles, o irony!
That part me from the vast blue infinite.

It is that sense of the independence and therefore unpredictability of the beloved that lends many of Baudelaire's love poems their edgy power, their sense of the transience of relationships, and their poignancy. Now, in this moment, we share something, but that proves nothing of the future. In Hugo's poetry, too, there are moments of sharing—the ecstatic moment of erotic love related in "Un soir que je regardais les étoiles (One evening when I was gazing at the stars)" offers a powerful example—but the sense of transience associated with these moments is based more on the indifference of nature and on the fragility of life than on the possible resistance of the woman. In this beautiful poem, the beloved urges the poet to turn his gaze and his thoughts away from the vast universe and back to her and to their love. "It's beautiful," she admits, "to see a star blaze out. The world is full of marvelous things. Sweet is the dawn and sweet the roses, but nothing is so sweet as the charm of loving. True light, like the best flame, is the ray that leaps from soul to soul!" This is a pretty potent argument, as the lover's ardent response reveals: "Our hearts were pounding, I was breathless with joy / The flowers of the evening were opening their buds . . ." But once the three dots have run their course, the questions arise: "What have you done with our words, O trees? / With our sighs, O boulders, what have you done? / How sad must be our destiny, / Since such a day flies away like the others!" Baudelaire seems to be responding to a longing for permanence similar to that expressed in Hugo's poem, and in many others like it—Lamartine's "Le Lac" and Musset's "Souvenir" for instance—in his beautiful poem "Le Balcon (The Balcony)." Where Lamartine and Hugo lament the fragility and ephemerality of human existence, however, Baudelaire explores the elusive relationship that links ecstasy, memory, and poetic recreation. The beloved, for the first two poets, functions above all as the initiator of the poet's meditations: Baudelaire's poem shares the meditation with her. The poem also gains power from its position within the collection, following "Duellum," where the lover invites his mistress to roll down to hell with him in order to eternalize the ardor of their hatred, and preceding "Le Possédé (The Possessed)," where the lover recognizes that every fiber in his body knows his beloved as the devil in disguise, and yet adores her. "Le Balcon" offers a rare moment of respite from such passionate intensity, a moment, in fact, where passion is infused with tenderness. As in Catullus's most powerful love poetry, we are eavesdroppers on an intimate conversation when the lover whispers to his beloved not just about his feelings for her, but about how moments of shared bliss can be preserved, caught in the amber of poetry. Here the beauty of nature is not asked to record the lovers' presence or to reveal the traces of their words and their kisses: nature heightens and intensifies the beauty of love, but the poet alone has the burden of summoning it back from oblivion. The kisses and vows may not themselves return—the poet here specifically puts that in doubt with his question, and its poignancy is thrust into prominence by the fact that the poem ends on the raising of doubt and not on the affirmation of a certainty—but what the poet can do is to capture the memories the lovers have shared.

LE BALCON

Mère des souvenirs, maîtresse des maîtresses,
Ô toi, tous mes plaisirs! ô toi, tous mes devoirs!
Tu te rappelleras la beauté des caresses,
La douceur du foyer et le charme des soirs,
Mère des souvenirs, maîtresse des maîtresses!

Les soirs illuminés par l'ardeur du charbon,
Et les soirs au balcon, voilés de vapeurs roses.
Que ton sein m'était doux! que ton cœur m'était bon!
Nous avons dit souvent d'impérissables choses
Les soirs illuminés par l'ardeur du charbon.

Que les soleils sont beaux dans les chaudes soirées!
Que l'espace est profond! que le cœur est puissant!
En me penchant vers toi, reine des adorées,
Je croyais respirer le parfum de ton sang.
Que les soleils sont beaux dans les chaudes soirées!

La nuit s'épaississait ainsi qu'une cloison,
Et mes yeux dans le noir devinaient tes prunelles,
Et je buvais ton souffle, ô douceur! ô poison!
Et tes pieds s'endormaient dans mes mains fraternelles.
La nuit s'épaississait ainsi qu'une cloison.

Je sais l'art d'évoquer les minutes heureuses,
Et revis mon passé blotti dans tes genoux.

Car à quoi bon chercher tes beautés langoureuses
Ailleurs qu'en ton cher corps et qu'en ton cœur si doux?
Je sais l'art d'évoquer les minutes heureuses!

Ces serments, ces parfums, ces baisers infinis,
Renaîtront-ils d'un gouffre interdit à nos sondes,
Comme montent au ciel les soleils rajeunis
Après s'être lavés au fond des mers profondes?
-Ô serments! ô parfums! ô baisers infinis!

(FM XXXVI)

THE BALCONY

Mother of memories, mistress of mistresses
All of my pleasures and all of my cares!
You will recall the beauty of caresses,
The sweetness of the hearth and the charm of the evenings
Mother of memories, mistress of mistresses.

Those evenings lit by the glow of the coals,
Those evenings on the balcony veiled in pink mists.
How sweet your breast! How kind was your heart!
How often we said things we will never forget,
Those evenings lit by the glow of the coals.

How beautiful the sun on those warm summer evenings!
How vast then is space! How powerful the heart!
In leaning toward you, queen of the adored,
I felt I was breathing the scent of your blood.
How beautiful the sun on those warm summer evenings!

The nights would grow as thick as the partition wall
And my eyes in the dark would seek out your eyes,
And I drank in your breath, o sweetness, o poison!
And your feet fell asleep in my brotherly hands.
The nights would grow as thick as the partition wall.

I know how to call up the moments of joy,
See my past once again nestled in your knees.
Where should one look for your languorous beauty
If not in your dear body and in your sweet heart?
I know how to call up the moments of joy.

Those vows, those perfumes, those infinite kisses,
Will they rise yet again from a gulf none may measure?
As the rejuvenated sun rises again to the heavens
After being washed in the depths of deep seas?
—O vows! O perfumes! O infinite kisses!

The woman evoked here is richly complex, uniting the mother and the mistress, the sister and the queen, the source of all the poet's pleasures but also the center of all his obligations. Perhaps most importantly, she is present in the poem, the vital listener to this whispered affirmation of the poet's power. Looking at the translations at this point helps to bring into sharp focus what is essential to the poem, elements of its density, aspects of its suggestions that may be impossible to weave into any one English version, but whose absence in a translation makes us suddenly aware of the role they play in the original. George Dillon's rhymed translation, however fine as poetry in its own right, gets much of the first verse wrong. He sets the memories in the past—"Like yesterday, it seems"—whereas it strikes me as essential that at least some of those memories are being produced now, and that part of the power and poignancy of the poet's triumphant affirmation that he can evoke them stems from the fact that his ability to do so is not yet put finally to the test. Dillon also glides over the cluster of images that introduces the woman in the opening lines, replacing their contrasting facets with a more banal picture: "Inspirer of my youth, mistress beyond compare, / You who were all my pleasures, all my hopes and dreams!" The maternal side needs to be there as well, and it needs also, I think, to be linked with the birth of memory, just as the idea of duty has to be present, not just "hopes and dreams" but the good Jansenist concept of duty, obligation, responsibility. F. P. Sturm loses this aspect, too, driven out by the exigencies of rhyme—and his choice of "thou" makes Baudelaire's modernism sound strangely archaic: "Mother of memories, mistress of mistresses, / O thou my pleasure, thou all my desire / Thou shalt recall the beauty of caresses, / The charm of evenings by the gentle fire." Beresford Egan and C. Bower Alcock sink to further depths than even they have before in their inappropriately archaic rendering: "Fled love of all loves, that brook'st no eclipse, amalgam compounded of pleasure and light, thou wilt remember the beauty of the caresses, the fire's near sweetness and evening's charm, fled love of all loves that brook'st no eclipse." Let's send them both to "that abyss which man may not fathom" and hope they do not spring to new birth. Richard Howard gives us beautiful rhythms and an imaginative version of "maîtresse des maîtresses" but abandons the moral overtones of duty, presenting Baudelaire's poet as Epicurean: "Mother of memories, absolute mistress, / in you my pleasure is my only task"—and it is a pity that a vodka advertisement threatens to shape our reading of "absolute mistress."

Looking at these translations, however, helps us focus on another question central to Baudelaire's poetry, that of the suggestive power of rhyme as well as its limitations and its bullying. "Oh who will tell of the wrongs of rhyme?" Paul Verlaine is to ask later in the century.[2] Duty is pushed out of these English versions of "Le Balcon," often in preference for "desire"—primarily, one has to assume, not because duty is misread or misunderstood, but far more banally because desire is so useful and apparently appropriate a rhyme for "fire." But the French word "foyer" here is broader and more multi-layered than "fire." After all, "la douceur du foyer" is a phrase the nomadic Baudelaire uses elsewhere to summon up all the attractions of a calm and stable home life. In "Le Crépuscule du soir (Evening Twilight)" he thinks of those who as evening falls will lose their struggle against illness and never again enjoy their soup by the fireside with someone they love, and he adds as a bleak afterthought, beautifully expressed here in James McGowan's translation: "Moreover most of them have never known the call / of friendly hearth, have never lived at all!" The *foyer* as focus of home life is what is at issue here, and it is an image that touches on the complex nature of the woman as friend and consolation as well as lover and inspiration.

While "Le Balcon" like many of the first cycle of love poems in *Les Fleurs du mal* (the group Baudelaire numbers XXII to XXXIX), evokes the beauty and intensity of erotic passion, with its surges of fury and its slumps of lethargic despair, the nine poems of the second cycle suggest a very different relationship, one in which the poet turns away from intense eroticism and yearns for a more spiritually fulfilling love. To some extent there is a degree of literary exercise going on here, an ambition to rival Dante and Petrarch through an idealization of a woman seen as pointing the direction to a love pure of physical passion. Although Baudelaire affirmed in a letter to Mme Sabatier that several of these poems were written for her, thus prompting some critics to term this her cycle, it is clear that the opening poem "Semper Eadem" (always the same), evokes women in general, and at least one of those he claimed she had inspired is already present in embryonic form in a letter sent earlier to a "Mme Marie" who may or may not have been the actress Marie Daubrun. In that letter, Baudelaire writes: "Through you, Marie, I will be strong and great. Like Petrarch, I will immortalize my Laura. Be my guardian angel, my Muse and my Madonna and lead me in the path of beauty" (CI 182). These poems are sharply different from the previous love poems, and not just in this reconsideration of the nature of love, but more vitally still in that all but one have as their central focus the lover rather than the couple. The exception, "Confession," is remarkable in allowing the woman to speak, although the critic Jean Prévost is not really correct in asserting that it is the only time in Baudelaire's poetry where the woman appears as a

[2] Paul Verlaine, *Œuvres poétiques complètes,* ed. Y. G. Le Dantec and Jacques Borel (Paris: Gallimard, 1962), 327.

thinking creature (the prose poems contain several examples of women who think). Typically Baudelairean, of course, is the irony that the confession itself is made necessary precisely because of the complicated relationships between the sexes in a culture that had been strongly marked by the misogyny of Napoleon's 1804 Civil Code, with its severe restrictions on women's freedoms, and by the gulf between the kind of education that Baudelaire had received and what passed for education for most women. "Confession" recounts a stroll during which the poet's beloved, whom the poet sees as radiantly happy and effortlessly beautiful, suddenly shocks him by her affirmation that beauty comes only at the cost of immense effort: "Nothing in this world is certain," she tells him, "human selfishness is present everywhere no matter how carefully it dresses itself up as something else. Being a beautiful woman is a demanding profession, the banal and brutal fact behind the dancer's mechanical smile." Building on hearts, she has learned, is folly; "everything shatters, love as well as beauty, until the moment when oblivion throws them into his basket to hand them over to eternity." But once you extract what is said from the beautiful underpinnings of the poem's rhetoric—the susurration and alliteration of "Ce silence et cette langueur, / Et cette confidence horrible chuchotée, / Au confessional du cœur" (this silence and this listlessness and this horrible confidence whispered in the heart's confessional) (FM, XLV), or the seductive scenery in which it is set, "Like a newly minted medallion, the full moon spread its light, and the solemnity of the night, like a river, streamed over sleeping Paris,"— you are left with what looks horribly like cliché. Worse still, the listener has no desire to hear this plaintive note, staggering into his awareness like a horrible, sickly child whose family would blush to see it out in public. Walter Martin's version captures beautifully the disturbing uneasiness of the poem, and what he translates as "the paradox / Of that painful intimacy of ours." If this poem draws attention to itself within this cycle, it is at least in part because Baudelaire is inviting us to read the poem as a paradox, an irruption into the idealized image of the woman when the lover's voice is briefly silenced. Hearing his voice stop, however briefly, makes us aware of just how much he has been holding the floor in this group. It is not that the woman talks more in the other cycles, but that there is a possibility of conversation, of shared experience, whereas here the idealization of the woman, whose exquisite harmony fuses all the senses into one, throws up a barrier between them—everything depends, in other words, on her remaining constantly ahead of him.

The tone of this group is perhaps best illustrated with the untitled sonnet XLII:

Que diras-tu ce soir, pauvre âme solitaire,
Que diras-tu, mon cœur, cœur autrefois flétri,
A la très belle, à la très bonne, à la très chère,
Dont le regard divin t'a soudain refleuri?

—Nous mettrons notre orgueil à chanter ses louanges:
Rien ne vaut la douceur de son autorité;
Sa chair spirituelle a le parfum des Anges,
Et son œil nous revêt d'un habit de clarté.

Que ce soit dans la nuit et dans la solitude,
Que ce soit dans la rue et dans la multitude,
Son fantôme dans l'air danse comme un flambeau.

Parfois il parle et dit: "Je suis belle, et j'ordonne
Que pour l'amour de moi vous n'aimiez que le Beau;
Je suis l'Ange gardien, la Muse et la Madone."

(FM XLII)

What will you say tonight, poor lonely soul,
And you my heart, heart withered long ago,
What will you say to the loveliest, best and dearest
Whose hallowed gaze has made you flower anew?

"Our pride will be to sing her praise
Nothing's so sweet as her authority;
Her spiritual flesh has the perfume of Angels
And her eye decks us out with a mantle of light."

Whether in the long lonely hours of the night
Or in the street where the crowds multiply,
Her phantom on high dances like firelight

And sometimes it speaks, saying: "I am beauty and I order
That for love of me you'll love Beauty alone;
I'm the guardian angel, the Muse and the Madonna."

There is a particular beauty in the French sounds of this poem, in the careful balance of the rhythm—"à la très belle, à la très bonne, à la très chère," "Que ce soit dans la nuit et dans la solitude,/ Que ce soit dans la rue et dans la multitude"—in the image of the phantom dancing like a flame, and in the triumphant build-up to the last line. But that formal beauty, the sharp attention devoted to ornamental qualities, fails to give this poem, or indeed most of the poems in this cycle, the striking originality and modernity of the first cycle of love poems. It retains throughout a quality of literary exercise and, however fine the results, it lacks that sudden irruption of felt experience that other Baudelaire love poems manage to convey.

With poem XLIX, *Les Fleurs du mal* turns to a third cycle, the evocation of a different kind of love, inspired by a different kind of woman. Intense erotic passion has given way to the desire for a purifying love. Now the poet again seeks an intense experience, one whose effect will be more powerful than wine or opium in plunging him into forgetfulness, intoxicating him to the point where he loses all sense of self. The woman here inspires thoughts of escape from humdrum reality, longings to set off on exotic voyages. It is in this cycle that we find one of Baudelaire's best-known poems, "L'Invitation au voyage (The Invitation to a Journey)," as well as "Le Beau Navire (The Lovely Ship)," that *blason* that sings of the various elements that make up this woman's particular blend of maturity and youthfulness. Above all, she invites a series of poems that attempt to suggest her nature by creating a landscape that represents her. And she forces the poet to recognize that the longing for a spiritual love, the fear of physical relationships and the yearning to be spared emotional pain, cannot withstand the force of her presence and her desires. These are not poems in which the woman shares with the poet a complex and changing relationship; rather, the focus is on the lover himself, and on his dawning awareness not just of a new love, but also of the eternal return of desire. Woman is catalyst, but she is also an individual. Her unusual blend of the childlike and the majestic, of physical strength and lethargy—she is a "molle enchanteresse," a yielding enchantress, a soft siren, soft enchantress, depending on the translation you choose—the changing color of her eyes (blue, gray or green? the poet asks in "Ciel brouillé") all make her personality stamp its mark on these poems, as that of the woman evoked in the second cycle does not. It remains the case that "Causerie (Conversation)" gives us just one voice, the lover's, but what he says is shaped, determined, and driven by her.

CAUSERIE

Vous êtes un beau ciel d'automne, clair et rose!
Mais la tristesse en moi monte comme la mer,
Et laisse, en refluant, sur ma lèvre morose
Le souvenir cuisant de son limon amer.

—Ta main se glisse en vain sur mon sein qui se pâme;
Ce qu'elle cherche, amie, est un lieu saccagé
Par la griffe et la dent féroce de la femme.
Ne cherchez plus mon cœur; les bêtes l'ont mangé.

Mon cœur est un palais flétri par la cohue;
On s'y soûle, on s'y tue, on s'y prend aux cheveux!
—Un parfum nage autour de votre gorge nue! . . .

Ô Beauté, dur fléau des âmes, tu le veux!
Avec tes yeux de feu, brillants comme des fêtes,
Calcine ces lambeaux qu'ont épargnés les bêtes!

(FM LV)

You are a lovely autumn sky, clear and pink!
But sadness rises in me like the sea,
And as it ebbs my gloomy lips still taste
The burning memory of its bitter silt.

—In vain your hand slides down my swooning chest.
There's nothing there, my love, but ruins left
By woman's claw and woman's wild tooth.
No longer seek my heart; foul beasts have eaten it.

My heart's a palace ravaged by the mob,
By drunkards and by killers, brawling louts
—Perfume swirls around your naked breast! . . .

O Beauty, harsh flail of souls, you want it so!
With eyes aflame, as if on holy days,
Burn to a cinder what the beasts have scorned to take!

She has no need to speak here, since her response to his longing to be left in peace finds so powerful a reflection in the final tercet, where the arousal of desire is so unambiguously conveyed and so beautifully attributed to her.

The richness and variety of these images of women are in part what makes Baudelaire's love poetry both so remarkable and so readable. But there is a further essential element in this depiction, one that concerns the significant variety of tone. Hugo had already, as he idiosyncratically expresses it, put a red beret on the old dictionary, invigorating a poetic language that had grown sclerotic. With Charles-Augustin Sainte-Beuve's poetry had come a sense of the potentially poetic nature of the quotidian, a realization that poetry did not have to concern itself uniquely with epiphanies and kings. Gautier and Banville had already flexed their muscles on virtuoso rhyming schemes and subtle rhythmic variations. What Baudelaire adds, in addition to his extraordinary and unrivaled range of subjects, is his ability to play on linguistic registers, to open French poetry up to the suggestive power and allusive strength of shifting and colliding tones. The formal diction and grammar at the end of "Remords posthume (Posthumous Remorse)," for instance, falls creatively apart as it collides with the down-to-earth curse of the final line: "'Que vous sert, courtisane imparfaite, / De n'avoir pas connu ce que pleurent les morts?' /—Et le ver

rongera ta peau comme un remords ('Of what use will it be to you, imperfect cour-
tesan, not to have known what the dead bemoan?'—And the worm will gnaw your
flesh like remorse)" (FM XXXIII). A similarly productive and unprecedented clash
of tones comes in "Une Charogne (A Carcass)" where the poet reminds his beloved:
"La puanteur était si forte, que sur l'herbe / Vous crûtes vous évanouir (The stench
was so strong, that on the grass, you feared you might swoon away)" (FM XXIX).
"Puanteur" (stench) and "évanouir" (swoon) are from different registers, one prosaic
and realistic, the other literary and euphemistic, just as the highly formal use in a
conversation of a tense generally reserved for formal writing ("Vous crûtes vous
évanouir—you feared you might swoon away") collides with the substance of what
is being said, the velvet glove of a courtly form of address suddenly snatched off to
reveal the steel fist of a brutal statement about mortality. In large measure this linguistic variety is closely connected to, if not demanded by, the range of images of
women that Baudelaire provides. Reading him one cannot help feeling a sense of
wonder at the overthrowing of stereotypes. Misogynistic though he often was in his
letters, his critical articles, and his diaries, and as he can be in his poetry, too, Baudelaire nevertheless, almost despite himself, one feels, breaks free from essentialism to
focus on the quiddity, the individuality of women.

In his article on Constantin Guys, whom he terms the painter of modern life, a
section entitled "Woman" insists—and Baudelaire here pulls out all the rhetorical
stops in a bravura passage that surely has more to do with his own esthetics than
with those of Guys or anyone else—on woman as "a divinity, a star that presides
over all the conceptions of the male brain; a glittering reflection of all the grace of
nature condensed into a single being; the object of the most intense admiration and
curiosity that the painting of life can offer the contemplative observer" (II 713). And
he goes on to explain that he is not just concerned here with harmony and perfection: "No, that would not be enough to explain her mysterious and complex enchantment" (II 713). Beauty, as he frequently argues, is always bizarre, stimulating
the curiosity of the observer, prompting a transformation of pleasure into understanding. That curiosity and enchantment can also be found, as the *Tableaux
Parisiens* reveal, in unexpected sources. Baudelaire's "Les Petites Vieilles (The Little
Old Women)" picks up that idea of enchantment and transforms the familiar trope
of the complex links among memory, experience, and art by bringing it to bear not
on erotic love but on the lives of old women. It is a poem many readers have found
difficult to like. Baudelaire himself confesses (sincerely or with false modesty, who
can tell?) that in this poem, as in "Les Sept Vieillards (The Seven Old Men)," he
feared he had "simply succeeded in going beyond the bounds set down for Poetry"
(CI 583). Hugo, to whom it was dedicated, sent a reply that was to become famous
but that does not indicate much more than a rapid reading: "What are you doing [in
these poems]? You're walking forward. You are providing art's heaven with some
macabre new ray. You are creating a new shiver" (LAB, 188). But in September

1859, when Baudelaire sent the poems to him, Hugo was completing the first series of his group of poems entitled *La Légende des siècles* (*The Legend of the Centuries*) and insisting in his preface on "the flowering of human kind from century to century, humanity climbing from the shadows to the ideal, the paradisal transformation of the earthly hell, the slow and supreme blossoming of freedom, rights in this life and responsibility for the next one."[3] Baudelaire's sardonic rejection of progress, implicit in the poems sent to Hugo, is stated with particular virulence in the notes collected for his never-completed book *Fusées* (*Rockets*): "What could be more absurd than Progress, since mankind, as is proved by what happens everyday, is always the same and always mankind's equal, that's to say, always at the stage of savagery. What are the perils of forest and prairie beside the daily shocks and conflicts of civilization? Whether man lassoes his dupe on the boulevards or pierces his prey in unknown forests, is he not man eternal, that is to say, the most perfect of all animals of prey?" (I 663). However rapidly he glanced at "Les Petites Vieilles," Hugo can hardly have failed to notice the gulf between his insistence on the relationship between art and progress, and Baudelaire's very different notion not just of each concept but also of the relationship between them.

Another reader who struggled with this poem is Marcel Proust, who commented in a letter to his mother:

It's certain that in a sublime poem like "The Little Old Women" not one of their sufferings escapes the poet's eye. [. . .] But the characteristic, descriptive beauty of the depiction means that he does not step back from any cruel detail. [. . .] These visions that, when you come down to it, must I'm sure have hurt him, he has conveyed in tableaux that are very powerful but from which all expression of feeling has been banished. [. . .] It may be that this subordination of sensitivity to the truth of expression is a mark of genius, of strength, of an art that is greater than individual pity. But there is something stranger than that in Baudelaire's case. In the most sublime expression that he has given to certain feelings, it seems that he has created an exterior painting of their form, without sympathizing with them. [. . .] He appears to be eternalizing through the extraordinary, exceptional power of the Word (a hundred times stronger, despite everything that has been said, than that of Hugo), a feeling that he does his best not to experience at the moment when he names it, when he paints it rather than expressing it.[4]

There is in this poem an awareness, bordering on the obsessive, of the loneliness of an industrial city, of the external details of old age, of the physical and emo-

---

[3] Victor Hugo, *La Légende des siècles* (Paris: Gallimard, 1950), 7.

[4] Marcel Proust, *Contre Sainte-Beuve* (Paris: Gallimard, 1971), 250–52.

tional suffering specific to old women. The language frequently strips them of their sex if not of their dignity, throws into sharp relief the contrast between past glories and present miseries, focuses unrelentingly on physical details, but for all that, if attentively read, it remains powerfully emotional. Much of that emotion derives precisely from the aspect Proust puts his finger on: the separation of narrative voice and narrative feeling, a reversal, if you like, of Stéphane Mallarmé's esthetic—depict not the thing but the effect it produces. Baudelaire would have found that technique already demonstrated in three of his immediate predecessors, Choderlos de Laclos, Prosper Mérimée, and Eugène Delacroix ("the great man," as Baudelaire himself notes, "is never a meteorite," but always prepared by predecessors [II 69]). Of *Les Liaisons dangereuses (Dangerous Liaisons)*, Laclos's novel of seduction as intellectual power game, Baudelaire affirms: "If this book burns, it can burn only as ice does" (II 67). Mérimée's short story "Mateo Falcone" with its dispassionate depiction of a father assassinating his son for blemishing family honor by betraying a wounded bandit to the police illustrates Baudelaire's judgment of the author, expressed in his study of Delacroix's life and works: "A man to whom one might legitimately compare Delacroix as regards his external appearance and his manners would be M. Mérimée. He had the same apparent, slightly affected, coldness, the same cloak of ice covering a restrained sensitivity, and a burning passion for good and for beauty" (II 757–58). Of course, here as in other passages defining Delacroix, Baudelaire is also tracing his own moral portrait. The gaze projected on the old women in Baudelaire's poem may suggest a cloak of ice, but the rhetoric frequently allows glimpses of restrained sensitivity, compassion, and a longing to understand how individuals develop, how they encounter their particular destinies, what they could have done to be different. The opening stanza is at once a summary of what will follow and yet another invitation to the reader. It suggests an artistic relationship with cities that is new in poetry and typically Baudelairean. When he sent his prose poems to the editor Arsène Houssaye, he argued that the genre of prose poetry was stimulated above all by city life, and here in his great verse poems about the city Baudelaire draws avidly on a source of inspiration that is of course not his alone, but that he exploits differently from all his predecessors (see chapter 8). The poet is depicted as a spy, lying in wait for a particular element of city life, and not just Parisian life—he specifically widens this to "old capitals." The surveillance, which includes both tenderness and distance ("de loin, tendrement"), takes place "in the sinuous folds" of the city, in its labyrinthine streets and alley ways, and it suggests that part of the poet's purpose is to explore not just the hearts and minds of the old women, but also the city itself. The parallel nature of women and city in this poem is suggested in the stress placed on the age of each and in the link made, in the fourth section of the poem, between the chaos of the city itself and the disarray of the women's lives, now that they have lost what previously gave that life meaning—beauty, talent, or love. What they retain unchanged from their far off childhood is their eyes, "piercing as a gimlet, gleaming like pools of water sleeping in the night," eyes that now in old age are "wells made of millions of tears." As in the case of Andromache in exile, or the swan stumbling through rough city streets, these old women symbolize humanity in general, and contemplating them, dreaming about how they come to be exiled in the present, the poet is able to "plunge into the multitude," as he puts it in the prose poem "Les Foules (The Crowds)." "Multiplied, my heart delights in all your vices," he insists, adding: "My soul glows bright with all your virtues." The second part of "Les Petites Vieilles" revels in that multiplicity in ways that illuminate the complexity of Baudelaire's vision of women, and particularly the suffering of women. Whatever misogynistic anger he may reveal elsewhere, here he creates an exceptionally powerful stanza that evokes, through a compression barely holding emotion in check, the vulnerability of women as citizens, wives, and mothers:

> L'une, par sa patrie au malheur exercée,
> L'autre, que son époux surchargea de douleurs,
> L'autre, par son enfant Madone transpercée,
> Toutes auraient pu faire un fleuve avec leurs pleurs!
>
> (FM XCI)

> One, whom her homeland had taught to suffer,
> Another, whom her husband had burdened with pain,
> A third, the Madonna pierced through by her child,
> And all could have made a river with their tears!

Andromache is again present here, in the reference to the river of tears, but so also is Baudelaire's own mother, the Madonna whose child has tortured her. Women beaten by their husbands are rarely acknowledged in contemporary literature, but Baudelaire suggests them here in his second line, which also undeniably evokes a more common motif, the woman betrayed by a philandering husband. (This motif had recently been powerfully, exuberantly, and ambivalently treated by Balzac in *La Cousine Bette*.)

The verse poetry conveys something of the richness of Baudelaire's vision of women, and of its inclusive nature, but the variety of tone and image demanded by that richness is almost at the edge of what was possible for poetry at the time. The prose poems, with their greater linguistic liberty, add to that image but demand rather different reading practices. The prose poem "Les Veuves (The Widows)," with its study of widows, shares some of the same elements as "Les Petites Vieilles," but its tone is more analytical, and in many ways more urbane, its address to the reader more open. Its vocabulary is that of philosophical meditation, its rhetoric that of an observer of curiosities, its opening invocation of the eighteenth-century French moralist, the marquis de Vauvenargues, an obvious (although perhaps therefore a deceptive) marker indicating how readers should approach this particular piece of writing. The verse poem with its suggestions of spying and stalking is deliberately disturbing, the relationship between viewer and viewed unnerving, because it transforms readers into peeping Toms. The prose poem sets out to legitimate the poet's observations as illustrations of Vauvenargues's dictum, which Baudelaire could have read in an 1857 number of the *Revue française*[5] and which he could consider at least moderately familiar to his readers. Two widows snap into sharp focus in the prose poem, prepared by an apparently philosophical question: which is the sadder and more saddening widow, the one who drags by the hand a child with whom she cannot share her reveries, or the one who is utterly alone? (PPP XIII). The urbanity of that seemingly innocent question and its nonchalant, apparently incomplete answer, "I don't know . . ." should not mislead us here. This is the point where the more general argument suddenly switches direction, where the broad sweep is abandoned in favor of a swiftly narrowed perspective, where the smoothness of the generalizations abruptly gives way to the grittiness of experienced reality and half-understood memories. The second widow is a version of one who also appears in the verse poem, the concert-goer who is lent an air of nobility by the martial airs to which she so avidly listens. But whereas in the verse poem she had only this function, in the prose poem her concert listening is the culmination of a day of utter solitude perceived and pondered on by the narrator. The old mountebank whose decrepitude the narrator laments as a symbol of his own future as a forgotten writer (PPP XIV) leaps into the mind here as we observe yet another symbol of the future, one the poet does not even find the courage to signal to us:

> She was obviously condemned through complete solitude to adopt the habits of an old bachelor, and the masculine nature of her habits lent their austerity a mysterious piquancy. She lunched in God knows what miserable café, God knows how. I followed her into a reading room and spied on her at length while her eyes, once burned with tears, ran busily down the gazettes seeking out news that had a powerful and personal interest for her.
>
> Finally, in the afternoon, under a charming autumn sky, one of those skies that rain down crowds of regrets and memories, she sat on her own in a garden, to hear, far from the crowd, one of those concerts that regimental bands bestow on Parisians.
>
> This was no doubt this innocent (or purified) old woman's little dissipa-

5 See Charles Baudelaire, *Petits Poèmes en prose,* ed. R. Kopp (Paris: Corti, 1969), 228–30.

tion, the well earned consolation for one of those heavy days without a friend, without a conversation, without joy, without a confidant, that God had been dropping on her perhaps for many years three hundred and sixty-five times a year.

(PPP XIII)

That concatenation of what is lacking in this woman's life (without a friend, without a conversation, without joy, without a confidant) sets up one of the many echoes that run through the prose poems, giving them an internal coherence despite the arbitrary order Baudelaire insisted should be allotted them in the letter to Houssaye that had spoken of the collection as being without head or tail. The Goya-like poem entitled "Chacun sa chimère (To Each His Chimera)" uses the same rhythm to set up a landscape of desolation: "Under a great gray sky, on a great dusty plain, without paths, without grass, without a thistle, without a nettle, I met several men who walked along bent over" (PPP VI). In "Les Veuves" the widow stands upright, bearing her personal burden with a stoic's pride, but the crushing rhythms of "Chacun sa chimère" are the same and the echoes reinforce the loneliness and pointlessness of her existence to which however she is able to attach some element of dignity by the strength of habit. She becomes here the symbol of a Sisyphean image of humanity, constantly beginning anew a pointless task, the task of getting through the loneliness of life.

The other figure in "Les Veuves" represents the widow with a child, triggering an exploration of degrees of loneliness. The resistance to memory, the difficulty of bringing to the surface a memory of childhood when the remembering adult simultaneously realizes and rejects the truth of what the child believed he or she had seen, is beautifully suggested here as the oily smoothness of the narrative voice gushes up to cloak the memory in the garb of a repeated and intellectual experience. The careful precision of diction, the stuffy separation of viewer and viewed, the sudden cluster of alliterating plosives should all alert the reader to something false here: "Je ne puis jamais m'empêcher de jeter un regard, sinon universellement sympathique, au moins curieux, sur la foule de parias qui se pressent autour de l'enceinte d'un concert public (I can never prevent myself from throwing a glance which, while it may not be universally sympathetic, is at least curious, on the crowd of pariahs who press around the barriers at a public concert)." It is a gaze, we are being urged to see, that is looking everywhere but where it most wants to look: at the glittering crowds, the darting glances, the richness and happiness of a well-off crowd. And here too warning bells sound, because the prose poem began by affirming that poets and philosophers disdain to visit the joy of the rich. Instead, we were informed, "they find themselves irresistibly pulled toward all that is weak, ruined, saddened, orphaned." Indeed, the speaker's eye turns away from the rich here, to look at the poor who crowd just outside the entrance. Once again a tawdry maxim is extracted: "It's always a matter of interest to see the reflection of a rich person's joy in the depths of the poor person's eye." But the resisting mind can no longer hold back the memory that surges forth, like Andromache, a memory that shares her majestic, noble demeanor. Sharing, too, something of the quality of Baudelaire's image of his mother when he was very young, as he describes it in his letter to her. This widow holds a child by the hand, a child in mourning as she is, and this provides the clue to why she has not paid to hear the concert, but stays outside the barrier with the plebeians. The price of the ticket could be better used to pay for a little toy for the child, now that her widowhood condemns her, as the widowed Madame Baudelaire was condemned, to suddenly straitened circumstances. There is a rapid change of tone in the final paragraph: the urbane narrator with his polished rhetoric is replaced by a voice that rings far more true in its bitter understanding of a truth now at last perceived by the adult who was that child: "And she will have returned home on foot, meditating and dreaming, alone, always alone; for the child is turbulent, selfish, with no gentleness or patience; and he cannot even like a true animal, like a dog or a cat, act as a confidant for her lonely grief" (PPP XIII). Woman as widow, one might say, is also within the context of the prose poems woman as suffering humanity.

The prose poems of *Petits Poèmes en prose* though, are thronged with women who are not just there to illustrate a certain common element in human experience, such as old age or bereavement or loneliness. Intensely individual, they leap off the page insisting that the poet stop mooning about clouds and eat his soup (PPP XLIV), or that he recognize that if men tend to group women into certain types, women can perform the same essentializing trick on men, lumping poets and doctors together for instance as Miss Scalpel does (PPP XLVII), or refusing to conform to the type into which she has been placed, as Benedicta does (PPP XXXVIII). They walk out under the noonday sun to sell their bodies in order to free their younger sister from slavery, as Dorothea does (PPP XXV), or force their men to acts of violence through their indifference, their virtue or their refusal to reflect exactly what the men want them to reflect (PPP XLII, XLIII, XXVI).

Leafing through the drawings of Constantin Guys, Baudelaire seized on the opportunity to evoke the enormous range and variety of the artist's figures of woman. The task Baudelaire attributes to him of explaining the beauty in modernity is also the task he himself has taken on, and when he talks of the galleries of women Guys depicts, it is easy to see an invitation to look at his own work in the same way. "In this immense gallery of London or Paris life, we will meet at every level different types of the wandering woman, the woman in revolt" (II 720), he affirms before launching into a bravura passage transferring Guy's plastic representation to words. But the point he is leading up to, and that has a particular bearing on the women of the prose poetry, is this: "what makes these images precious, what consecrates them, is the innumerable thoughts they provoke, thoughts that are generally severe and black" (II 722). The wonderful variety of Baudelaire's women, their quirks and their perversity, their individuality and their courage are there above all to force the reader to contemplate them, to meditate on them, and to extend that meditation into an exploration of self and the world.

Figure 1. Emile Deroy. *Portrait of Charles Baudelaire.* © *Réunion des Musées Nationaux / Art Resource, N.Y. Châteaux de Versailles et de Trianon, Versailles France.*

Figure 2. François Baudelaire's illustrated Latin vocabulary. Courtesy the Lilly Library, Bloomington.

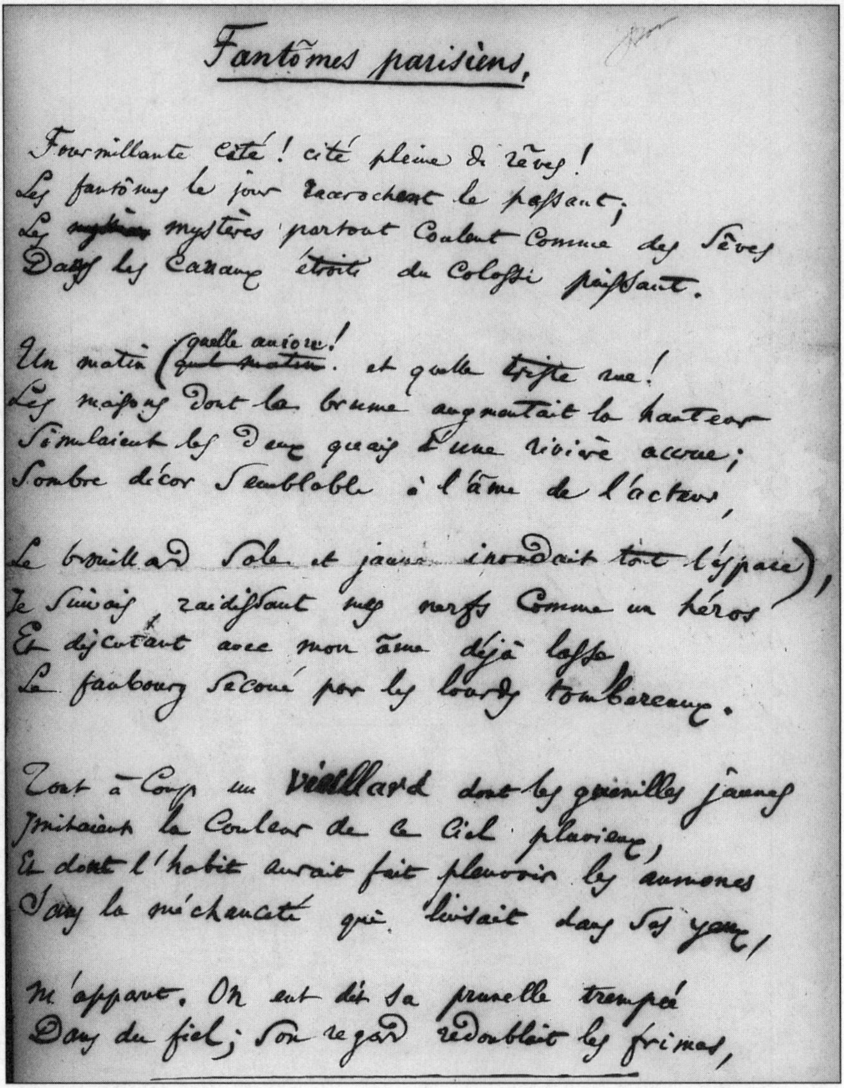

Fantômes parisiens,

Fourmillante cité ! cité pleine de rêves !
Les fantômes le jour raccrochent le passant ;
Les mystères partout coulent comme des sèves
Dans les canaux étroits du colosse puissant.

Un matin (quelle auront !) et quelle triste rue !
Les maisons dont la brume augmentait la hauteur
Simulaient les deux quais d'une rivière accrue ;
Sombre décor semblable à l'âme de l'acteur,

Le brouillard sale et jaune inondait tout l'espace),
Je suivais, raidissant mes nerfs comme un héros
Et discutant avec mon âme déjà lasse
Le faubourg secoué par les lourds tombereaux.

Tout à coup un vieillard dont les guenilles jaunes
Imitaient la couleur de ce ciel pluvieux,
Et dont l'habit aurait fait pleuvoir les aumônes
Sans la méchanceté qui luisait dans ses yeux,

M'apparut. On eut dit sa prunelle trempée
Dans du fiel ; son regard redoublait les frimas,

Figure 3. Baudelaire's manuscript "Les Fantômes" (later, "Les Sept Vieillards"). Courtesy the Lilly Library, Bloomington.

Figure 4. Alfred Déhodencq. Drawing of Théodore de Banville. Courtesy the Lilly Library, Bloomington.

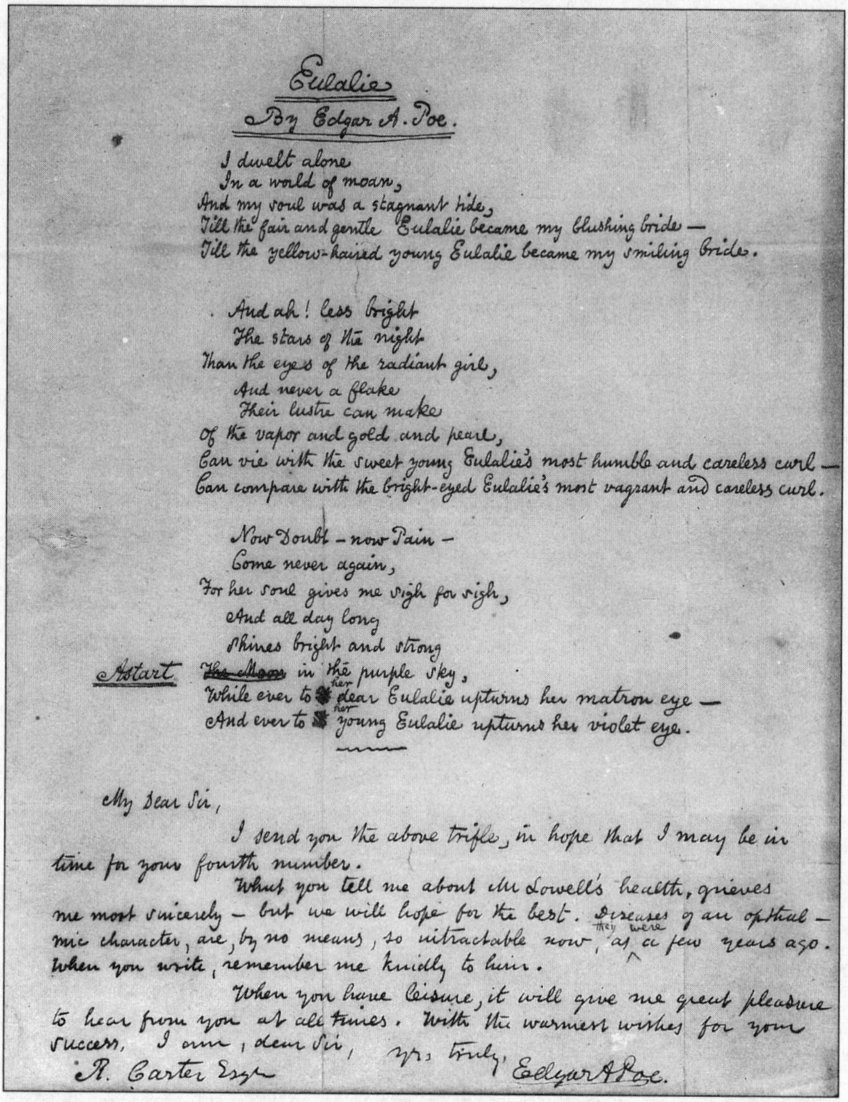

Eulalie

By Edgar A. Poe.

I dwelt alone
In a world of moan,
And my soul was a stagnant tide,
Till the fair and gentle Eulalie became my blushing bride —
Till the yellow-haired young Eulalie became my smiling bride.

And ah! less bright
The stars of the night
Than the eyes of the radiant girl,
And never a flake
Their lustre can make
Of the vapor and gold and pearl,
Can vie with the sweet young Eulalie's most humble and careless curl —
Can compare with the bright-eyed Eulalie's most vagrant and careless curl.

Now Doubt — now Pain —
Come never again,
For her soul gives me sigh for sigh,
And all day long
Shines bright and strong
Astart ~~The Moon~~ in the purple sky,
While ever to her dear Eulalie upturns her matron eye —
And ever to her young Eulalie upturns her violet eye.

My dear Sir,

I send you the above trifle, in hope that I may be in time for your fourth number.

What you tell me about Mr Lowell's health, grieves me most sincerely — but we will hope for the best. Diseases of an opthalmic character, are, by no means, so intractable now, as they were a few years ago. When you write, remember me kindly to him.

When you have leisure, it will give me great pleasure to hear from you at all times. With the warmest wishes for your success, I am, dear Sir, yr. truly, Edgar A Poe.

R. Carter Esqr

Figure 5. Manuscript of Edgar Allan Poe's "Eulalie." Courtesy the Lilly Library, Bloomington.

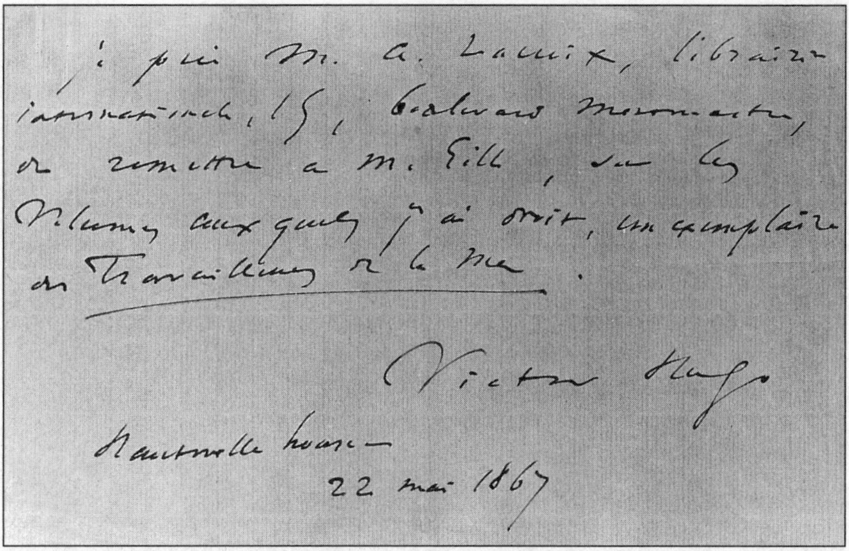

je prie M. A. Lacroix, libraire international, 15, boulevard Montmartre, de remettre à M. Gill, sur les volumes auxquels j'ai droit, un exemplaire des Travailleurs de la mer.

Victor Hugo

Hauteville house —
22 mai 1867

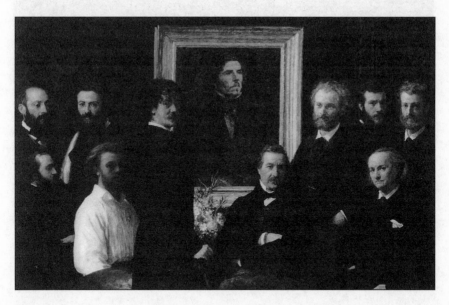

Figure 6. Manuscript of Victor Hugo's letter to the Belgian publisher Albert Lacroix. Courtesy the Lilly Library, Bloomington.

Figure 13. Henri Fantin-Latour. Hommage to Delacroix. Portrayed are Cordier, Duranty, Legros, Fantin-Latour, Whistler, Champfleury, Manet, Bracquemond, Baudelaire, and A. de Balleroy. Baudelaire is seated on the far right of the canvas. © Réunion des Musées Nationaux / Art Resource, N.Y. Musée d'Orsay, Paris, France.

Figure 7. Jean-Baptiste Clésinger. Portrait of Théophile Gautier. © Réunion des Musées Nationaux / Art Resource, N.Y. Louvre, Paris, France.

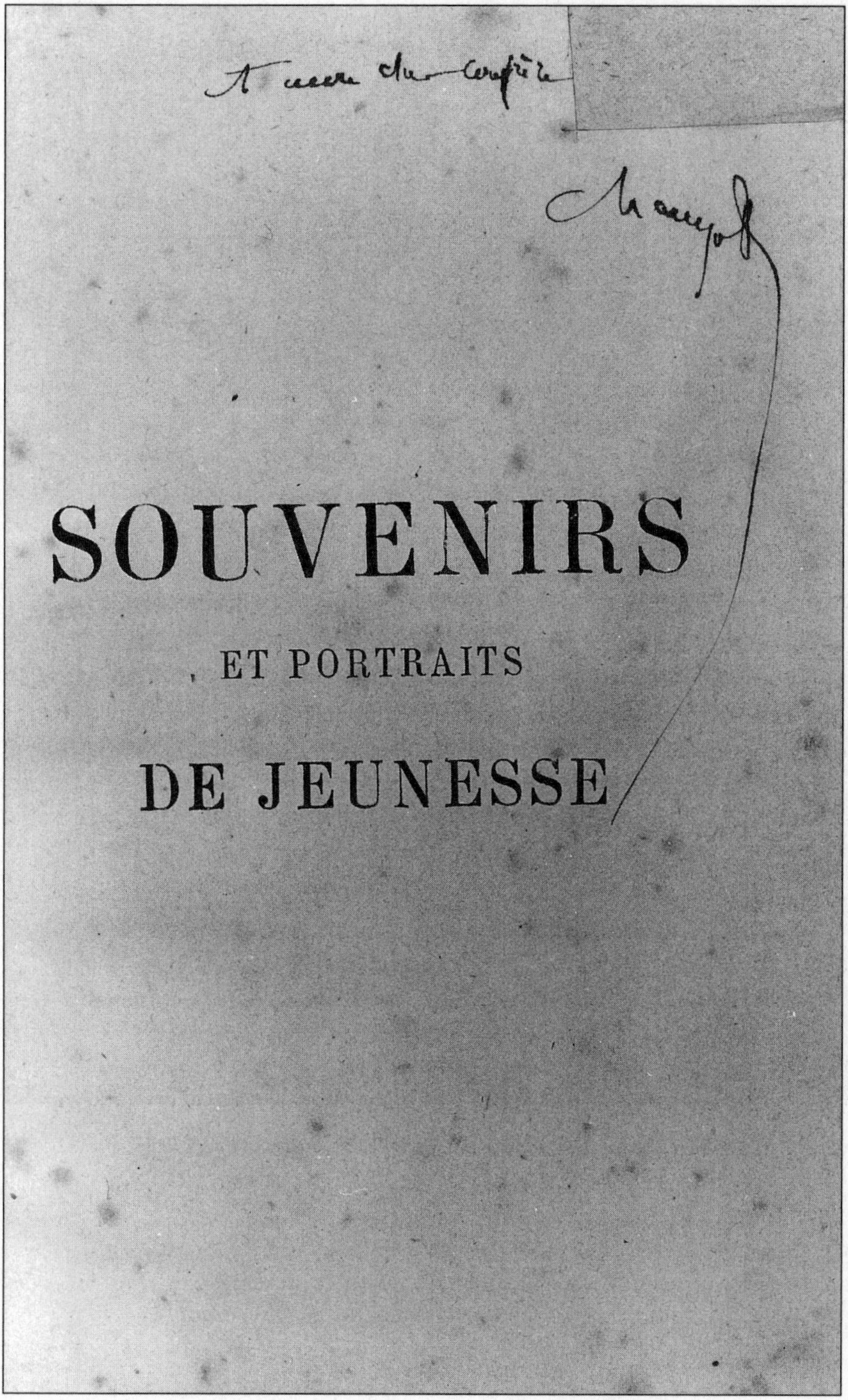

Figure 8. Autograph of Champfleury (Jules Husson) in his *Souvenirs et Portraits de jeunesse*. Courtesy Main Library, Indiana University.

Figure 9. Félix Nadar. Photograph of Charles Asselineau. © Réunion des Musées Nationaux / Art Resource, N.Y. Musée d'Orsay, France.

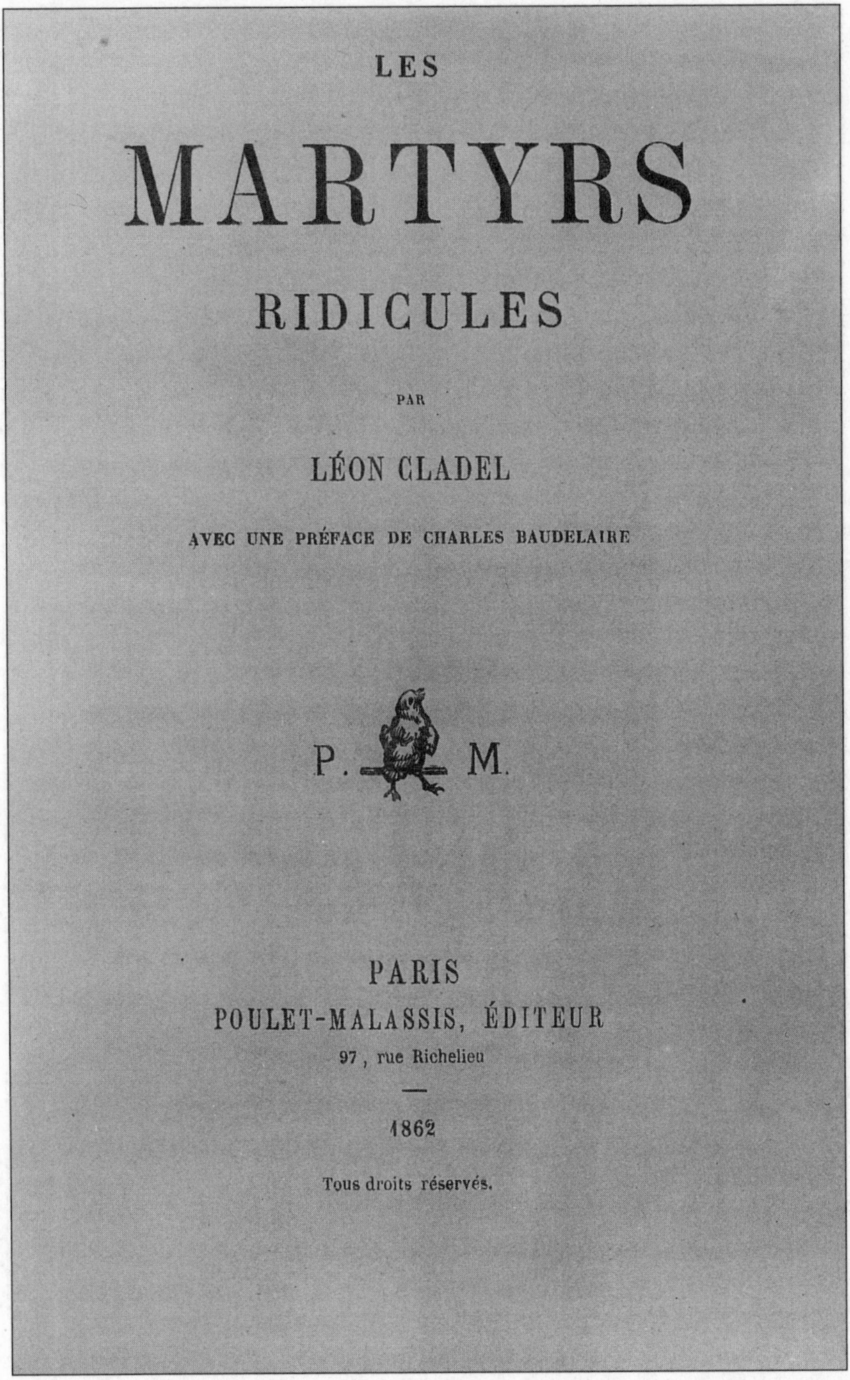

LES

MARTYRS

RIDICULES

PAR

LÉON CLADEL

AVEC UNE PRÉFACE DE CHARLES BAUDELAIRE

P. M.

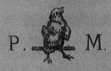

PARIS

POULET-MALASSIS, ÉDITEUR

97, rue Richelieu

1862

Tous droits réservés.

Figure 10. Poulet-Malassis's press symbol in Léon Cladel's Les Martyrs ridicules with Baudelaire's preface. Courtesy the Lilly Library, Bloomington.

Figure 11. Etienne Carjat. Caricature of Richard Wagner. © Réunion des Musées Nationaux / Art Resource, N.Y. Collection fonds Orsay. Louvre, Paris. France.

Figure 12. Félix Nadar. Photograph of Baudelaire. © Réunion des Musées Nationaux / Art Resource, N.Y. Musée d'Orsay, Paris, France.

*Figure 14. Constantin Guys. Men in top hats speaking with women. Collection fonds Orsay. ©
Réunion des Musées Nationaux / Art Resource, N.Y. Louvre, Paris, France.*

CHAPTER SEVEN

Talking to Friends

The poems about crowds and the poems about women might seem to present us above all with the poet's voice. But Baudelaire's writing is also marked, often profoundly marked, by conversations with friends, remembered or still on-going. In his biography of the poet, Baudelaire's friend Charles Asselineau (see figure 9) makes the following claim: "Every generation, every family of writers joined by a community of ideas and tastes, finds or creates a place, a journal or a review, to reveal its program. This journal was, after 1840, the *Corsaire-Satan*." Although Baudelaire contributed relatively little to the periodical, Asselineau argues convincingly that "the office of the *Corsaire-Satan* was above all for him a conversation salon."[1] In cafés and bars, in his friends' apartments or in the offices of periodicals and printing houses, in artists' studios and at concerts, he carried on conversations and arguments that leave their trace in his writing. "My first conversation with Gautier hugs the depths of my being," he tells us (II 107); Eugène Delacroix's conversation is an "admirable blend of philosophical solidity, witty lightness and ardent enthusiasm" (II 611); Charles Marie Leconte de Lisle's is "solid and serious, always seasoned by that mockery that is a proof of strength" (II 176), and Charles Augustin Sainte-Beuve is credited with "a conversation whose capricious, ardent, subtle, but always rational eloquence has no equivalent, even among the most famous conversationalists" (II 189). In a witty bravura passage, Baudelaire describes the kind of discussion that took place between Delacroix and the painter and great conversationalist Paul Marc Joseph Chenavard: "It was a real pleasure to see them throw themselves into an innocent battle, the words of the one striding heavily along like an elephant in full war regalia, while those of the other vibrated with all the sharpness and flexibility of a fencing blade" (II 766). From Belgium Baudelaire writes to complain of the lack of conversation, which he portrays as "that great—indeed, sole—unique pleasure of an intelligent being" (L 208, CII 409).

Yet, while it is true that his writing reflects conversations and arguments carried on with friends and enemies and strangers, Baudelaire is neither a poet of friend-

---

[1] J. Crépet and C. Pichois, *Baudelaire et Asselineau* (Paris: Nizet, 1953), 81.

ship nor someone for whom friendship came particularly easily, except perhaps in those first heady years of freedom in Paris. In one of his articles on Edgar Allan Poe, he suggests revealingly that the American poet was a man whose company was worth seeking out for "those who measure friendship according to the spiritual gain that they can acquire from frequenting someone" (II 270). This indicates a rather solemn measure of friendship, one that has little to do with companionship or easy-going camaraderie, but an ideal focused on and measured by spiritual growth. There is a telling passage in his article on Delacroix's life and work where you feel that yet again, in talking about the painter, he is also talking about himself: "Delacroix seemed to reserve all his sensitivity, which was deep and manly, for the austere sentiment of friendship. There are people who grow easily attached to everyone they meet; others reserve the use of that divine faculty for great occasions" (II 767–68).

It is also true, of course, that with the passage of time, with the increasing difficulty of his daily existence and with the growing shadow of his legend, it became less and less easy for him to use that divine faculty. In a letter to Sainte-Beuve dated January 1862, he touches on that sense of growing isolation: "I was deeply hurt, although I said nothing about it, to hear myself described over several years as a werewolf, an impossible and rebarbative man. Once, in a malicious newspaper, I read a few lines about my repulsive ugliness, just the sort to drive away any sympathy (that was hard for a man who has so loved the perfume of women)" (L 182, CII 219). Here we find the ugly man of one of the prose poems (PPP XL), gazing at his reflection in the mirror, and insisting on his right to do so, however little pleasure it might bring him. But this is again the mask that clings to the face, the legend that becomes a reality. The finicky Edmond and Jules de Goncourt depict him in 1857, dining near them in the Café Riche: "He is not wearing a tie, his neck is bare, his head shaven, looking exactly like someone who's been guillotined. [. . .] And a maniac's head, a voice that cuts like steel, and an elocution that aims at the ornate precision of a Saint-Just, and achieves it." [2]

Nevertheless, the more one looks at the close relationships Baudelaire built in the course of his adult life, the more complex the image of friendship becomes, and the more obvious it is that Baudelaire did have friendships that were much closer and more companionable than his own definitions might suggest. What is more, there were some friendships on which he was indeed willing to work. Although he set aside the mask only occasionally, he did make a few very close friends, whose conversation and achievements have left their trace on his writing. In this chapter I want to follow a few of the complex and interlocking lines of conversation and friendship that help create the context for Baudelaire's writing.

---

[2] Quoted in W. T. Bandy and C. Pichois, *Baudelaire devant ses contemporains* (Paris: Editions du Rocher, 1967), 38.

We can understand Baudelaire's somewhat prickly, somewhat formal, capacity for friendship rather better if we set it against other more or less contemporary images of friendship. The great nineteenth-century French poet of friendship is Stéphane Mallarmé, born some twenty years after Baudelaire, and whose witty quatrains used to address envelopes to friends reflect a warmth and a sense of humor quite alien to the poet of *Les Fleurs du mal.* In particular, Mallarmé's celebration of the Belgian poets he met in Bruges displays all the power of a sonnet to evoke the delight in a friendship that not only seems to find its physical correlative in the little medieval city in which it began, but also, despite its recent date, strikes the new friends as having its roots deep in the distant past. But the poetry of friendship so beautifully deployed by Mallarmé is perhaps dependent on a sense of security not just as a poet but also as a friend that Baudelaire rarely seems to have had, or indeed greatly to have valued.

It is a security certainly felt by Victor Hugo, and indeed several of Hugo's finest poems suggest a community of minds—his poems to Alphonse de Lamartine or to François-René Chateaubriand, Charles-Augustin Sainte-Beuve or the painter Louis Boulanger, as well as many others, have the air of a conversation, a sharing of ideas, experience, and goodwill that evoke the atmosphere of the circle of Romantic poets, painters, and thinkers who gathered for talk and argument and support. Hugo is particularly good at transforming his friends into symbols of courage in the face of adversity, or of beleaguered art struggling on despite the violence of the acts to which it was subjected. Here is how he addresses the young Sainte-Beuve, before the latter's metamorphosis into the influential and respected critic nicknamed "l'oncle Beuve," in the days when he was striving to make his way as a poet:

> Rayonne, il en est temps! et, s'il vient un orage,
> En prisme éblouissant change le noir nuage.
> Que ta haute pensée accomplisse sa loi.
> Viens, joins ta main de frère à ma main fraternelle.
> Poëte, prends ta lyre; aigle, ouvre ta jeune aile;
> > Etoile, étoile, lève-toi![3]

In English this seems to demand a more ample rhythm, something in the manner of Matthew Arnold or George Meredith:

> Shine, for now the time has come! and if the storm should break,
> Across the dark and lowering cloud a dazzling prism shake.
> Impose your thinking's lofty law upon the threatening skies.
> Come, brother, put your hand in mine. Take up your lyre and sing,

---

[3] Hugo, *Œuvres poétiques,* ed. P. Albouy (Paris: Gallimard, 1964), 446.

Young eagle, now's the time for you to open wide your wing;
Come star, come star, arise!

It is hard to imagine Baudelaire writing anything either so elevated or so vague—I cannot help thinking of Baudelaire's comment in a letter to Sainte-Beuve about *"that vagueness, beloved by the great"* (L 182, CII 220). Although Baudelaire mentions Hugo among the group of literary connections he made after his return from the sea journey to Mauritius and Reunion (I 785), the two poets were never to become friends, meeting rarely in person and more rarely still in mind. Writing to Asselineau to thank him for a copy of the latter's biography of Baudelaire, Hugo noted, somewhat pensively: "I met rather then knew Baudelaire. He often shocked me and I must often have offended him; I'd like to discuss him with you. I share all your praise of him, with some reservations" (LAB, 185).

Less portentous poems of friendship represent Théodore de Banville's image of the poetry of modernity, witty, supple, and full of virtuoso rhymes. His wonderfully varied book, *Odes funambulesques* (*Tightrope Odes*), for instance, is rich in tributes to friends and in joyous paeans to friendship. In the following triolet he wrote for the witty journalist Henri de La Madelène, with whom both Banville and Baudelaire had rubbed shoulders while working on various newspapers in the late 1840s, you can hear the affection and the pleasure in finding the rhymes:

J'adore assez le grand Lama
Mais j'aime mieux La Madelène.
Avec sa robe qu'on lama
J'adore assez le grand Lama.
Mais La Madelène en l'âme a
Bien mieux que de damas de laine.
J'adore assez le grand Lama,
Mais j'aime mieux La Madelène[4]

—the lightness and wittiness of which is, of course, almost impossible to seize in English. It might go something like this:

I'm wild about the Great Lama
But I'm wilder still about La Madelène.
With his robes all lama-
Nated, I'm wild about the Great Lama.
But La Madelène is ana-

---

[4] Théodore de Banville, *Œuvres poétiques complètes,* ed. Peter J. Edwards (Geneva: Slatkine, 1992–2001), III: 187.

Mated by better than this woolly damascene.
I'm wild about the Great Lama,
But I'm wilder still about La Madelène.

Other tributes to friends are scattered through Banville's writing. Here is the opening of his *Ballade* to the English poet John Payne, who had just published his translation of the medieval French poet François Villon:

A toi salut, cher Payne! En vers anglais
Tu mets Villon, que notre vigne inspire?
Entre les fous, aïeux de Rabelais,
O bons rythmeurs du pays de Shakspere,
Vous en pouviez, je crois, choisir un pire.[5]

Greetings to you Payne! In English verse
You set Villon, whose verse our vine inspires.
Among old Rabelais's eccentric sires,
Great rhymesters of Will Shakespeare's shires,
You could, I think, have chosen worse.

Although he is a curious absence from the list of literary connections in the bio-
bibliographic notes Baudelaire assembled for Antonio Watripon, and although the
correspondence leaves little trace of their friendship, Banville was one of Baudelaire's
earliest friends, one of those with whom he carried on the most enthusiastic literary
debates, at least, in his early twenties (see figure 4). Traces of their conversation are
clearly detectable through their poems. In an exchange of sonnets written in the
spring of 1845, Baudelaire and Banville debate the value poets should place on materialism in their writing.[6] We are in the midst of a conversation here, as if the two
young men had separated after an animated discussion, either in Banville's rooms in
the rue Monsieur-le-Prince or in Baudelaire's apartment on the Ile Saint-Louis, with
each of them now eager to set his ideas down on paper. When, in an article he published in 1861, Baudelaire was to glance back to those happy years of his youth, he
would admit just how much Banville had already accomplished in his first volume,
Les Cariatides, but he nevertheless allowed himself the following *caveat:* "His work as
a whole, with its radiance and its variety, did not at first reveal the particular nature
of its author, either because that nature was not yet sufficiently formed or because the
poet was still under the fascinating charm of all the poets of the great age of French

[5] Ibid., VIII:288.
[6] On this see my article " 'Le Réseau mobile de quelque toile d'araignée': Banville et la conversation poétique," in *Poésie et Poétique en France,* ed. Peter J. Edwards (New York: Peter Lang, 2001).

verse" (II 162–63). This is the nub of the issue: how do you forge your own identity at a time so dominated by great poets? It is also a statement that sheds particular light on Baudelaire's ambivalent attitude to friendships with poets, on his determination to stay apart and stamp his own highly individual mark on the age. Reading the first line of Banville's 1845 poem "A Charles Baudelaire" in the light of this article, one can detect the major elements of the debate: "Oh poet, since we must, let's honor matter's role." How can one free oneself from the poets of the great years of Romanticism in order to create a truly modern poetry? What would be the role in that poetry not only of the emotions and the intellect, but also of matter, and above all of physical and erotic love? If Banville pays mere lip-serve to honoring materialism, Baudelaire's reply summarily dismisses the image in which Banville shows the poetic soul visited by inspiration. He, on the contrary, grabs the Goddess of poetry by the hair to pull her abruptly into the modern world (just as Banville himself will do later on, for example, in "La Malédiction de Cypris [The Curse of Venus]," which appears in his volume *Le Sang de la coupe* published in 1857, the same year as the first edition of *Les Fleurs du mal*). The poet in Baudelaire's poem transforms himself into a muscle-bound ruffian who hurls his mistress brutally to the ground. For Banville, "honoring" physical reality is merely the first step that needs to be taken before giving free rein to the imagination. For Baudelaire, who, one week before writing his letter, had attempted (or pretended) to kill himself, physical reality loomed as the most menacing threat to the imagination's very existence, posing a danger that was at the same time imagination's most ferocious stimulus. Banville was to continue this conversation on matter even after the death of his longtime friend, in a poem that is simply entitled "Baudelaire" and dated September 1874. The lines in which Banville returns to the old theme of matter are exceptionally rich:

> La Matière, céleste encor même en sa chute,
> Impuissante à créer l'oubli d'une minute,
> Pâture du Désir, jouet du noir Remord,
> Et souffrant sans répit jusqu'à ce que la Mort,
> Apparaissant, la baise au front et la délivre.[7]

> Celestial even in its fall,
> Matter finds no oblivion,
> Food for desire, remorse's toy,
> Death's kiss alone its suffering ends.

These lines, deeply nourished by Banville's reading of *Les Fleurs du mal,* reveal the extent to which he had understood the role of remorse in the thinking of Baude-

---

[7] Banville, IV:184.

laire, but they reproduce, in a far more complex way, the spiritualization of matter that was already present in his 1845 poem. Baudelaire, in "Le Voyage," transforms death into a captain and the soul into a traveler eager to plunge into the abyss, regardless of what might be found there. Banville, on the other hand, presents Matter not just as celestial but as feminized, a victim of desire and remorse, and passively accepting death. Just as Baudelaire, reading E. T. A. Hoffmann or Thomas de Quincey, for instance, seeks out doubles of himself, so Banville here, even while he struggles to rediscover Baudelaire, projects onto the universe of *Les Fleurs du mal* a Banvillian light. In his funeral oration for Baudelaire, Banville claimed that *Les Fleurs du mal* was the work "not of a poet of talent, but of a poet of genius, and with each passing day we'll have a clearer view of the great place held in our tormented and suffering age by a work which is essentially French, essentially original, essentially new."[8]

Another of the early friendships Baudelaire formed while frequenting the office of the *Corsaire-Satan* was with the writer and art-critic Jules Champfleury, whose love of the fine arts led him later to become director of the ceramic works at Sèvres (see figure 8). In February of 1848, Champfleury and Baudelaire would found a short-lived journal, *Le Salut public,* whose second and final number would be illustrated by the realist painter Gustave Courbet. Champfleury's respect for Delacroix, his enthusiasm for pantomime, his interest in caricature, and his love of cats are all traits he shared with Baudelaire. Moreover, in 1856 he translated a selection of short stories by E. T. A. Hoffmann, whose witty or terrifying tales of the fantastic and whose impassioned writing on music strongly attracted Baudelaire in the years before he encountered Poe. Champfleury, like Gautier and Baudelaire, wrote a review of Wagner's *Tannhäuser* when it was performed in Paris. An amateur violinist, he also wrote the occasional short story about violins. He wrote histories of caricature in the Middle Ages and the Renaissance and published memoirs of the famous Funambules Theater whose mimes are so lovingly re-created in Jacques Prévert and Marcel Carné's great film *Les Enfants du paradis.* He shared Baudelaire's interest in eccentrics, devoting to them a little book that came out in 1852. His memoirs contain a carefully drawn portrait of Baudelaire, suggesting that Champfleury found him more intriguing than endearing. "Sometimes Baudelaire's enthusiasms struck me as hoaxes," he confesses bemusedly at one point.[9] Yet, he admits rather stuffily: "Baudelaire's conversations were nonetheless a fertile source of information for me, since I would listen attentively to the man who had read and researched a great deal, and thanks to my twenty-year-old intellectual stomach, I had no difficulty digesting these

[8] Quoted in Crépet and Pichois, 151–52.

[9] Champfleury, *Souvenirs et portraits de jeunesse* (Paris: Dentu, 1872), 132.

strange fruit.''[10] Champfleury's depiction of his friend concludes with a parallel drawn from an area both appreciated, the pantomime.

> I couldn't find a better way of describing Baudelaire physically and intellectually than by comparing him to a certain *Sprit* [*sic*: for Sprite?] from an English pantomime that we watched together. This Sprit appeared throughout the play and usually appeared with his legs in the air and his head upside-down, and he was above all remarkable for a brilliant flame on the tip of his nose. From time to time I glanced at the place next to mine, wondering if Baudelaire had not escaped unbeknownst to me to perform the role of this extraordinary Sprit. [11]

The community of interest between Baudelaire and Champfleury contained, however, sharp distinctions in terms of how those interests were best served, distinctions that set up a series of echoes and conversations reflected in their letters and in their publications. Champfleury's championing of realism in the early 1850s stung Baudelaire into drafting his notes for an article which remained unpublished but to which he had given the tentative and provocative title: "Puisque réalisme il y a" ("Since Realism Exists"). Baudelaire uses it to explore the ways in which literary and artistic movements get underway, and to suggest that they can do so with such impetus that those who had initiated them are swept away despite themselves. "Confess, perverse child," he snarls at Champfleury, "that you are taking pleasure in the general confusion and even in the weariness that writing this article causes me" (II 57). It all came about, Baudelaire argues, teasingly and belligerently, because Champfleury believed that any movement needed a word, a flag, a joke, and that such words have magic potency. The problem is, he adds, that once you have launched such a hoax, you have to believe in the magic. You can overhear the conversation between the two men at this point, with Champfleury protesting that art should convey the real world, that this is what modern literature and art should make their main goal, and Baudelaire responding that the world is a hieroglyphic dictionary, one that art needs to translate and transpose, and that, "Poetry is what is most real, what is completely true only in *another world*" (II 59).

In 1865, when Baudelaire was in Brussels, Champfleury wrote with news of his study of modern caricature, devoted above all to Honoré Daumier, whom Baudelaire also greatly admired. In his letter, Champfleury asks Baudelaire for a poem to accompany a portrait of Daumier that would appear in his study, clarifying what he wanted in the following revealing terms:

[10] Champfleury, 134.
[11] Champfleury, 146.

I'm not asking you for an improvisation or a quatrain or some occasional verse. I know that for you the slightest poetic conception demands a lengthy meditation, and I see how much that proves the respect you have for your art. But you are full of Daumier and his work, the man and his pencil. The poetry I need for this subject lies dormant in you and I'm awakening it by writing to you, as I woke up this morning drawn to my work.

(LAB 82)

There is perhaps more courtesy here than deep warmth, but it successfully milked a common interest. In writing his poem, Baudelaire thought back to his own distinction, explored in his 1855 article *On the Essence of Laughter,* between laughter as a satanic conviction of superiority and laughter as an outburst of joy. The terrible laughter of Melmoth, the central character in Charles Robert Maturin's gothic novel of that name, reflects the man's duality, while Daumier's humor, on the contrary, stems from the joy of creating, and, more specifically, from the delight in showing the grotesque in everyday life. The poem Baudelaire wrote for Champfleury is both a somewhat nostalgic echo of the studies on caricature he had written in the previous decade and a tribute to their friendship. The letter he sent Champfleury claimed that he had written the poem within an hour of receiving the request, and he explained: "If you find in these lines a degree of hardness and platitude, even clumsiness, it is *intentional.* I wanted to imitate the sententious tone and the epigraphic, legendary style of lines you find under old engravings" (NL 97). In translating this little poem, I've attempted to seize this same tone, sententious and epigraphic, as Baudelaire claims.

Celui dont nous t'offrons l'image,
Et dont l'art, subtil entre tous,
Nous enseigne à rire de nous,
Celui-là, lecteur, est un sage.

C'est un satirique, un moqueur;
Mais l'énergie avec laquelle
Il peint le Mal et sa séquelle,
Prouve la beauté de son cœur.

Son rire n'est pas la grimace
De Melmoth ou de Méphisto
Sous la torche d'Alecto
Qui les brûle, mais qui nous glace.

Leur rire, hélas! de la gaîté
N'est que la douloureuse charge;

Le sien rayonne, franc et large,
Comme un signe de sa bonté!

(I 167)

He whose portrait on this page,
And whose gifts in all he draws,
Makes us laugh at our own flaws,
That man, reader, is a sage.

Though he plays the mocker's part,
Still his energetic wrath
At Evil and its aftermath,
Proves the beauty of his heart.

Melmoth or Mephisto's sneer
Lit by Alecto's flaming torches,
Freezes us but them it scorches
Daumier's art shines far more clear.

Their laugh alas is but deception,
Just joy's painful counterfeit,
His is radiant pleasure's seat,
Symbol of his deep compassion.

Although they remained on relatively good terms, and although Champfleury's letters contain occasional words of praise for Baudelaire's poems, after his friend's death Champfleury reached the following melancholy conclusion: "I leafed through all Baudelaire's works again recently, and despite my friendship for the man, I found very few ideas and my reading left me sad and empty" (LAB, 78). Ah, but, as Mallarmé might have replied, it is not with ideas that one makes poetry, but with words.

Two of Baudelaire's friendships with artists stand out: that with Delacroix, in which the painter sometimes treats the poet with a degree of suspicion that may surprise modern readers, knowing the crucial role Baudelaire played in making the artist's work more familiar to the reading public; and that with Edouard Manet, whom Baudelaire is seen by some critics as treating with similar ambiguity. By the time they met, in 1847, Delacroix was in his late 40s, no longer the ardent and sometimes eccentric young man we find in the early passages of his journal. He records Baudelaire's first visits with a tinge of amused and distant irony, as if observing an exuberant puppy dog. And there is something bumptious about Baudelaire's allusion, in his 1846 article titled *Conseils aux jeunes littérateurs (Advice to young writers)*, to the painter's advice to him: "E. Delacroix was saying to me the

other day: 'Art is something so ideal and so fleeting that our tools are never sufficiently appropriate nor our means sufficiently expeditious.' It's the same with literature. That's why I'm not in favor of rewriting—it disturbs the mirror of thought"
(II 17). The formula "Delacroix was saying to me the other day" seems to have been
a catchword of Baudelaire's in those days, one that was caricatured in the newspaper *La Silhouette* in the same year as the *Conseils aux jeunes littérateurs*. In *La Silhouette,* Baudelaire is in conversation with his friend, the journalist Auguste Vitu. "You
see, Vitu, creditors are like women. You can't love them enough. Eugène Delacroix
was saying to me the other day . . ." (II 1087). But at that point the editor arrives
and we hear no more.

Nevertheless, in 1847 Delacroix jotted down Baudelaire's address, recorded several visits, and lent him 150 francs (April 4, 1847). Political differences separated
them in 1848, yet we find Delacroix noting Baudelaire's name and address again in
the Journal of 1855.[12] Armand Moss's study of their relationships suggests that
Baudelaire invented much of what he says about his acquaintanceship with the
great painter, but in a diary entry of May 30, 1856, Delacroix pays Baudelaire the
rare accolade of quoting with approval some of the remarks he made about his art.
Here we find the artist reading Poe, analyzing the sense of the mysterious it creates
in him, and moving on to sharpen the comparison between himself and Poe by
drawing on Baudelaire: "Baudelaire says in his preface that my painting recalls this
sentiment of the ideal which is so strange and so pleasing when combined with the
terrible. He's right, but the kind of disconnected and incomprehensible element that
accompanies Poe's visions does not suit my turn of mind."[13] What is more, regardless of how little real friendship Delacroix might have felt for Baudelaire, he certainly understood and appreciated his talent both as critic and as translator. Michele
Hannoosh, who is currently preparing a new edition of Delacroix's journals, argues
that there are also statements in Baudelaire's essay on Delacroix which only someone
who knew him well would have been able to produce at that period.[14] Certainly
Delacroix appreciated his comments on his art, suggesting that Baudelaire had indeed seized the essence of what he was attempting to do. In June 1859, for instance,
he wrote to thank Baudelaire for his remarks in the review of that year's salon, which
had provoked some negative criticism from certain quarters, notably Henri De-
laborde and Maxime du Camp (Baudelaire somewhat tongue-in-cheek dedicated
his poem "Le Voyage" to this inveterate traveler). "You have come to my aid,"
Delacroix acknowledges to Baudelaire, "at a moment when I found myself berated
and vilified by a fair number of serious critics—or at least they proclaimed them-

---

[12] I am very grateful to Michele Hannoosh, who is preparing a new edition of the journals, for providing
me with this information. The reference to Baudelaire in the 1855 Journal was omitted from the Plon version. Eugène Delacroix, *Journal,* ed. André Joubin (Paris: Plon, 1938).

[13] Delacroix, *Journal,* II:450–51.

[14] Private email to author on April 25, 2001.

selves to be serious. [. . .] Having had the good fortune to please you consoles me for their reprimands. You treat me as only the great dead are treated. You make me blush while pleasing me greatly. We are made like that." And he adds, in a paragraph that turns away from himself and to his correspondent: "Publish something often. You put yourself in everything you do, and those who are friends of your talent complain only of the rarity of your appearances."[15] Delacroix's thank you note for Baudelaire's review of the paintings in the church of Saint Sulpice is more specific and just as enthusiastic. "My sincere thanks both for your praise and for the reflections that accompany and confirm it, on those mysterious effects of line and color, effects that unfortunately are felt by only a few aficionados."[16]

Most important, Delacroix served as a model for Baudelaire's image of a certain kind of Romanticism, the movement he saw as the expression of the modern in art, and writing about him allowed Baudelaire to explore what it was that made Delacroix so great a colorist and so perfect a vehicle for the mood of the age. What is more, because of his admiration for the man and his work, he developed a critical language of particular power and beauty, as if fired up by the painter's extraordinary achievements to find a counterpart for them in a rhetoric that was at once precise and intense, subtle and resonant, capable of depicting tiny details and of drawing back to offer the wide sweep that sets him against the backdrop of his age.

Baudelaire's relationship with Manet was different both in its sense of equality and in the warmth it shows. Manet first met Baudelaire in the 1850s, at the time when the painter was studying with Thomas Couture and both poet and painter frequented the Rôtisserie Pavard and the Restaurant Dinocheau (a punning name meaning dine on something warm). He has left us a couple of portraits of the poet, glimpsed in profile wearing a top hat in the oil painting entitled "A Concert in the Tuileries," and again, in profile and in a top hat, in the little etching that accompanied Asselineau's biography. He painted Jeanne Duval, in an 1862 oil known as "Baudelaire's Mistress," and did two portraits of Poe, as if in a conscientious attempt to please and flatter the translator of Poe's tales. Antonin Proust's memoirs depict the two men wandering through the parks and gardens of Paris, with Baudelaire watching as Manet sketched or painted the crowds. Manet shared Baudelaire's enthusiasm for Constantin Guys, whose portrait he painted, and several of whose sketches he owned.[17] Like Delacroix (and many others), Manet lent the poet money—an IOU dated January 4, 1863 indicates a loan of 1,000 francs. But Manet relied much more on Baudelaire's good

---

[15] Eugène Delacroix, *Correspondance générale,* ed. André Joubin (Paris: Plon, 1938), IV: 111.

[16] Delacroix, IV:276.

[17] On this, and the question of why Baudelaire chose Guys rather than Manet as his painter of modern life, see Lois Boe Hyslop and Francis Hyslop, "Baudelaire and Manet," *Baudelaire as a Love Poet* (University Park: Pennsylvania State University Press, 1969), and Lois Boe Hyslop, *Baudelaire, Man of His Time* (New Haven: Yale University Press, 1980).

wishes and looked to him much more for guidance and support than Delacroix ever did. A letter Baudelaire sent Manet in April of 1864, for instance, warns him to change a work he must have been planning to submit to the Salon that year. Baudelaire points out that the wound inflicted on Christ by the lance was on the right side, and that the painter should be careful not to give ill-wishers a chance to laugh at him by getting this wrong (CII 352). Most importantly, in June of 1864 Baudelaire wrote to the art critic Théophile Thoré, reminding him of the discussions they used to have, and thanking him for his defense of Manet, published in the Belgian newspaper, *L'Indépendance belge*. (Thoré was another of those outspoken republicans forced into exile during the Second Empire.) Baudelaire is, however, eager to correct Thoré's judgment that Manet's painting represented a pastiche of certain Spanish artists, notably Goya and El Greco. It is certainly the case that early Manet, with its dark tones and its barely repressed violence, recalls the intensity of the Spanish artists. And it is not surprising that in a letter of September 1865 when Manet had just returned from Madrid, where for the first time he had seen paintings by Velasquez, he should express his enthusiasm in the following exuberant terms:

> At last dear friend I know Velasquez, and I can tell you that he is the greatest painter there ever was. In Madrid I saw 30 or 40 of his canvases, portraits or pictures, and all of them masterpieces. He's worth more than his reputation and on his own he is worth the weariness and the impossible difficulties you encounter on a trip to Spain. I saw some interesting things by Goya, some of them very lovely including a portrait of the duchess of Alba dressed as a *majo*, which is extraordinarily charming
>
> (LAB 236).

As this letter suggests, their friendship was deep and supportive. So much so, indeed, that critics have sometimes misunderstood the nature of the letter Baudelaire sent his friend in May 1865. Seen out of context, the letter may seem harsh, even derogatory, as if the great supporter of Delacroix had failed to understand Manet's gifts and above all his potential. But that letter needs to be considered as a response to a not untypical missive in which the painter laments the harsh treatment he had received from critics. "I wish you were with me, my dear Baudelaire," Manet writes, reeling under the attacks provoked by the two works he had sent to the Salon, his *Jesus insulted by the soldiers* and *Olympia*: "Insults are pouring down on me like hail, I've never before found myself in such a party.[. . .] I would have liked your sensible judgment on my paintings for all these shrieks get on my nerves, and it is clear that someone is wrong here" (LAB, 233–34). Baudelaire, only too familiar with the derision that originality can provoke, could see that sinew-toughening was in order, and sent a bracing letter, which Manet clearly treasured since many years later he was to show it to his friend Mallarmé. Here is what Baudelaire wrote, and in these lines we can hear not just the voice of friendship, but something more, the echo of long and frequent conversations, and underlying that, something of what Baudelaire must have said to himself in times of doubt and depression.

> So I have to talk to you about yourself again. I have to set myself to show you your own worth. What you demand is really stupid. *People tease you; their jokes* get under your skin; no one knows your real worth, etc. etc. Do you think you're the only person to be placed in that position? Do you have more genius than Chateaubriand and Wagner? But they were jeered at, weren't they? It didn't kill them. And to avoid turning your head, I'll add that those two were models, each in his own way, and in a very complex world, whereas you, *you're only the first in the decadence of your art.* I hope you won't bear me a grudge for my lack of formality. You know my friendship for you.
>
> (L 227, CII 496–97)

Manet was not, of course, so silly as to bear any grudge. He knew how to read this, as critics who read too quickly or too seriously, did not. After all, Baudelaire begins his *Notes nouvelles sur Edgar Poe* (New Notes on Edgar Poe) with the following lines: "*Literature of decadence!*—Empty words that all too often we hear falling with the tone of an emphatic yawn from the mouths of those riddle-less sphinxes that guard the holy gates of classical Esthetics. Each time the irrefutable oracle rings out, it can be affirmed that what is at issue is a work that is more amusing than the *Iliad*"(II 319). Champfleury, as we have seen (chapter 3) depicts Baudelaire often speaking of a certain art of decadence, but an art that nevertheless has its laws. And Baudelaire himself was frequently accused of decadence. No doubt Manet had heard him ironically associating both Poe's work and his own with decadence, sardonically turning a term of abuse to his own purposes, as the impressionists were later to do with a word initially coined to mock them.

The warmth of Manet's affection for Baudelaire can be seen in letters he wrote while the poet was in Belgium. In the May 1865 letter in which he lamented the attacks on his painting, he nevertheless found time and heart to write: "Your prolonged stay in Belgium must be tiring you. I'm eager to see you return, and that's moreover what all your friends here want. What's happening with the business you were working on with Lemer? [Baudelaire was attempting to get Julien Lemer, a literary agent, to try to find publishers for his works.] I'd love our newspapers and reviews to give us something of you more often, some poems for instance. You must have written some in the last year" (LAB 234). And only then does he add in a throwaway line that the Royal Academy in London had rejected his paintings for the annual art show. It is clear that he tried to make Lemer take up Baudelaire's case, though Baudelaire warned him in a letter of September 1865 not to hurt Lemer's feelings, given what the poet described as Manet's irritable nature (NL 109); however, in a letter written later that month, Manet sent the following advice, in terms only a close and trusted friend could have used: "Believe me, your affairs will be done well by no one better than you yourself, don't count on others" (LAB 236–37). And in a last, moving letter of March 27, 1866, he expresses his deep concern at not having heard from his friend for some time:

> It's a good while since you sent me any news of you. Tell me without delay how you are and what's happening to you. I'm still waiting for the book you told me was coming—it made my mouth water to think of reading something new by you. I sent two paintings to the exhibition. I'm planning to get them photographed and send you copies. There is a portrait of Rouvière in the role of Hamlet. I call it The Tragic Actor to avoid the criticism of people who'll say it is not enough like him. And there is a Fife player of the light infantry guard, but you need to see the paintings to get a real idea of them. [. . .] Farewell my dear Baudelaire. We all send you our love and would love to see you back here
> (LAB 239).

Philibert Rouvière was an actor both men admired—indeed, Baudelaire had published a study of him in 1855 and wrote an obituary of him when he died in 1865. The choice of subject was, therefore, also a homage to friendship. As it happened, the jury refused both paintings, and by the time he received this letter, Baudelaire had already suffered the attack that led to his death.

Two of Baudelaire's closest friendships leave their complex mark on the last twenty years or so of his life and his writing.[18] He met the first of these devoted friends, Charles Asselineau, in 1845, and they were to remain close for the rest of Baudelaire's life (see figure 9). Baudelaire wrote an article on Asselineau's collection of short stories, *La Double Vie,* and Asselineau for his part devoted four articles to Baudelaire's translations of Poe, and to *Les Fleurs du mal* and the prose poems. Moreover, Asselineau wrote a biography of his friend in which he concluded resolutely and unashamedly that "Charles Baudelaire, [. . .] is, after the great masters of 1830 [a reference to the French Romantics] the only writer of this time whom one can without ridicule describe as a genius."[19] Together with Banville, he became Baudelaire's literary executor after the poet's death. Asselineau certainly was one of those who most valued friendship and worked hardest at making it succeed. When he died, Banville said in his eulogy for him: "Loving those he admired, admiring those whom he loved, that was the faithful watchword, the sole preoccupation, and the constant religion of Charles Asselineau."[20]

---

[18] His relationship with Sainte-Beuve, and the latter's possible influence on Baudelaire's writing, has been explored in depth by Norman Barlow, *Sainte-Beuve to Baudelaire* (Durham, N.C.: Duke University Press, 1964). Their friendship seems rather one-sided, with Baudelaire working to keep the powerful critic favorable to him, and while Sainte-Beuve's *Joseph Delorme* does seem to point the way to *Les Fleurs du mal* as Baudelaire claimed, what is most striking is that the older writer never appeared aware of how radically Baudelaire was changing the face of modern poetry.

[19] Crépet and Pichois, 151.

[20] Crépet and Pichois, 33–34.

As a result, of course, he found himself frequently helping Baudelaire out of financial predicaments. A letter Baudelaire wrote probably at the end of 1855 is typical: "I took the liberty of borrowing your key. I even think that, given my great weariness, I violated the bed. I told your concierge that tomorrow morning someone would bring a packet bearing my name to your apartment. Could you push devotion to the point of personally taking the packet immediately to a *good* pawnshop and trying to get 50 francs for it? In any case, the *top price* you can get" (CI 333). And he adds: "Dear friend, you keep everything, and when one thinks of posterity, one doesn't sign letters like these." A later letter asks for a similar favor: "This morning, have the greatness of heart to put *one* franc in a pair of socks, the socks in a handkerchief, the handkerchief in a shirt, and all of that into the hands of this messenger" (CI 361). And this time he does sign.

There are traces of conversations between Baudelaire and Asselineau in the review of the Salon of 1845. Together with the young painter Emile Deroy they had wandered through the Louvre hotly debating the quality of the artists there, and they shared many enthusiasms, especially for Delacroix. In his own account of the 1845 Salon, Asselineau modestly stated that readers could find his ideas on Delacroix "more knowledgeably and more openly developed" in Baudelaire's review.[21]

Asselineau was an enthusiastic and energetic book collector, acknowledged by Banville as deeply knowledgeable about poetry,[22] and Baudelaire did not hesitate either to borrow books from him or to ask for his opinion on poetic matters. He was the one who advised the addition of the third stanza of "L'Albatros," for example. In a letter written late in February 1859, he asserts, in a judicious blend of praise and suggestions: "The *Albatross* poem is a diamond!—Except that I'd like to see a stanza between the second and the last, to insist on the clumsiness or at least the difficulty of the albatross, and to give a picture of its predicament. It seems to me that this would make the last stanza stand out all the more powerfully" (LAB 18). Baudelaire responded by adding the following verse, with its tense and elliptical depiction of the contrast between the bird flying and walking, and showing it ridiculed by the sailors:

> Ce voyageur ailé, comme il est gauche et veule!
> Lui, naguère si beau, qu'il est comique et laid!
> L'un agace son bec avec un brûle-gueule,
> L'autre mime, en boitant, l'infirme qui volait.
>
> (FM II)

McGowan translates this as: "This voyager, how comical and weak! / Once handsome, how unseemly and inept! / One sailor pokes a pipe into his beak, / Another

---

[21] Quoted II 1266: see also Crépet and Pichois, 69.
[22] See Théodore de Banville, *Petites Etudes* (Paris: Charpentier, 1882), 288–303.

mocks the flier's hobbled step." Howard, as usual translating more loosely, writes: "How weak and awkward, even comical / this traveler but lately so adroit—one deckhand sticks a pipe stem in its beak, / another mocks the cripple that once flew!" Walter Martin manages both rhythm and rhyme gracefully here to give: "This noble traveler, so graceful then, / So awkward now, and comical, and meek— / One sailor apes the sea-sick alien, / Another sticks a pipe stem in his beak!" Carson gives us: "This wingèd voyager, now bedraggled, ugly, awkward, how pathetic! / Someone pokes a pipe into his mouth, and someone else who mimics him is paralytic." But it is perhaps Wilbur who succeeds best in conveying the original while retaining the rhyme: "This rider of the winds, how awkward he is, and weak! / How droll he seems, who lately was all grace! / A sailor pokes a pipe stem into his beak; / Another, hobbling, mocks his trammeled pace."

Yet something is inevitably lost in these translations, given the impossibility of finding an English word as striking and suggestive as the word here translated as pipe or pipe stem. The French slang term Baudelaire uses, "brûle-gueule," is literally "throat burner" or, better yet, "gullet burner," and next to that the neutral "pipe" lacks not only the echo of colloquial speech but also the intensity of the image. But this is insurmountable, at least until English comes up with and assimilates a slang term as powerful as "brûle-gueule." In any case, Asselineau was certainly right in his judgment, even if many might also have liked him to urge Baudelaire to leave off the final stanza, with its somewhat heavy-handed explanation of the image. We knew, before being told, that "the poet is like this prince of the clouds." But the fact that Baudelaire accepted Asselineau's suggestion so readily indicates the depth of friendship and trust between them, a trust reflected in the letter in which Baudelaire describes the strange brothel he visited in a dream (see chapter 5) or in the request he made in December 1856 that Asselineau come and advise him on writing a contract involving the publisher Poulet-Malassis (CI 367). And in February 1866, in response to a letter from Asselineau reproaching him for leaving his friends worried about him because of his silence (LAB 20–21), Baudelaire wrote to ask for his advice and help concerning the growing seriousness of his physical condition.

It is clear, moreover, that money, dreams, health, and literature were not the sole subjects of conversation. These two friends also talked of friendship, and it seems likely that Baudelaire was touched by Asselineau's sense not just of what was due to friendship, but also what was needed to maintain it. Writing from his mother's house in Honfleur in February 1859, Baudelaire alludes to the critic and novelist Hippolyte Babou's attempt to stir up trouble between himself and Sainte-Beuve: "Babou knows I'm very closely tied to uncle Beuve, and that I greatly value his friendship. He knows that *I* go to great lengths to hide my opinion when it goes against Sainte-Beuve's." And he adds, in what is a tribute to Asselineau's image of friendship, "Now, there are some thoughts that are made to meet your approval" (CI 555). Indeed, their continuing friendship must have obliged Asselineau to temporize on many subjects, especially politics. In politics he was a moderate, more likely to support a return of the monarchy than to long for a republic; in religion he was hostile to Catholicism and mysticism; his taste in literature did not extend to Poe, and he provoked Baudelaire's mockery for refusing to hear Wagner because the composer was reported to be a republican.[23]

We can hear something of the tone of their conversation in the marginal comments Baudelaire wrote on Asselineau's preface to his collection of short stories, *La Double Vie*. These comments are also arresting in the sharply focused glimpse they give us into Baudelaire's reading habits. At one point Asselineau describes the esthetics of a certain editor as being "a complicated and labyrinthine composition of a crowd of little nuances," provoking from Baudelaire the tart rejoinder, "Composition *implies complication*" (II 93). No doubt Baudelaire agreed with the sentiment, if not its expression, since he remarks in his notes for the never completed *Mon cœur mis à nu (My Heart Laid Bare),* "On editors and pedantry. The immense pleasure all French people find in pedantry, and in dictatorship" (I 685). His sharp eye for cliché picks up Asselineau's hackneyed expression, "you've been accepted; your article is on the marble," meaning the marble of the printing press. But this is too much of a commonplace for his friend's taste and is summarily rejected as "an old marmoreal saying" (II 93). Sloppy constructions attract his red ink, too. Here is Asselineau, getting carried away in discussing the tribulations of a critic: "A critic who lives on current events can take his manuscript up again only in order to destroy it. The hour and the place of appearance must be right, or suicide is the sole answer." Baudelaire, unmoved by the critic's plight, zeroes in on the grammar to ask: "Is it the critic that has to *appear* and commit suicide, or the manuscript?" (II 94). And when Asselineau's modesty leads him to write, "Do not think I exaggerate. I am abbreviating ridiculously. I have friends (alas!) who are full of talent and whom necessity nails to their harsh task," Baudelaire, unflattered, leaps in to ask "why ridiculously"? "Why alas?" At one point Asselineau scribbles a question for Baudelaire in the margin, "can you say the slope of a valley?" to which Baudelaire laconically replies, "No." Baudelaire comments on the grammar, on the use of suspension points, remarks that a sentence is incomprehensible, explains how the expression, "the school of good sense," came into being, and, with a speaking exclamation mark, points out the silliness of writing that "I attach enough importance to my frail personality to envelope it in some movement or other" (II 96). Asselineau took most of these corrections in good part, accepting Baudelaire's suggestions or acting on his criticisms in revising his preface. And of course as the title of Asselineau's collection, *La Double Vie,* suggests, it is dominated by a concept of human nature that is very close to Baudelaire's own. In his review, indeed, Baudelaire raises a question central to both of them, illustrating it with a quotation from the admired De Quincey: "Who among

---

[23] See Crépet and Pichois, 19.

us is not a *homo duplex?* I am referring to those whose mind has been since childhood 'touched with pensiveness'; always double, action and intention, dream and reality; always one half harming the other, one half usurping the other's share" (II 87). And from here he takes off, in one of those extraordinary and intense passages where suddenly the difference between critical and creative voice disappears, and Baudelaire seems to merge with the writer whose works he is discussing:

> The intention abandoned en route, the dream forgotten in an inn, the project blocked by obstacles, misfortune and weakness springing from success like venomous plants from a rich and neglected soil, regret mingled with irony, the glance thrown behind like that of a tramp who meditates for a moment, the unceasing mechanism of earthly life, teasing and tearing at every instant the fabric of ideal life: these are the principal elements of this exquisite book which, through its nonchalance, its unstudied, friendly garb and its suggestive sincerity, recalls a monologue or an intimate letter entrusted to the mailbox for far off countries.
>
> (II 87)

He is not claiming for the author of *La Double Vie* the status of a great writer, but he is claiming something that Asselineau may well have valued rather more: shared convictions, the quality of unstudied friendship, the capacity for sincerity and intimacy. In its understated way, this is a considerable tribute. Asselineau strikes one as the most endearing and perhaps also the most hardworking of Baudelaire's friends—hardworking in terms of keeping the friendship on an even keel.

Nevertheless, the friend who grew closest to Baudelaire was almost certainly his publisher, Auguste Poulet-Malassis, who was some four years younger than the poet. He came from a family that had long been in the printing business, in Alençon, which is in Normandy. As Claude Pichois affirms in his biography of Malassis, only a few of the letters he wrote to Baudelaire have been preserved, and then only those written after 1857, so their friendship has to be traced primarily through Baudelaire's letters. It is a friendship that Baudelaire had to work at, especially in the early phases. Early in 1850 the two men met through their mutual acquaintance Champfleury. At this stage Malassis was cooling his heels in Paris, ostensibly attending the Ecole des Chartes, which prepares students for careers as archivists and paleographers. The letters we have from Baudelaire in these years suggest that he was eager to secure the friendship. Soon after their first meeting, Baudelaire writes to Nerval requesting tickets for Malassis to see a show created by Nerval and Joseph Méry, and in mid-July 1850 we find him planning to visit Malassis in Alençon during the summer.

After the coup d'état in 1852, Baudelaire wrote him an unusually revealing letter, which shows not only how close he felt Malassis' politics were to his own, but also how much at ease he was in discussing his literary plans with him. After a rapid review of the current situation, dominated, he argues, by folly and individual passions, Baudelaire sums up: "All this amuses me very much. But I've decided that henceforth I'll remain aloof from all human polemics. I've become more determined than ever to pursue the loftier dream of applying metaphysics to the novel" (L 46, CI 189). There is, in this relatively expansive letter, a tone, rarely found in Baudelaire's correspondence, of relaxed confidence and friendly trust. (A week later he was to write to his mother a much more typical letter, complaining of how little time he had to himself, how much he was forced to waste his time on feeble articles dashed off merely to gain money, how he was forced to lead a mad, painful life, tormented by his mistress and so forth.)

From 1853 to 1855 Malassis was back in Alençon, working in the family printing house, and playing an active role in a local paper, *Le Journal d'Alençon,* in which he published an article on Edgar Allan Poe, which concludes with a judgment that must have astonished Baudelaire, given the stress he had placed in his letter to Malassis on metaphysics and the novel. "We refer those who would like to know more about Poe to the article published by M. Baudelaire (*Revue de Paris,* March and April 1852). The biographical part is very brilliant, but the philosophical part should be completely rewritten."[24] This is a tease, but Baudelaire, clearly wanting to keep this independently minded young man onside, refrained from replying to Malassis' jibe until the end of the year, when, typically, he wrote primarily to beg for a loan. In a postscript to this begging letter, Baudelaire complains: "You say [in the *Journal d'Alençon* article] that my categories, my psychological explanations are unintelligible—and even, if I'm remembering correctly, —that I have no philosophical bent. — It's possible that I'm a little obscure in work I have to do in haste, when need drives me on and romantic brutes hound me [. . .] For my part, I'm convinced that you haven't understood the GENIUS in question. You spoke, taking flashy pleasure in your wit, of a man you've not frequented" (L 59, CI 239–40). And he adds, again in characteristic style, "Don't let my little outburst prevent you from doing what you can for me" (L 59, CI 240). Malassis was to be useful to Baudelaire not just in financial terms, for in January of 1854 the *Journal d'Alençon* printed two of his cat poems ("Les Amoureux fervents (Fervent lovers)" and "Viens, mon beau chat (Come, my fine cat)"). Later, in the same month, his study "La Morale du joujou (The Moral of the Toy)" appeared, while in May his translation of Poe's *Philosophy of Furniture* was published, alas, with the translator's name misspelled, to his fury, as Beaudelaire.[25]

In 1855 Malassis and his brother-in-law Eugène De Broise took over the family publishing house and established their own imprint. Short-lived though it may have

---

[24] Quoted in Claude Pichois, *Auguste Poulet-Malassis* (Paris: Fayard, 1996), 56.
[25] This so enraged Baudelaire that he destroyed the entire print run (which was in any case very small.)

been, this imprint was to become associated with many of the most dynamic young writers of the decade. In the seven years before he was forced to go into exile in Belgium, Poulet-Malassis succeeded in publishing a remarkable crop of works, including Baudelaire's *Les Fleurs du mal,* both Banville's *Odes funambulesques* and his *Poésies,* Charles Monselet's *La Lorgnette littéraire* and Emile Montégut's *Le Génie français*—all in 1857. But the openness and energy of Malassis' publishing policy carried a serious price: for *Les Fleurs du mal* a fine; for Antonin Lauzun's *Mémoires,* condemned for "outrages to public morals," a fine and a stay in prison; for Ernest Hamel's *Saint-Just,* with its outspoken praise for the revolutionary hero, an order to destroy all copies of the book; for Francis Lacombe's *La France et l'Allemagne sous le premier Empire,* with its less than favorable presentation of Napoleon I, yet another order to destroy the entire print run.[26] Something of the character of Malassis comes across in the choice of books published, in his enthusiastic rather than judicious championing of young talent, and in his buoyant return after each brush with the censors.

Writing to him early in 1857, when *Les Fleurs du mal* was being prepared, Baudelaire reveals a warmth and a trust that show how important this friendship was to him. Poulet-Malassis had raised a question about fonts, and Baudelaire responds: "It's impossible for me to guess if your *nine* would be better. [. . .] But I can tell you something that will put you permanently at your ease. In all questions of this kind, as you know infinitely more about the matter than I do, *in every case when there is no radical repulsion on my part,* FOLLOW YOUR OWN TASTE" (CI 376). This seems generous enough, but the problem was that on very many occasions Baudelaire would indeed reveal radical repulsion. He insisted that the dedication should be lower on the page—unconvincingly adding, "but I leave this to your good taste" (L 91, CI 382). He also complained about the appearance of quotation marks, wanting to maintain the old-fashioned spelling of *poëte,* where Malassis preferred the modern *poète,* and pleading to substitute words while there was still time—"boredom, son of dull incuriosity," should read "boredom, fruit of dull incuriosity," since this correction "though it may appear puerile, is important to me,"(L 94, CI 395). It is clear, too, that Malassis urged Baudelaire (in vain) to write a preface for *Les Fleurs du mal* in which he explained his aims and means in writing his poems, and the intention and method behind the book as a whole (I 185). Even the trial and the fine imposed on the house of Malassis and De Broise did not lead to a cooling of their relationships. On the contrary, Malassis went on to publish Baudelaire's *Paradis artificiels* in 1860 and the new edition of *Les Fleurs du mal* in 1861.

In the late 1850s, moreover, they were bound by closer or at least more intricate ties than friendship, for they became involved in a complex borrowing system meant to help each of them find the funds he needed, but inevitably driving still fur-

---

[26] See Pichois, *Poulet-Malassis,* 76.

ther into debt not only Malassis and Baudelaire but also the friends and acquaintances who joined them in this frequently frenetic shuttling of loans from one money-lender to another. An exchange of letters between Baudelaire and Malassis in March 1861 reflects the seriousness of the situation. Here's Baudelaire writing to Malassis:

> I'm sorry to distress you, but despite the terrible and frequently repeated expression—*We'll go under*—I'm forced to ask you what may perhaps be impossible, in a word a great act of devotion, *with the reservation nevertheless that after payment I'll go on the great expedition of errands and within a couple of days I'll close either partially or completely the hole made in your private affairs.* You can be the judge:
>
> 25 March 1,000 Tenré (impossible)
> 25 March 500 Schwartz (impossible)
> 25 March 350 Gélis (impossible)
> 1 April 500 Lemercier (impossible)
> 10 April 1,100 Hetzel
>
> So our shuttle is impossible since all the moneylenders appear this time in the total. You could perhaps, at Lemercier's or Gélis's, get a note accepted if it is signed by someone other than me, for I must tell you that, to crown my misfortunes, I'm at present being sued for 1,900 francs' worth of disputed IOUs (of which only 600 concern me directly). Schwartz and Gélis are mixed up in this so you can see the danger.
>
> (L 162, CII 135)

Malassis' reply is remarkably forbearing: "I've always had the superstition that this unfortunate debt would be the cause of our collapse and I'm more afraid than ever, for it is impossible to pay it this month. I understand moreover just from looking at your list of names that you for your part can do nothing" (LAB 308).

They survived this particular crunch, but in 1861 de Broise, much less easygoing, much more concerned about his good name than was his brother-in-law, withdrew from the firm, leaving Poulet-Malassis to publish under his own name, and to use the canting trademark of a chicken (*poulet*) apparently on the point of falling from its perch (*mal assis* = poorly seated) (See figure 10). Poorly seated, indeed, for by the summer of 1862 he was forced to declare bankruptcy, and in 1863 he left France for Brussels, knowing by then that Baudelaire had treacherously sold his works to the publisher Pierre Jules Hetzel.

When the two men met again in Brussels in 1864, whatever bad feeling there might have been on Poulet-Malassis' part seems quickly to have been forgotten. As Malassis wrote, endearingly, to Asselineau: "I've seen Baudelaire again, not without pleasure as you can well imagine. All we had to do was see each other again, and everything was forgotten" (Pichois 326). Baudelaire celebrated Malassis' gift for conversation in a witty if unpretentious little poem written in the spring of 1865, which also names their mutual acquaintance, Alphonse Lécrivain:

Mon cher, je suis venu chez vous
Pour entendre une langue humaine;
Comme un, qui, parmi les Papous,
Chercherait son ancienne Athêne.

Puisque chez les Topinambous
Dieu me fait faire quarantaine,
Aux Sots je préfère les Fous
—Dont je suis, chose, hélas! certaine.

Offrez à Mam'selle Fanny
(Qui ne répondra pas: Nenny
La salut n'étant pas d'un âne,)

L'hommage d'un bon écrivain,
—Ainsi qu'à l'ami Lécrivain
Et qu'à Mam'selle Jeanne.

(NL 99)

Dear friend, I came to visit you
To hear a human language spoken,
As one exiled in Timbuktu
Might seek his old Athena's token.

Since I amongst the Topinbou
Must live until the curse is broken,
The mad (like me) I much prefer to
Those whose heads are wholly oaken.

Offer to your dear Miss Frances
(For *no no no* she never answers—
The greeting not being from an ass)

The homage that a writer sends.
The same, please, offer to our friends
Lécrivain and Jeanne his lass.

In Belgium, Malassis had set up business again, now publishing pornographic books and attacks on France's Second Empire. But he was still desperately short of money and eager to have Baudelaire repay the 5,000 francs he owed. In June 1865 Baudelaire made a brief journey to Honfleur and Paris to beg his mother and Narcisse Ancelle, the lawyer in charge of his money, to help him repay this loan, returning with 2,000 francs (see NL, 100). Malassis would not be repaid the rest until after Baudelaire's death. In August 1865 Malassis revealed a certain degree of coldness, no doubt as a result of this financial situation. In a letter to Asselineau he wrote, with sad foresight:

> I hardly see Baudelaire these days. It doesn't worry me too much for although I never see him without pleasure, on the other hand, the way he drags things out, his doggedness and his ramblings have assumed such proportions that it would be more than boring if he visited every day. He will have wasted his time in Belgium as you can easily imagine. His studies consist in forcing everything into his preconceived ideas.[27]

When Baudelaire suffered his stroke, Malassis wrote numerous letters to their friends in Paris and offered to help Baudelaire's mother accompany the dying poet back to Paris. A photograph taken by Charles Neyt in 1864 carries this dedication from Baudelaire: "To my friend, Auguste Malassis, the only being whose laughter lightened my Sadness in Belgium." Malassis, when he received word from Asselineau that Baudelaire had died, wrote back: "Though I was prepared, your letter gripped me by the throat, and I felt anguish, even tears. You know how much I loved him" (Pichois 362).

But the last word in a study of Baudelaire's friendships belongs, I think, to Asselineau, whose biography of Baudelaire includes this wonderfully worded tribute:

> It is certain that Baudelaire, if he was often bored, was never boring. Above all, he never bored others. He was one of those rare men—very rare—beside whom one can live every day without knowing a moment's boredom. His virtues were intimate and secret. Moreover, he hid them through modesty, or was driven by pride to profess the opposite of what he really thought. That is why he had as enemies only those people who did not know him. Whoever knew him loved him.[28]

---

[27] Quoted in Pichois, *Poulet-Malassis*, 186.
[28] Crépet and Pichois, 154.

CHAPTER EIGHT

City of Dreams

Think of Baudelaire in his late adolescence, the "horror of school" (I 295) behind him, supposed to be studying law but devoting his energies, like so many before and since, to a study of cafés and bars and streets. Don't imagine the well lit and carefully groomed Paris of today. Baudelaire's Paris is dirty and ill lit, but perhaps all the more fascinating for being so. Like the Victor Hugo he describes in an essay written for Eugène Crépet's anthology of contemporary writers, Baudelaire already had that "sublime but dangerous taste for strolling and dreaming" (II 129). This is *flânerie*, a word for which there is no truly satisfying English equivalent (and which, surprisingly, comes from the ancient Scandinavian, not, one would think, a culture leaving much time for this particular activity). It's a ramble without an aim, more active than hanging out, more passive than going for a walk. It's a loitering without intent, an extension of window-shopping to cover the whole spectacle a city can offer.

We can picture Baudelaire as *flâneur*, again like Hugo, "ceaselessly, everywhere, under the light of the sun, in the torrents of the throng, in the sanctuaries of art, by dusty libraries exposed to the wind" inviting everything to "enter into [his] eyes so that [he] can remember [them]" (II 129). He sees the "chaos of mud and snow, crossed by myriad carriages, sparkling with toys and candies, bristling with greed and despair" (PPP IV), the baby screaming at the old woman's smiling but unknown and wrinkled face (PPP II), the sun-drenched parks with their statues of Venus (PPP VII), the window-seller whose glass is shattered to smithereens by a customer furious not to have been offered panels of glass that presented a rose-colored view of life (PPP IX). He gazes at fairgrounds and imagines cages holding not animals, but wild women put on display by their equally monstrous men-folk. He meditates on the eloquent juxtapositions of rich and poor, beggars and cheapskates, gamblers and dreamers. He becomes aware of "the profound and complex charm of an ancient capital grown old in the glories and tribulations of life" (II 666). He watches the old and suffering, and he realizes that it is often more productive to stay in one's room, close the curtains and project on their dark and uniform surface images that draw their sustenance from reality but that go beyond, transforming reality in metaphor and allegory.

In 1861, thinking back twenty years to the publication of Théodore de Banville's first collection of poetry in 1841, he offers a sharply-delineated contrast between past and present: "Paris in those days was not what it is now, a hurly-burly, a shambles, a Babel populated by the imbecilic and the useless, with little delicacy as concerns how they kill time, and completely rebellious to the joys of literature. In those days, the Parisian elite consisted of a select group of men charged with shaping the opinions of the rest, and who, when a poet was born, were the first to know about it" (II 162).

In the carefree nature of these early experiences of freedom in a great city lie the inevitable seeds of nostalgia. He could not long hope to escape the attention of a stepfather who expected him to gain the qualifications he would need to earn a living. His personal situation would soon alter radically, but that change would only make him more sensitive to the enormous transformations taking place in Paris itself. Much of that change, at least in terms of the physical disposition of the city, was politically motivated, a calculated attempt to make the center of the city less vulnerable to riots in an age marked by a series of climactic uprisings and revolutions. And much of the bitterness Baudelaire reveals about that change stems from a complicated involution of private experiences and public events in the years leading up to Napoleon III's coup d'état and the declaration of the Second Empire in 1852. 1847 was one of his most difficult years, a time of poverty and of increasing irritation with the difficulties of establishing his name as a writer. He had been commissioned to write articles on caricature and the history of sculpture, but found himself constantly frustrated by his own characteristic procrastination and the practical difficulties of writing while leading the bohemian existence he had chosen. His mother, from whom he frequently begged money, refused to meet him, and he was forced to accept the humiliation of going cap in hand to Narcisse Ancelle whom the *conseil judiciaire* had appointed to manage his finances.

The political situation was growing rapidly worse, as King Louis-Philippe, advised by the reactionary Prime Minister François Guizot (notorious or illustrious, depending on your politics, for urging people to "get rich"), became increasingly entrenched in a conservative rearguard position. His rejection of electoral reform and the banning of a banquet planned in protest stung the National Guard into turning against the government. Guizot resigned on February 23, 1848, and the following day Louis-Philippe abdicated. Baudelaire's step-father, Jacques Aupick, recently promoted to head the *École polytechnique*, had the sagacity to recognize that there was no going back to the House of Orléans and added his name to those who rallied to the provisional republic (Pichois 158–59).

On the morning of the twenty-fourth a friend found Baudelaire on the barricades, brandishing a gun, and shouting that Aupick must be shot. Looking back at this time in the notebooks now called *Mon cœur mis à nu (My Heart Laid Bare)*, Baudelaire refers rather ruefully to his "intoxication in 1848" and, with that desire to analyze his reactions that is typical of him, he adds: "What was the nature of that intoxication? A taste for revenge. The *natural* pleasure of demolition. Literary intoxication; memory of readings" (I 679). The three elements touched on here with such brilliantly suggestive conciseness—the longing for personal vengeance, the more general tendency to revel in destruction, and the influence of his reading of writers as diverse as Charles Fourier, Pierre Joseph Proudhon, and Joseph de Maistre, among many others—reveal how little Baudelaire was really interested in politics. Although he might later claim that he had been "depoliticized" by these events, it is clear that his personality was too self-centered and his thinking too shaped by a belief in the natural aristocracy of an intellectual elite to have much understanding of the compromises and flexibility needed in politics. Jean-Paul Sartre's somewhat cynical acceptance of the need to get your hands dirty, as he shows in the play of that name, seems far removed from the consciousness that shapes *Les Fleurs du mal*.

The coup d'état that transformed Louis-Napoleon from president of the new republic to head of the new empire may have filled Baudelaire with brief rage, but looking back at it in his notes books what he stresses is the rapid passage from anger to analysis: "My fury at the coup d'état. How many rifle shots I had to brave. Another Bonaparte! How shameful! And yet everything calmed down. Doesn't a president have a right to invoke? Description of the emperor Napoleon III. What he's worth. Find the explanation of his nature and his providentiality." (I 679) Baudelaire's response to the changing face of politics is like his reaction to the changing face of Paris. It is the highly personal vision of a man watching from the margins, and of a mind that believes itself to be in exile, even at home.

Paris has changed, the poet laments in "Le Cygne." The old city is no more. Certainly by the 1850s Paris had undergone immense changes, in both physical and social structure. Its population had doubled between 1800 and 1850. The industrial revolution, which came later to France than to England, may not have transformed Paris into a city of factories, but its changes in working patterns had brought a much larger proletariat to the city's center and transformed the patterns of its productivity. The ambitious plans of Napoleon I, inspired in large measure by the architecture of imperial Rome, had left their mark on the city's shape and on its monuments. This was all the more clear, perhaps, in that the abrupt abandonment of those plans in 1812, when Napoleon was exiled to Elba, had not given rise to a similarly ambitious or imaginative program on the part of the Restoration monarchy that replaced him.

The Louvre is emblematic of those changes. The idea of using part of the vast palace as a museum had already been envisaged in the reign of Louis XIV and first took form in 1793 with the opening to the public of the Grand Gallery. Napoleon not only enriched the Louvre with tributes exacted from nations he had defeated, but also had a triumphal arch built in the Place du Carrousel. In the area around the

Place du Carrousel, with the Louvre on its North West side, on the South East the Tuileries Palace, which was to be destroyed during the Paris commune of 1870–71, and on the North the Palais royal, there lingered on through the Restoration a huddle of streets and dilapidated houses. The "Plan Turgot," that wonderful three-dimensional map of Paris made in the eighteenth century, gives some idea of the crush of buildings that crowded into what is now an open space. It was an area frequented by, among others, bohemian artists and writers. Gérard de Nerval and Théophile Gautier, for instance, both lived in the rue du Doyenné (literally: street of the Deanery), which was part of this cramped and populous area. Nerval describes it in his *Châteaux de Bohème* in a passage tinted by warm memories of youth:

> The dean's old drawing room, with its four doors, each with two panels, with its ceiling depicting rockeries and serpents—restored through the care of so many painters, our friends who have since become famous—echoed with our poems of love, frequently interspersed with the joyful laughter or wild songs of our Cydalises. [. . .] We were young, always merry, often rich . . . But I've just struck a somber chord: our palace has been razed. I strode through the debris last fall. Even the ruins of the chapel which stood out with such grace against the green of the trees, and whose dome had crashed to earth one day in the eighteenth century, on six unfortunate canons gathered to say mass, had not been respected. The day they cut down the trees around the Carrousel I'll go and read on the square Ronsard's poem of the forest under the axe: "Woodman, spare that tree."[1]

Balzac depicts the area with a far bleaker eye in his novel *La Cousine Bette*:

> A description of this corner of present-day Paris will certainly not be a hors-d'œuvre, for later no one will be able to imagine it; and our nephews, who will no doubt see the Louvre completed, would refuse to believe that such a barbaric thing survived for 36 years, in the heart of Paris, opposite the palace where three dynasties have received, during those same 36 years, the elite of France and of Europe.
>
> From the wicket gate that leads from the Carrousel Bridge to the rue du Musée, visitors to Paris, even those who come only for a few days, notice a dozen houses with ruined facades, where the disheartened landlords carry out no repairs. This is the residue of an old quarter, which has been in the process of demolition since the day when Napoleon resolved to complete the Louvre. The rue du Doyenné, and the cul-de-sac of the same name, are the sole roads

---

[1] Gérard de Nerval, *Œuvres* (Paris: Gallimard, 1974), I:66–67. "Cydalise" is the term Nerval uses to refer to the mistresses of the artists and poets who were his friends.

within this dark and deserted block of houses, where the inhabitants must be phantoms, for one never sees a soul there. [. . .] Darkness, silence, glacial cold, and the cavernous depths of the soil all conspire to make these houses like crypts, like living tombs. [. . .] This problem, terrifying in itself, becomes horrible when one sees that these so called houses are surrounded by a marsh on the rue de Richelieu side, an ocean of foaming paving stones on the Tuileries side, little gardens, sinister cabins on the side where the shops are, and the steppes created by the stone cutting and the demolitions on the side of the old Louvre. [. . .] For nearly 40 years the Louvre has been crying out through all the mouths made by those disemboweled walls and gaping windows: strip these warts from my face! [2]

Balzac laments the unchanging nature of these endlessly deferred repairs. As it happened, shortly after this passage was published, those dilapidated houses were demolished in the first stage of Haussmann's transformation of the city. For the poet of "Le Cygne," walking through this region after the demolition, the removal of what Balzac had termed warts opens the floodgates for a stream of memory, carrying with it debris from other cities: Troy, Rome, the Paris of the past.

With this flood of memory comes the realization that our surroundings, despite the durability of their stone, marble, and brick, alter more rapidly and less predictably than the ephemeral human heart. Contingency has entered the poet's experience all the more powerfully in that cities seemed to offer a promise of permanence. Haussmann's transformations yoked the promise of greater salubriousness and beauty with the pragmatic and primarily political desire to move the working classes out of the city center and widen the streets to prevent crowds from easily throwing up barricades against the forces of order. For Baudelaire, bitter enemy of the facile belief in progress, Haussmann's cynicism itself made his newly transformed Paris an allegory. The critic Richard Burton, in his study *Baudelaire in 1859*, reminds us that two years before writing "Le Cygne" the poet had angrily noted in a preface to his translations of short stories by Edgar Allan Poe:

Is it not truly stupefying to see a nation, several nations, soon all of humanity, saying to its wise men, to its magicians: "I will love you and magnify you if you persuade me that we are progressing without even wanting to, inevitably, in our sleep; free us of the responsibility, veil from us the humiliation of comparisons, whitewash history, and you can call yourselves the wisest of the wise"? Is it not astonishing that such a simple idea does not burst into every brain: that Progress (in so far as there is any progress) perfects suffering in the same proportion as it refines pleasure, and that if the epidermis of the races

---

[2] Honoré de Balzac, *La Cousine Bette* (Paris: Gallimard, 1972), 77–78.

grows ever more delicate they are obviously pursuing merely an *Italiam fugien-tem* (an ever-receding Italy), a conquest lost the minute it is gained, a progress that always negates itself?[3]

(II 325)

One thinks here of W. H. Auden in his "Recitative by Death":

Ladies and gentlemen, you have made most remarkable
Progress, and progress, I agree, is a boon;
You have built more automobiles than are parkable
Crashed the sound-barrier, and may very soon
Be setting up juke-boxes on the moon:
But I beg to remind you that, despite all that,
I Death, still am and will always be a Cosmocrat.[4]

Paris as embodiment of the despised and simplistic image of progress collides in "Le Cygne" with the phantoms of other lost cities, cities in which apparent progress had merely been a road to destruction. In his attitude to progress, Baudelaire is strikingly different from many of his contemporaries: Gautier, in an article published in *La Presse* (August 11, 1851) speaks in rapturous tones of "printing, steam, electricity, all those marvelous means of almost instantaneous communication," while Hugo's preface to his *Légende des siècles* asserts that his poems are connected uniquely by "the great mysterious thread that runs through the human labyrinth, Progress."[5] Here Gustave Flaubert, as in many other aspects, is closest to Baudelaire. He comments dryly that "industrialism has developed the ugly in gigantic proportions," and exclaims: "In what an absence of esthetic sense our fine nineteenth century reposes."[6]

Yet however much, after his stepfather's death in 1857, Baudelaire may have professed his pleasure in his mother's little house in Honfleur on the coast of Normandy, Paris was what shaped his sensibilities and defined his image of life. Exiled to Lyon as a schoolboy—his four years there were to be his longest absence from the capital—he wrote poignantly of what he missed about Paris—the boulevards and Berthellemot's candies, Giroux's general store and "those rich bazaars where you have such an ample choice of wonderful presents" (CI 23). As an adult there were times when he hated Paris, bemoaned the fact that he spent too much money and time living there, railed at its mud-splattered streets in winter and its stifling heat in summer, berated it for "never having treated me justly, never having paid me, either

[3] Richard Burton, *Baudelaire in 1859* (Cambridge: Cambridge University Press, 1988), 153.
[4] W. H. Auden, *Collected Poems,* ed. Edward Mendelson (New York: Vintage, 1991), 720–21.
[5] Hugo, *La Légende des siècles* (Paris: Gallimard, 1950), 4.
[6] Flaubert, *Correspondance* (Paris: Conard, 1926–33), IV:20, 87.

in esteem or money, WHAT IS OWED TO ME" (L 236, CII 553). But Paris also gave him the companionship of artist and writer friends, the easy familiarity of coffee houses and cabarets, the relatively inexpensive entertainment provided by fairs and popular theaters. These were to provide the sites for many of Baudelaire's poems and prose poems, with their images of gambling dens where one can lose one's soul to a supremely urbane Devil, theaters where mimes, clowns, and tightrope walkers suggest parallels with the high seriousness of politics, streets where the traffic is so dangerous that in crossing them you may lose your halo forever, and walk away liberated from any tokens of your status and reputation. There was the café Momus, made popular by Henri Murger's novel *La Vie de Bohème* (*Bohemian Life*), where Baudelaire met painters such as the realist Gustave Courbet and was once involved in a violent quarrel, which would have led to a duel, had the seconds not resigned. We find him reciting his poem "Les Chats (The Cats)" at the café called the Divan Le Peletier, providing the subject of one of Banville's *Odes funambulesques* (*Tightrope Odes*):

On voit le doux Asselineau
Près du farouche Baudelaire,
Comme un Moscovite en traîneau,
On voit le doux Asselineau.
Plus aigre qu'un jeune cerneau,
L'autre est comme un Gœthe en colère.
On voit le doux Asselineau
Près du farouche Baudelaire.[7]

You'll see the gentle Asselineau
Beside the savage Baudelaire,
Like someone fresh in from Moscow,
You'll see the gentle Asselineau.
Angrier than a baited bear,
The other's like Goethe in his lair.
You'll see the gentle Asselineau
Beside the savage Baudelaire.

Edouard Manet depicts him listening to an outdoor concert in the painting called "The Concert in the Tuileries Gardens." The journalist Charles Monselet describes meeting him at one of his favorite haunts, the dance hall Casino Cadet, where Baudelaire explained that he was watching the death's heads go by. He portrays himself fleeing the cold and lonely boredom of his room to go and write in the library or a reading room, a wine shop or a café (L 48, CI 191–92). But although he might

---

[7] Banville, *Œuvres poétiques complètes,* ed. Peter Edwards (Geneva: Slatkine, 1995), III:191.

complain, it is clear that it is precisely "in the midst of noise, card games and billiards" that he can "be calmer and think more clearly" (L 47, CI 190). Above all, he is aware that much of what he writes is "specifically Parisian," written for and speaking to a specific urban milieu.

Paris was indeed where he drew his greatest inspiration. It was above all, he claimed in the letter he sent to the editor Arsène Houssaye introducing his prose poems, from frequenting vast cities, from the intersection of their countless connections that arose the obsessive image of prose poetry. Plunging into the multitude, imagining the lives of others, responding to the allegorical force of the human bric-a-brac encountered daily in crowded urban environments, these were Baudelaire's prime sources of material and inspiration. It is not just at the anecdotal level that mingling with the crowd furnished benefits to him as poet. It is also at a profounder level of the creation of his poetic identity, a kaleidoscopic combination of multiple and contrasting elements.

Part of the contrast comes from the variety of Paris itself. He knew it well and had lived in many of its quarters because of the frequent changes of address inflicted on him by the fact that he was so often in debt, by his restless spirit, by his sense that things would be better, that inspiration would come more easily, and that work promised long ago might find a swifter completion if he could only find a better place to live. His letters show him torn between the imagined attractions of a Bohemian lifestyle and a bitter awareness of the realities such impermanence enforced. His impression of his own "poverty, unending poverty" is harshly painted in a letter to his mother of December 4, 1847. Whatever bad faith there may be in his frequent protestations, there is in this letter a sense of raw humiliation that rings horribly true. "On occasion," he tells his mother in this letter, "I've had to spend up to three days in bed, sometimes because I had no clean linen, sometimes because there was no wood" (L 30, CI, 143). He even appears to contemplate an invitation from people he met on his sea voyage to act as tutor to their children in Reunion:

> Indeed, despite the terrible pain I'd feel at leaving Paris and bidding farewell to so many fine dreams, I've taken the sincere and violent decision to do so, if I can't force myself to live and to work for some time on the money I'm asking you to send. People I met on the "Ile de France" [the ship on which he traveled] have been kind enough to remember me. I'd find with them a post whose duties I could easily fill, with a generous salary in a country where the living is easy once one is established there, and the boredom, the horrible boredom and the intellectual decay of warm blue countries.
>
> (L 32, CI, 145)

Anything would be better than facing that fate, and particularly abandoning his ambitions, which he felt depended on being in Paris, near to art galleries and exhibitions, publishing houses and reviews. The relative luxury of the apartment on the Ile Saint-Louis where he lived when he first came into the inheritance he so rapidly squandered contrasts sharply with the cheap boarding rooms and sleazier *quartiers* he came to know later on. From the fall of 1845 we find him in a bewildering gallop through cheap hotels and furnished rooms, occasionally recuperating from illness by staying with his mistress Jeanne Duval. At one point in the spring of 1855, he claimed to have had to move to new lodgings six times in a month, "living among plaster and sleeping among fleas," his letters pursuing him from hotel to hotel (CI 311). Claude Pichois's beautiful book entitled *Baudelaire à Paris* includes a map of the poet's lodgings in the city, showing him moving with amazing frequency from the Latin Quarter to Neuilly, from the area around Montmartre to that around the Arc de Triomphe. One has the feeling that Baudelaire, like the sun in one of his poems "would enter like a king, without noise, without valets / All of the hospitals and all of the palaces" (FM LXXXVII).

Pierre Citron's magisterial thesis, *La Poésie de Paris dans la littérature française de Rousseau à Baudelaire*,[8] reveals that Baudelaire was not the first to choose Paris and the Parisian crowd as a poetic motif. Nevertheless, it seems indisputable he was the first to make that motif so rich and so complex a symbol of contemporary existence. Virgil, according to Richard Jenkyns, was the originator of the feeling that landscapes reveal the long history and social evolution that have gone into their creation: "It is [Virgil] who first finds how the mind's eye and the literal eye may work together, so that landscape may give us an understanding of our past and our identity, and history enhance our apprehension of the visible scene."[9] Baudelaire is the first to do this for Paris, to present it as both a physical object and a rich compendium of the past that enabled an understanding of identity. He remains the most powerful of all those who have taken Paris as their subject, however much he draws on his predecessors.

Auguste Barbier was one of the most powerful of those predecessors, or at least those from the nineteenth century. Barbier was one of the writers to whom Baudelaire devoted an article in the collection entitled *Réflexions sur quelques-uns de mes contemporains* (*Reflections on My Contemporaries*). It is an irate piece, crossly deploring the fact that Barbier's natural gifts as a poet have been diminished and tarnished by his determination to make his poetry serve a cause other than beauty. Baudelaire attributes to him not just a false concept of poetry, but also, yet greater source of irritation for this proponent of modernism, a skewed idea of what constituted modernity. He ascribes to Barbier this credo: "The aim of poetry is to spread illumination among the people, and, with the help of rhymes and numbers, more easily fix scientific discoveries in men's memories" (II 145). On the pretext of writing sonnets in

---

[8] See Pierre Citron, *La Poésie de Paris dans la littérature française de Rousseau à Baudelaire,* 2 vols. (Paris: Minuit, 1967).

[9] Richard Jenkyns, *Virgil's Experience* (Oxford: Clarendon Press, 1999), 370.

honor of great men, Baudelaire angrily affirms, Barbier has sung of the lightning conductor and the weaving machine. Curiously, the indignant Baudelaire also condemns Barbier for so frequently being inspired by indignation. The world, he somewhat snidely insists, "is full of highly indignant people who will nevertheless never succeed in writing great poetry" (II 142). Coming from a poet as often indignant as Baudelaire this may seem surprising. What he means is that indignation may be the spur but should never be the result, and that the poet's task is not to spell things out but to suggest, not to tell but to show.

The poem on Paris entitled "La Cuve (The Vat)," from Barbier's collection *Iambes*, may well have filled Baudelaire with an equally explosive mix of admiration for Barbier's potential and rage at the misuse of his gifts. Its evocation of Paris as a nauseous pit of decay and vice, its simplistic use of metaphor, its unrelenting condemnation of the city, its blindness to that curious mixture of the beautiful and the bizarre that stamps Baudelaire's own vision all suggest why Barbier's poetry so enraged the poet of "Le Cygne." It also indicates why Baudelaire considered the motif of the city so important. The first verse is typical:

Il est, il est sur terre une infernale cuve,
On la nomme Paris; c'est une large étuve,
Une fosse de pierre aux immenses contours
Qu'une eau jaune et terreuse enferme à triples tours.
C'est un volcan fumeux et toujours en haleine
Qui remue à longs flots de la matière humaine;
Un précipice ouvert à la corruption,
Où la fange descend de toute nation,
Et qui de temps en temps, plein d'une vase immonde,
Soulevant ses bouillons, déborde sur le monde.

There is, there is on earth a hellish vat
Its name is Paris; and this mighty pot,
This stone clad ditch, this vast prodigious heap,
A muddy yellow stream enfolds in triple sweep.
Volcano belching smoke without reprieve
Its rumbling makes its human magma heave,
A precipice of sleaze and filth and dearth
And vile mud that comes from all the earth
From time to time in bubbling overflow
It belches out across the world to grow.

And so on in unrelenting alexandrine couplets.

Alphonse Esquiros, whom Baudelaire lists in his bio-bibliographical notes among the literary friends he met after his return from his sea voyage (I 785), also devotes some lines to Paris. This champion of socialist humanitarianism called one of his poems "Paris aux réverbères (Paris lit by streetlights)" and used it to set up a series of contrasts—the crowd and the lonely individual, the ugliness of reality and the splendor of dreams ("Oh! que Paris est laid! Sous ses sombres nuages / Que j'ai souvent rêvé de longs et beaux voyages! (how ugly Paris is! Under its dark clouds / how often I've dreamed of long and splendid journeys)")—that lead to his affirmation of the importance for the poet of remaining aloof from the corruption of contemporary life. Like Barbier, Esquiros plays on the motif of the fraudulence of city life, and depicts the city as a drunkard snoring in a filthy gutter:

> Paris dort: avez-vous, nocturne sentinelle,
> Gravi, minuit sonnant, le pont de la Tournelle,
> C'est de là que l'on voit Paris de fange imbu;
> Et comme un mendiant ivre près d'une cuve
> Le géant est qui ronfle et qui râle, et qui cuve
> Le vin ou le sang qu'il a bu. [10]

> Paris sleeps: have you climbed, watcher of the night
> To the Tournelle bridge when midnight chimes?
> It's from there you see a Paris mud-befouled
> And like a drunken beggar sleeping by a cask
> The snoring, gasping giant's sleep ferments
> The wine or blood that he has just devoured.

But the city in Esquiros's poem is merely background and its depiction realistic if jaundiced. There is none of the variety and multiplicity of Baudelaire's Paris and no metamorphosis of the city's bric-a-brac into the allegories that transform *Les Fleurs du mal* into modernist poetry. In fact there is little difference between the Paris of Barbier and Esquiros and that of Paul Scarron (1610–1666), writing this snappy little sonnet two centuries before them:

> Un amas confus de maisons
> Des crottes dans toutes les rues
> Ponts, églises, palais, prisons
> Boutiques bien ou mal pourvues

> Force gens noirs, blancs, roux, grisons
> Des prudes, des filles perdues,

---

[10] Adolphe Esquiros, *Les Hirondelles* (Paris: Renduel, 1835), 105.

Des meurtres et des trahisons
Des gens de plume aux mains crochues

Maint poudré qui n'a pas d'argent
Maint filou qui craint le sergent
Maint fanfaron qui toujours tremble,

Pages, laquais, voleurs de nuit,
Carrosses, chevaux et grand bruit
Voilà Paris que vous en semble?

Hugger-mugger houses, prisons,
Streets of dung and refuse smelling,
Churches, bridges, regal dwellings,
Shops with, and without, provisions.

Black folk, white folk, red and gray,
Prudishness and lechery,
Murderers and treachery,
Writers—hands like claws of prey,

Many in wigs with empty purses,
Many a crook who fears the forces,
Braggarts with a coward's stink,

Pages, lackeys, thieves by night,
Carriages, horses, noisy flight—
Now, that's Paris, don't you think?

Baudelaire does—however fleetingly—pay tribute to one poet of the city, Hugo, a fragment of whose ode to the Arc de triomphe he includes in his account of the Salon of 1859 (II 667). Nevertheless, Hugo's great evocation of contemporary Paris comes in *Les Misérables,* published in 1862, at the moment when Baudelaire was trying to launch several of his own volumes (L 187, CII 238). However much Baudelaire may find in it aspects that excite his admiration and enthusiasm, he sees it as too steeped in its author's belief in progress and too shaped by the desire to inspire its readers to charity to conform to his own conviction of the preeminent importance of beauty. His review of the novel does not even touch on the role Hugo allocates to the city. Moreover, in a letter to his mother, he angrily describes the novel as "disgusting and inept" and adds in reference to his review: "I showed that I possess the art of lying" (L 190, CII 254).

Baudelaire found in Hugo a rival who set his teeth on edge: novelist Honoré de Balzac arouses in him a far more straightforward enthusiasm, and there is no doubt that he admired the novelist's creation of a Paris that is not only quintessentially modern, but that is partly anchored in reality and partly shaped by Balzac's determination to suggest a creative symbiosis between individual and surroundings, people and their dwellings. Some of that movement between inner and outer worlds is reflected in Baudelaire's own re-creation of Paris. Nerval, too, offers a familiarity with Paris and an awareness of its power as a forest of symbols that suggest close affinities with Baudelaire's. His *Nuits d'Octobre, Promenades et souvenirs,* and his novella *Aurélia* bear potent witness to a fascination with the city and with what it offered in terms of poetic and personal inspiration. But Nerval is attracted above all by the picturesque, which frequently turns to the fantastic, and his style in many of the pieces he devotes to Paris is whimsical, journalistic, gently ironic or self mocking in ways that contrast sharply with Baudelaire's often bitter but always conscious determination to extract from what he sees something deeper, more powerful, more allegorical. In a letter of March 1865, Baudelaire told Charles-Augustin Sainte-Beuve that the latter's *Vie, poésies et pensées de Josephe Delorme (Life, Poetry, and Thoughts of Joseph Delorme)* was *Les Fleurs du mal* of yesterday, adding, as if in fear of offending the famous critic: "The comparison is glorious for me" (CII 474). While Sainte-Beuve may have fussed over what he saw as the incorrectness of Baudelaire's phrase, "a bath of the multitude,"[11] his poems certainly do, on occasion, presage Baudelaire's own fascination with the crowd. "Les Rayons jaunes (The Yellow Rays)," a poem influential for focusing on the inspiration of the everyday—sunlight through curtains, memories of the past and so forth—ends with the poet seeking solace and company from the anonymous crowd:

—Ainsi va ma pensée; et la nuit est venue;
Je descend; et bientôt dans la foule inconnue
     J'ai noyé mon chagrin;
Plus d'un bras me coudoie; on entre à la guinguette,
On sort du cabaret; l'invalide en goguette
     Chevrotte un gai refrain.

Ce ne sont que chansons, clameurs, rixes d'ivrogne;
Ou qu'amours en plein air, et baisers sans vergogne,
     Et publiques faveurs;
Je rentre; sur ma route on se presse, on se rue;

---

[11] On this see CII 493, Baudelaire's letter to Sainte-Beuve, dated May 4, 1865.

Toute la nuit j'entends se traîner dans ma rue
    Et hurler les buveurs.[12]

So run my thoughts. Night falls. I go downstairs,
Among the unknown crowds in the thoroughfares
    My grief's soon drowned.
Elbows rub mine. Doors open, doors close, cabarets
And dance halls beckon. The tipsy cripple warbles away
    The gay song resounds.

Nothing but songs, shouts, drunken clashes,
Love in the open, shameless kisses,
    Caresses on show.
I come back home. My route is thronged with the swarming crowd.
All night drunks stumble and roar out loud
    In the street below.

In a letter written to Sainte-Beuve, late in Baudelaire's life, he again indicates a similarity between his own perceptions and those of Sainte-Beuve's poet-hero Joseph Delorme in terms that clarify what he saw as the essential element to be extracted from the inspiration of Paris: "I hope one of these days to be able to show a new Joseph Delorme strolling along, hitching his rhapsodic thought to everything he happens upon, and drawing from every object a disagreeable moral" (L 244, CII 583). What Baudelaire understood, with an intensity and a clarity no other writer of his time except perhaps Flaubert came near approaching, was that strolling through Paris could no longer be a picturesque or sentimental exercise. As Priscilla Parkhurst Ferguson puts it: "Flânerie posed the fundamental problem of the ways of knowing and being that are possible, even necessary, in the modern city, and only in the modern city. The practice of flânerie turned the artist's unique, and uniquely modern, relationship to that city into a spectacle, a projection of the imperative need to make sense of the city. Ultimately, flânerie was a strategy of representation."[13] That stress on representation suggests that it is not just against the backdrop of other poets who had attempted to address Paris as poetic subject that Baudelaire's Paris poetry needs to be seen. He also drew inspiration—positive and negative—from a range of artists. And his representation of Paris appears more sharply individual when

---

[12] Sainte-Beuve, *Vie, Poésies et Pensées de Joseph Delorme*, ed. Gérald Antoine (Paris: Nouvelles Editions latines, 1956), 71.
[13] Priscilla Parkhurst Ferguson, *Paris as Revolution* (Berkeley: University of California Press, 1994), 81.

seen against theirs. Imagination, as he so forcefully argues in reviewing the Salon of 1859, is what makes a landscape painting great (II 665). It is also what he sees as central to a cityscape, a genre that, from an early stage in his critical career, he clearly considers important, and whose absence he laments in the Salon of 1859. The section of *Les Fleurs du mal* entitled *Tableaux parisiens (Parisian Paintings)* asks to be read as a determinedly imaginative recreation of a contemporary city. The opening poem of the section is called "Paysage (Landscape.)" It is a title that insists on the visual suggestions already set in train by the use of the term *tableaux* (paintings) in the section title, and the poem sets out a program for transforming the traditional genre of the eclogue, the pastoral poem, into its modern equivalent:

> Je veux, pour composer chastement mes églogues,
> Coucher auprès du ciel, comme les astrologues,
> Et, voisin des clochers, écouter en rêvant
> Leurs hymnes solennels emportés par le vent.
> Les deux mains au menton, du haut de ma mansarde,
> Je verrai l'atelier qui chante et qui bavarde;
> Les tuyaux, les clochers, ces mâts de la cité,
> Et les grands ciels qui font rêver d'éternité.
> [. . .]
> Car je serai plongé dans cette volupté
> D'évoquer le Printemps avec ma volonté,
> De tirer un soleil de mon cœur, et de faire
> De mes pensers brûlants une tiède atmosphère.

(FM LXXXVI)

> I want to compose pure pastoral poems
> Lying close to the sky as star-gazers do,
> With church towers for neighbors I'll listen and dream
> As their solemn refrains are blown into the blue.
> My chin in my hands, from my high attic casement,
> Through the clock towers and pipes, those masts of the city,
> I'll watch factory yards with their songs and their chitchat;
> While the vast arching skies inspire dreams of infinity.
> [. . .]
> I will be deep in that exquisite pleasure
> Of summoning the spring with my will power alone,
> Dreaming of plucking a sun from my heart
> And warming the world with the fire of my art.

Translating "Tableaux" as "Scenes," as some translators do,[14] shifts the emphasis to theater, certainly an interest of Baudelaire's and certainly part of his complex image of the city. But what is made clear by this poem, set at the beginning of the section, is that the poet is figured here as painter: painter of fantastic architecture, in the style of Hubert Robert (there will be fairy-like palaces with gardens and fountains); painter of seascapes (the city is transformed into a port, by the representation of pipes and bell towers as masts); painter of skies draped in coal fumes, or bathed in moonlight. The title of the book needs to be translated in a way that puts the emphasis on painting as something like *Parisian Paintings*.

There are close parallels between "Paysage (Landscape)" and Baudelaire's review of the Salon of 1859, with its insistence on the need for a painting to represent the poetic impression the subject had initially inspired, a poetic impression recalled by an effort of will (II 665). The fascination with skies and clouds suggested in the poem and found in much of Baudelaire's writing is also present in the review, for instance, in a passage where language rivals painting (see chapter 10), but more to the purpose here, Baudelaire laments the absence from the salon of "landscapes of great cities." To illustrate what he means, he chooses the engraver Charles Meryon (1821–1868), Baudelaire's contemporary. In a remarkably taut and powerful passage Baudelaire extracts the essence of Meryon's cityscapes:

> I have rarely seen depicted with more poetry the natural solemnity of a vast city. He had forgotten neither the majesty of accumulated stone, the bell-towers "pointing their fingers to the heavens," the obelisks of industry vomiting into the sky their congregations of smoke, the prodigious scaffoldings on monuments that are being repaired, applying to the solid architectural forms their open-air architecture whose beauty is so paradoxical, the tumultuous sky, heavy with anger and rancor, the depth of perspectives made greater still by the thought of all the dramas held within it, nor any of the complex elements that create the painful and glorious decor of civilization.
>
> (II 666–67)

All of this reappears in Baudelaire's city poems, from the suggestive power of the stone, through the wild skies and the fusion of the ephemeral and the permanent symbolized by the scaffoldings on old buildings. Here is the allegorical blend of transience and changelessness that Baudelaire evokes in "Le Cygne."

It is hardly surprising that in 1862, when he reviewed the work of certain engravers, he was able to perceive the promise of a young artist whose career was just beginning, James McNeil Whistler. Baudelaire depicts his engravings as "subtle, as

[14] See for instance McGowan, Howard, and Martin.

alert as improvisation and inspiration, representing the banks of the Thames; a wonderful jumble of rigging, yardarms, ropes; a chaotic amalgam of fog, furnaces, and corkscrew fumes; the profound and complex poetry of a vast city" (II 740).

That fascination with what he terms elsewhere the intoxication engendered by great cities (I 651) is also something he attributes to his painter of modern life. Constantin Guys is associated both with modernism and with the artist par excellence through the intense curiosity he reveals for the masses that throng contemporary urban existence. The crowd, Baudelaire insists, is his domain: "His passion and his profession is that of *espousing the crowd*. For the perfect stroller, for the passionate observer, it is an immense delight to make one's home among the masses, in the inconstant, in the fugitive and in the infinite. To be away from home and yet to feel oneself always at home; to see the world, to be at the world's center and yet hidden from the world, these are some of the slightest pleasures of those independent, passionate, impartial spirits, those whom language can define only imperfectly" (I 691–92). And Baudelaire makes Guys cry out in an affirmation that heightens our sense that this painter, like Edgar Allan Poe and Thomas de Quincey, is yet another of the poet's doubles: "Any man who is [. . .] *bored in the bosom of the crowd* is a fool! a fool! and I despise him!" (I 692).

The joy and the tyranny of the crowd are part of the bric-a-brac that the poet reassembles in his great city poems, part of the dross that his alchemy turns to gold. In this he resembles that quintessentially urban figure, the rag picker, so vividly depicted by Baudelaire in his essay on wine and hashish: "Here is a man whose task it is to gather the detritus of a day in the capital. Everything the great city throws away, everything it loses, everything it disdains, everything it breaks, he catalogs and collects. He consults the archives of debauchery, the clutter of refuse. He makes a selection, an intelligent choice. Like a miser gathering up treasure trove, he gathers garbage for the god of Industry to chew over and transform into objects of use or pleasure" (I 381). And just to make sure we succeed in reading this symbol correctly, he adds: "He stumbles over the paving stones, like young poets who spend their entire day wandering in search of rhymes" (I 381). There are echoes of this image in "Le Soleil (The Sun)," one of the *Tableaux parisiens*:

Je vais m'exercer seul à ma fantasque escrime,
Flairant dans tous les coins les hasards de la rime,
Trébuchant sur les mots comme sur les pavés,
Heurtant parfois des vers depuis longtemps rêvés.

(FM LXXXVII)

My fantastic swordplay I'll practice alone,
Sniffing out in lost corners the chance of a rhyme,
Bumbling over words as over paving stones
Stumbling across lines sought in dreams of past time.

And we find him again in "Le Vin des chiffonniers (The Rag Pickers' Wine) collected in *Le Vin:*

Souvent à la clarté rouge d'un réverbère
Dont le vent bat la flamme et tourmente le verre,
Au cœur d'un vieux faubourg, labyrinthe fangeux
Où l'humanité grouille en ferments orageux.

On voit un chiffonnier qui vient, hochant la tête,
Butant, et se cognant aux murs comme un poète.

(FM CV)

Often in the street lamp's bright red fire,
The flame whipped by the wind as it rattles the cover,
In the heart of the old town, that labyrinth of mire,
Where humanity swarms in stormy disorder,

You'll see an old rag picker, shaking his head,
Stumbling, and thumping on the walls like a poet.

From the Romantics' image of the poet as Magus, leading the people on the route of progress, through the Parnassians' picture of the artist as impassive observer, we are brought sharply down to Baudelaire's identification with the old rag and bone man, shambling along in a drunken dream of glory, picking over the city's detritus to refashion it into the work of art. Like some stormy tide, the city throws up other images of the poet, too, and of the search for inspiration. In the prose poems the simple pleasures of the crowd enjoying a holiday fair, for instance, can set up striking contrasts between the entertainers whose acts delight and those whose stage attracts no one. "Le Vieux Saltimbanque (The Old Mountebank)" sets out this dichotomy with characteristically muscular force. A paragraph depicts all the stock figures of a city fair, the kind we see as the camera sweeps down the Boulevard du Crime in Prévert and Carné's tribute to nineteenth-century Paris, *Les Enfants du paradis.* The language here bristles with alliteration and onomatopoeia, paralleling the shouts of the barkers and the laughter of the onlookers. The booths, we're told,

were vying formidably with each other: they squawked and bellowed and howled. There was a hullabaloo of shouting, a thundering of brass instruments, explosions of rockets. The red-ribboned clowns and the dupes contorted faces tanned and hardened by the wind, the rain and the sun; with the steady nerves of comedians sure of getting their laughs, they flung off jokes and quips that were as weighty and solid in their fun as those of Molière. The strong men, proud of their huge limbs, even if their brows were as low and their skulls as shriveled as orangutans', lounged about majestically in costumes washed the previous day to be ready for the fair. The ballerinas, as beautiful as fairies or princesses, leaped and capered under the glow of lanterns that set their skirts sparkling.

(PPP XIV)

In bitter contrast with the sights, tastes, and smells of this pleasure is the booth of the old mountebank, a figure "bent over, obsolete, decrepit, the ruin of a man." No lights here apart from some squalid and guttering candles, no inviting booth, but merely a wretched hovel. The only spectacle is that of absolute misery, physical and psychological. Returning home the narrator finds himself obsessed with this image: "I struggled to analyze my sudden grief," he tells us in a typically Baudelairean transformation of experience into understanding, "and I said to myself: I have just seen the image of the old man of letters who has outlived the generation for whom he was the brilliant entertainer; of the old poet with neither friends nor family nor children, degraded by his poverty and by the ingratitude of the public, and into whose booth the forgetful world no longer deigns to enter!" (PPP XIV).

Seeing oneself multiplied and refracted in other people is one of the many pleasures and pains Baudelaire suggests are provided by the theater, itself a vital element of Baudelaire's city. This is not the grand theater, the elegant spaces and the highbrow plays associated with, say, the *Comédie française*. This is the more popular entertainment of the boulevards or the street, of the small theatres limited by law to presenting mimes, or to works inspired by the Italian *commedia dell'arte*. Baudelaire's fascination with it is associated, too, with the attraction he felt to the actress Marie Daubrun, the "girl with the golden hair" whose memory colors some of his love poems. The poem "L'Irréparable (The Irreparable)" in *Spleen et Idéal* beautifully evokes the apparent simplicity and the spur to the imagination of this kind of theatre:

—J'ai vu parfois, au fond d'un théâtre banal
    Qu'enflammait l'orchestre sonore,
Une fée allumer dans un ciel infernal
    Une miraculeuse aurore;
J'ai vu parfois au fond d'un théâtre banal

Un être, qui n'était que lumière, or et gaze;
    Terrasser l'énorme Satan;
Mais mon cœur, que jamais ne visite l'extase,
    Est un théâtre où l'on attend
Toujours, toujours en vain, l'Être aux ailes de gaze.

(FM LIV)

—I've sometimes seen, in the depths of an ordinary theatre
Set afire by a sonorous orchestra
A fairy illumine in an infernal sky
A miraculous dawn;
I've sometimes seen, in the depths of an ordinary theatre

A being, made of nothing but light and gauze,
Lay low the enormous Satan;
But my heart, which ecstasy never visits,
Is a theater where you wait
And wait in vain for the Being with wings of gauze!

If the street actor and the play actor are both to some extent refractions of the poet, figures allowing Baudelaire to explore and develop his own poetic persona, so also—unexpectedly—is the seller of glass panels who figures in "Le Mauvais Vitrier (The Bad Glazier)." This figure, wandering through the city streets, advertising his wares in a symbolically discordant and piercing voice, is transformed into the poet who refuses to give his readers a rose-tinted view of reality. Accosted by a client who obliges him to clamber up to his sixth-floor apartment, he negotiates his way through the narrow stairwell, at every moment risking damage to his fragile merchandise. But when he arrives, the client, who, ironically, is the narrator of this prose poem, berates him for not offering "colored panes," "glass that's pink or red or blue, magic glass, glass of paradise" (PPP IX). And when the window seller, after scrambling down the stairs again, makes his way to the street, the narrator hurls a flower pot down upon him, "an engine of war" that destroys the panes he carries on his back, making, as it does so, the noise of a "crystal palace shattered by lightning" (PPP IX). Whatever political resonance this poem may have, written as it was at a time of considerable unrest, it also carries an ironic vision of a reading public that would have preferred pretty glosses to evocations of reality, the *Fleurs de mai* (*Flowers of May*) the young Verlaine thought he was purchasing, rather than the *Fleurs du mal*.[15]

In many of these allegories and symbols, Baudelaire is drawing on—more precisely is making profoundly his own—a relationship between crowd and poet that runs through most of his favorite writers, from the German Romantic E. T. A. Hoffmann and the American Edgar Allan Poe, to Balzac and De Quincey. The prose poem "Les Foules (The Crowds)" evokes this relationship with a characteristic blend of cockiness and angry self-defense: "Not everyone has the gift of taking a bath of the multitude: delighting in crowds is an art, and the only ones who can extract a binge of vitality at the expense of humanity are those in whom a fairy has instilled at birth the love of dressing up and of masks, the hatred of home and the passion for traveling." And he goes on to depict the poet as one who "enjoys the

---

[15] Verlaine tells this story in his memoirs.

incomparable privilege of being at will himself and other people. Like those wandering souls in search of a body, he enters, when it pleases him to do so, into everyone's persona. For him alone, everything is vacant and if certain places appear to be closed to him it is because in his view they are not worth visiting" (PPP XII). The image recalls his early fascination with the German writer of the fantastic, Hoffmann, but it also suggests some of that writer's more realistic tales. Hoffmann's characters wandering through crowds, or watching them from corner windows, are constantly launched into imaginary encounters or adventures. For his part, Poe opens his tale "The Man of the Crowd" with a quotation from Jean de La Bruyère: "Ce grand malheur, de ne pouvoir être seul (This great misfortune of not being able to be alone.)" What is more his protagonist is in "one of those happy moods which are so precisely the converse of ennui—moods of the keenest appetency, when the film from the mental vision departs"[16]—one hears a premonition of Baudelaire's own phrase: "There are days when an individual awakens with a youthful and vigorous genius. Hardly have his lids been freed of the sleep that enchained them than the outer world offers itself to him in powerful relief, with a clarity of contours, an admirable richness of colors" (I 401). Poe's narrator finds himself absorbed in the contemplation of the sea of human heads that surges past his window seat in a London coffee house, fascinated by their variety and filled with curiosity about their purposes. As it grows darker, the narrator peers ever more intently into the crowd: "With my brow to the glass, I was thus occupied in scrutinizing the mob when suddenly there came into view a countenance (that of a decrepit old man, some sixty-five or seventy years of age)—a countenance which at once arrested and absorbed my whole attention, on account of the absolute idiosyncrasy of its expression." Following him through the night and all through the next day, the narrator is eventually forced to conclude that this old man is "the type and genius of deep crime. He refuses to be alone. He is the man of the crowd."[17] He is to reappear multiplied and intensified in one of the most Parisian of Baudelaire's poems, "Les Sept Vieillards (The Seven Old Men)" (see figure 3).

This is a poem that also reflects De Quincey's response to the crowds of a big city, a response in which the excitement of taking a plunge into the multitude gradually turns, under the influence of opium, into something far more terrifying and sinister. "Our author," Baudelaire comments, "had too deeply loved the crowd, had too deliciously plunged into the seas of the multitude, for the human face not to assume in his dreams a despotic role. And then there manifested itself what has been called *the tyranny of the human face*" (I 483). This is the negative side of that experience of multiplicity that Baudelaire evokes in his notebooks: "The pleasure of being in crowds is a mysterious expression of the delight in the multiplication of numbers" (I

---

[16] Edgar Allan Poe, *Works* (New York: Walter J. Black, 1927), 245.
[17] Ibid., 251.

649). Indeed, however much Baudelaire draws his inspiration from the crowds, however much he may delight in the multiple possibilities they offer for imaginative escape from his own personality, it is equally important to him to be able to withdraw and to find solitude. In his notebooks he jots down the following acidic commentary: "Invincible taste for prostitution in the human heart, whence the horror of solitude.—Man wants to be two. The genius wants to be one, thus solitary. Glory consists in remaining one while prostituting oneself in a special way" (I 700). It would not be too cynical to say that the crowd is above all a poetic concept, best enjoyed from the safety of high attic windows, most constructively remembered when walking through deserted streets in the depths of night or before the working day starts again:

> At last! Alone! You can no longer hear anything but the rumble of a few belated and exhausted cabs. For a few hours, we'll lay claim to silence, if not rest. At last! The tyranny of the human face has disappeared and there'll be no one to cause me suffering but myself.
>
> At last! So at last I'm allowed to relax in a bath of shadow! First, a double turn of the lock. It is as if that turn of the key will increase my solitude and strengthen the barricades that now separate me from the world.
>
> (PPP X)

This is the other side of the coin, the inevitable antithesis that Baudelaire's duality sets up as equally important to him as the stimulus of the crowd. The poem's final paragraph, moreover, shows that fear of inferiority, that sense of being judged by those the poet himself judges so harshly, that underpins this sharply conflicting vision of the crowd:

> Annoyed with everyone and annoyed with myself, I would love to redeem myself and gather a few scraps of pride in the silence and solitude of night. Souls of those I've loved, souls of those I've sung, strengthen me, support me, drive far from me the lies and the corrupting vapors of the world, and you, Lord God!, grant me the grace to produce a few fine lines that will prove to myself that I am not the last of men, that I am not lower yet than those I despise!
>
> (PPP X)

That fear of being judged and found wanting is a potent element in the bitterness of "Les Sept Vieillards (The Seven Old Men)," a poem in which the narrator encounters seven identical old men who seem to project onto him such personal animosity that he staggers back to his room, his soul dancing on the monstrous ocean of his bewilderment and his sense of inadequacy. The poem's opening stanza encapsulates the city seen as symbol:

Fourmillante cité, cité pleine de rêves,
Où le spectre en plein jour raccroche le passant!
Les mystères partout coulent comme des sèves
Dans les canaux étroits du colosse puissant.

(FM XC)

Ant-seething city, city full of dreams,
Where in broad day the specter seizes passersby,
Mysteries flow through you like sap through a tree's veins
Fills your narrow gutters, Colossus reaching to the sky!

The subject leaps from the page in this magnificent evocation of the city. The opening line, pivoting around the repetition of "city," immediately establishes the two central themes. The swarming crowds that live in the metropolis, thronging it in such numbers that they resemble more the uniformity of insects than the individuality of humans, fill the air with their dreams, dreams that hinge on their being seen precisely as individuals. The power of dreaming splendidly that De Quincey had seen as one of the promises of opium quickly degenerates, however, into the tyranny of the human face that was also a product of opium. Past and present collide in the city, memories cling to it like mud, and the passerby cannot escape the ghosts of the past, summoned up by associations as unpredictable and as intricate as the bond linking Andromache and the swan. People seen in the street—the widows, the old women, the prostitutes—carry with them invisible but powerful invitations to imagine their pasts, to understand how they have become what they are. Old men, like old actors, offer symbols of a future that often defies deciphering. To the poet for whom everything can become allegory, even the city's gutters seem to be running with passions and emotions.

The poem goes on to tell the story of this strange encounter with the phantasmagoria of a city that is also a labyrinth through the past and through the self:

Un matin, cependant que dans la triste rue
Les maisons, dont la brume allongeait la hauteur,
Simulaient les deux quais d'une rivière accrue,
Et que, décor semblable à l'âme de l'acteur,

Un brouillard sale et jaune inondait tout l'espace,
Je suivais, roidissant mes nerfs comme un héros
Et discutant avec mon âme déjà lasse,
Le faubourg secoué par les lourds tombereaux.

Tout à coup, un vieillard dont les guenilles jaunes,
Imitaient la couleur de ce ciel pluvieux,
Et dont l'aspect aurait fait pleuvoir les aumônes,
Sans la méchanceté qui luisait dans ses yeux,

M'apparut. On eût dit sa prunelle trempée
Dans le fiel; son regard aiguisait les frimas,
Et sa barbe à longs poils, roide comme une épée,
Se projetait, pareille à celle de Judas.

Il n'était pas voûté, mais cassé, son échine
Faisant avec sa jambe un parfait angle droit,
Si bien que son bâton, parachevant sa mine,
Lui donnait la tournure et le pas maladroit

D'un quadrupède infirme ou d'un juif à trois pattes.
Dans la neige et la boue il allait s'empêtrant,
Comme s'il écrasait des morts sous ses savates,
Hostile à l'univers plutôt qu'indifférent.

Son pareil le suivait: barbe, œil, dos, bâton, loques,
Nul trait ne distinguait, du même enfer venu,
Ce jumeau centenaire, et ces spectres baroques
Marchaient du même pas vers un but inconnu.

A quel complot infâme étais-je donc en butte,
Ou quel méchant hasard ainsi m'humiliait?
Car je comptai sept fois, de minute en minute,
Ce sinistre vieillard qui se multipliait!

Que celui-là qui rit de mon inquiétude,
Et qui n'est pas saisi d'un frisson fraternel,
Songe bien que malgré tant de décrépitude
Ces sept monstres hideux avaient l'air éternel!

Aurais-je, sans mourir, contemplé le huitième.
Sosie inexorable, ironique et fatal,
Dégoûtant Phénix, fils et père de lui-même?
—Mais je tournai le dos au cortège infernal.

Exaspéré comme un ivrogne qui voit double,
Je rentrai, je fermai ma porte, épouvanté,
Malade et morfondu, l'esprit fiévreux et trouble,
Blessé par le mystère et par l'absurdité!

Vainement ma raison voulait prendre la barre;
La tempête en jouant déroutait ses efforts,
Et mon âme dansait, dansait, vieille gabarre
Sans mâts, sur une mer monstrueuse et sans bords!

(FM XC)

One morning in the gloomy street
Its houses swollen by the mist
Like quays along a flooding river
—A backdrop for an actor's soul—

Where dirty yellow fog lay thick,
I screwed my nerves up, what a hero,
Whipped up my soul already drained
And walked between the heavy barrows.

An old man clad in rags stained yellow,
Reflection of the yellow sky,
Appeared—no rain of alms would greet
The malice glinting in his gaze.

His eye you'd think was steeped in bile,
His glance a knife that cut the cold,
And from his chin a beard that jutted
A hairy sword, like that of Judas.

Not bent but broken, his backbone made
A perfect right angle with his legs.
His walking stick topped off the picture,
Gave him the look and clumsy stride

Of an infirm beast or a three legged Jew.
In the snow and the mud his feet were entangled
As if he were crushing dead men with his shoes,
Hostile to the world, not just indifferent.

His double behind him: beard, eye, back and rags
No feature was different, from the same hell they came,
These antique twin brothers, these weird old phantoms
Pursuing the same path to an unknown goal.

What hideous plot had made me its victim?
What evil fate had chosen to mock me?
For I counted seven times from moment to moment
This sinister ancient reproducing himself.

Let those who laugh at my disquiet
Who are not filled with brotherly qualms
Remember that despite their decrepitude
These seven monsters seemed eternal.

Could I have looked on the eighth and not died,
Inexorable double, ironic and fatal,
Sickening Phoenix, each son his own father
—But I turned my back on this cortege from hell.

Mad as a drunk seeing double I went home,
Banging my door, stricken with horror,
Ailing and frozen, fevered, disturbed,
Mystery's victim, absurdity's prey!

Vainly my reason grasped at the rudder,
The tempest in playing derided my efforts,
And my soul was sent dancing, a battered old hulk,
Without masts on a sea that was monstrous, unending!

(FM XC)

Baudelaire drafted two epilogues for the 1861 edition of *Les Fleurs du mal,* one of which seems to be the outline while the other begins to transpose that initial sketch into verse. The verse form chosen, that of stanzas of three lines each, appears to have proven inadequate to the innovative and imaginative sketch and the epilogue was never completed. Nevertheless, it projects a powerful light on the importance of Paris to the whole of the collection, and it suggests the extent to which Baudelaire saw this representation of the city as central to his transforming vision of poetry. This is the poet speaking directly to the city, seeking a creative reconciliation between his rage against what it represented socially and politically, and his knowledge that nevertheless his own identity and his own history were not only deeply rooted in it, but also epitomized in its multiple characteristics. It is also the poet recognizing the tight symbiosis that ties him to Paris and that makes the city dependent on him to give it expression, to transmute its banality into gold:

> Tranquil as a sage and gentle as the damned, I said:
> I love you, o my most lovely, my charming . . .
> How many times . . .
> You carouse without thirst, you make love without love
>   Your taste for the infinite,
> Which everywhere, even in evil, declares itself . . .
> Your bombs, your daggers, your victories, your fetes,
> Your melancholy suburbs
> Your furnished rooms,
> Your gardens full of sighs and intrigues,
> Your temples vomiting out prayers and music
> Your childish despairs, your old madwoman's games,
>   Your discouragements,
> And your fireworks, eruptions of joy,
> That bring laughter to the sky, mute and gloomy.
>
> Your venerable vice displayed in silk
> And your laughable virtue, with its suffering eyes,
> Gentle, ecstatic over the luxury vice unfolds.
>
> Your principles saved and your laws spat upon,
> Your lofty monuments where the fog clutches on,
> Your domes of metal flaming in the sun,
> Your queens of the stage with their seductive voices
> Your alarm bells, your canons, your deafening orchestra,
> Your magic paving stones built up into fortresses,
> Your little orators, with their rococo periods,
> Preaching of love, and then your sewers full of blood,
> Rushing down into Hell like Orinocos,
> Your sages, your clowns, brand new in old clothes.
> Angels clad in gold, in crimson and hyacinth,
> O you, bear witness that I've done my duty
> Like a perfect chemist and like a holy soul.
> For I have extracted the quintessence of everything,
>   You gave me your mud and I turned it into gold.

(I 191–92)

CHAPTER NINE

Nature, the Pitiless Enchantress

My dear Desnoyers,
You ask me for some poetry for your little collection, poems on Nature, I believe? On
woods, great oaks, greenery, insects—the sun, too, if I'm not mistaken? But you know
very well that the vegetable kingdom fails to move me and that my soul rebels at the
strange new religion that will always be, so it seems to me, rather shocking to any
spiritual being. I'll never believe that the soul of the gods inhabits plants, *and*
even if it did, it's not something for which I could really work up much enthusiasm. I
would consider my own soul as of much more importance than that of the sanctified
vegetables. What's more, I've always thought that Nature, *flourishing, rejuvenated*
Nature, possessed something impudent and painful.

(L 59, CI 248)

Thus Baudelaire in late 1853 or early 1854, provocatively replying to an invitation
to participate in a collection celebrating F. C. Denécourt, the man who had done so
much to make the Fontainebleau Forest a popular and accessible pleasure space for
Parisians. Baudelaire is mocking the somewhat vapid pantheism of contemporaries
like the poet Victor de Laprade whose poem "A un grand arbre (To a Tall Tree)" of
1843 had suggested that "L'esprit calme des dieux habite dans les plantes (The calm
spirit of the gods lives in plants)." It is a limp statement of a belief Gérard de Nerval
conveyed more powerfully a couple of years later in his "Vers dorés (Gilded Lines),"
which adjured humanity to:

Respecte dans la bête un esprit agissant:
Chaque fleur est une âme à la Nature éclose;
Un mystère d'amour dans le métal repose:
"Tout est sensible!"—Et tout sur ton être est puissant![1]

Respect in each animal a spirit in action:
Each flower is a soul that Nature unfolds;

---

[1] Nerval, *Œuvres*, edited by Albert Béguin and Jean Richer (Paris: Gallimard, 1974), I, 8.

A mystery of love lies asleep in each metal:
"Everything can feel!"—And commands your soul.

Baudelaire's irate response to this recrudescence of pantheism can be found not just in the letter to Desnoyers, but also in his notes for a study of what he termed "L'Ecole païenne (The Pagan School)." His irritation stems partly from the refusal of the modern in such an attitude, the derivative recycling of the themes and images of antiquity, rather than the imaginative rejuvenating we find in, for instance, "Le Cygne (The Swan)" or "Le Tonneau des Danaïdes (The Barrel of the Danaides)." His study mocks one of the adherents of the school for insisting that Pan was not dead but would return: "He spoke of the God Pan as if he were the prisoner of Saint Helena" (II 44). Substitute King Alfred or Abraham Lincoln, Robin Hood or Gough Whitlam, it hardly matters—such an attitude reveals a lack of awareness of the realities of modern life that Baudelaire derides in a passage vibrant with his personal experience of patching together a living from writing. Harking back to the past, looking for Venus, raising alters to Bacchus or Priapus will hardly help to feed and console you. "Can you drink ambrosia soup? Or eat Paros cutlets? How much do the pawn shops offer for a lyre?" (II 47). But his criticism goes deeper than such pragmatism, since the affectation of the past and the denigration of the present mean looking at life and at Nature askew. Above all, he argues, "the world will appear to you only in its material shape. The springs that make it move will long remain hidden from your sight" (II 47). The article is so slippery with irony that it is sometimes difficult to interpret, but what it does indicate is that Nature, for Baudelaire, is something quite different from what it was for most of his contemporaries and not just those of the Pagan School. What is more, we can hear yet again, as so often in Baudelaire, that determination to transform an emotional response into understanding. For it is understanding the mechanisms that drive the world—and particularly the social world—that underpins much of his thinking, even when he does turn to subjects and motifs more usually linked with Nature.

Baudelaire's "Nature," however, is both limited and idiosyncratic. Felix Leakey, in his meticulous study, *Baudelaire and Nature,* suggests a complex and shifting attitude across time, with an early love of Nature later repudiated, and then, as the poet became increasingly misanthropic, an attraction to those aspects of Nature that are most removed from human contact: seas, clouds, stars. This provides a useful grid for thinking about Baudelaire's representation of Nature, provided we bear in mind that people—the bath of the multitude—remain essential to his creativity, even if, or especially if, they are kept at some remove. Above all, perhaps, his vision of Nature is always associated with a city-dweller's perspective. We can, for instance, hear further echoes both of the letter to Desnoyers and of Baudelaire's search for ideal surroundings, in his prose poem "Any Where out of the World" when the narrator suggests to his soul that they live in Lisbon: "Tell me, pour soul, pour frozen soul, what would you think about living in Lisbon? The warmth there would make you perk up like a lizard. It's a town by the sea. I'm told it's made of marble and that the people have such a hatred of the vegetable world that they tear down all the trees. Now there's a landscape that would be to your taste; a landscape made of light and minerals, and there'd be the liquid to reflect it" (PPP, XLVIII). Light, minerals, reflection: these are the elements we find again and again dominating Baudelaire's image of the ideal living space, not the mountains and wild rivers, the craggy cliffs and belling stags of an earlier generation.

Romanticism came relatively late to France, and it did not inspire in the majority of French Romantics the sense of Nature that we find in either its English or its German counterparts. Indeed, to find a sense of the independent beauty of Nature one needs to turn to its late-eighteenth-century precursors, but even then it is clear that the ecstatic joy in Nature expressed by, say, Rousseau or Chateaubriand is quite alien to Baudelaire's thinking. Even those poems that do seem to offer an intense delight in the natural world recount above all not the close inspection of Nature's beauties that stimulated Rousseau's ecstasy, but a movement up and away into a sphere far beyond the earthly. Like Rousseau, Chateaubriand demonstrates an intense joy in natural beauty, especially as he found it in America, but Wordsworth's sense that "Nature then to me was all in all," like the intensely religious sentiment of German Romanticism's *Waldeinsamkeit* (the solitude of the woods), was unknown to most of those who made up the French Romantic school. It is not that they are insensitive to natural beauty, but they tend to use it either as a projection of their own emotions or as a symbolic or metaphorical depiction of human Nature. Sounding cataracts rarely haunt them like a passion. They are more likely to represent the cataracts as analogies of human virtues and vices. Baudelaire, in his exploration of Hugo, puts this with characteristic force:

> The poetry of Victor Hugo is able to translate for the human soul not only the most direct pleasures that it extracts from visible nature, but also the most fleeting, the most complex and the most moral sensations (I use the word moral advisedly) that the visible creation transmits to us through inanimate nature, or what is termed inanimate nature. Not merely the figure of a being that is external to humans, either vegetable or mineral, but also its physiognomy, its gaze, its sadness, its sweetness, its radiant joy or its repulsive hatred, its enchantment or its horror. To put it differently, all that is human in everything, and also all that is divine, sacred or diabolical.
>
> (II 132)

The anthropocentrism of this depiction of the natural world seen as constituting a repertory of analogies for human experience is central not just to Hugo's writing but to much of French Romanticism, and extends also to Baudelaire's own thinking and writing. In 1856, for example, Baudelaire sent a letter to Alphonse Toussenel, that ardent supporter of the utopian thinker Charles Fourier, thanking him for sending a copy of his book, *L'Esprit des bêtes. Le Monde des oiseaux. Ornithologie passionnelle* (*The Spirit of the Animals. The World of the Birds. Passionate Ornithology.*) Fourier's concept of universal analogies, which provided a way of reading the world as a series of physical representations of human interests, passions, and virtues, a concept reflected in Toussenel's work, seems to have sharpened Baudelaire's own search for analogies and for metaphors capable of giving a visible and concrete form to abstractions. In the letter to Toussenel, he denies the influence of Fourier, but insists on the parallelism of thought: "*Rational men* didn't await Fourier's arrival on earth to realize that Nature is a *language,* an allegory, a mold, an *embossing,* if you like. We know all that, and it's not through Fourier that we know it. We know it through our own minds and through the poets" (L 80, CI 337).

Hugo was certainly one of the poets who reveal those analogies most clearly, and while it is in his later poems that he does so most consistently and forcefully, his taste for the allegorical is evident from early on. Baudelaire responds to this tendency in the essay he devoted to Hugo for Eugène Crépet's anthology of contemporary French poets. Everything is hieroglyphic, he asserts in this article, and the poet's role is that of translator and decoder of that secret language. Hugo, he insists, is one of the few poets in whose work the reader finds a truly "magnificent repertory of human and divine analogies" (II 133). Moreover, where Nature is concerned, Hugo can do it all: "The transparency of the atmosphere, the cupola of the sky, the form of the tree, the gaze of the animal, the silhouette of the house are painted in his works with the brush of a consummate landscape painter" (II 135).

With Leconte de Lisle, born only two years before him and seventeen years after Hugo, Baudelaire detects a palpable change in the presentation of nature, "a certain completely novel thread that is characteristic of him and unique to him." This new thread is found in poems where the poet has described natural beauty for its own sake, without setting it in the context of a religion or a philosophy: "The imposing and crushing power of nature, the majesty of the animal in movement and in repose; [. . .] the divine serenity of the desert or the redoubtable magnificence of the Ocean" (II 178).

This image of Nature is much closer to what Baudelaire notes in some of the artists he most admires, Camille Corot, Alexandre Decamps, Eugène Delacroix. What arouses his highest admiration in their landscapes, however, is what is most available to him as a city dweller, what most strikes his largely urban sensibility, that is, light and color. In Corot, for instance, he appreciates a keen sensitivity to different shades of light: "That patch of sunlight in the middle distance, illuminating the grass and giving it a different color from the foreground, is certainly audacious and what is more highly successful" (II 390). Decamps, too, is praised above all for his "meticulous taste for nature, studied in all its luminous effects" (II 448). Much of Baudelaire's response to landscape painting, however, is marked by a sense that the artist has done nothing more than copy and reproduce, rather than transform Nature. (Here we can already perceive his later fulminations against current applications of photography: "I am convinced that the poorly applied progress of photography has greatly contributed, like, moreover, all purely materialist progress, to the impoverishment of the French artistic genius" [II 618].) It is for reasons like this that the creator of medallions, David d'Angers, is condemned for merely reproducing Nature: "This child clinging to a bunch of grapes [. . .] is a curious object to examine. It is true that you would swear it was flesh. But it is as stupid as nature, and yet it is an undisputed truth that the aim of sculpture is not to rival life-masks" (II 403).

It is Delacroix's landscape painting that comes closest to Baudelaire's dual demand for a rapid notation that seizes the ephemeral while conveying the eternal, and for an intellectual and emotional interpretation of Nature. For Delacroix, he affirms as early as his account of the 1846 Salon, "nature is a vast dictionary whose pages he thumbs through and consults with a sure and profound gaze, and his painting, which arises above all from memory, speaks above all to memory" (II 433). In a later article he finds the term he has been searching for: *mnemonic.* Nature transposed by the artist's temperament, Nature seen as a storehouse of memories rather than Nature seen for its own sake—here we find again the poet looking at a cityscape and reading its layers of personal and human history. He puts it most trenchantly in his account of the 1859 Salon, when he opens his section on landscape with what amounts to an artistic credo: "If a certain grouping of trees, mountains, rivers, and houses, that is, what we call a landscape, is beautiful, then it is not beautiful by itself. What makes it beautiful is me, my personal grace, the idea or the sentiment that I attach to it. Which expresses sufficiently clearly, I think, that every landscape artist who is unable to convey a feeling through a grouping of objects from the vegetable or mineral kingdoms is no artist" (II 660).

His poem "Elévation," placed early in the development of the poet whose experiences from birth to death Baudelaire traces in *Les Fleurs du mal,* conveys this sense of analogies and correspondences in Nature. At the same time, it makes clear the differences between Baudelaire's vision of Nature and that, say, of Rousseau or the English poets of the Lake District. The poem opens with the poet's spirit soaring above ponds, valleys, mountains, woods, and seas, to reach the vast immensity of space from which he can gain both serenity and an understanding of "the language of flowers and speechless things" (FM III). The elements of Nature mentioned here are generic, not specific. When Wordsworth, for instance, wants to convey a similar conviction, he brings to his verse an intensity of vision and expression that suggests that, however universal the aspects he names, he has specific instances sharply in mind, precise memories stamped ineradicably in his brain:

The immeasurable height
Of woods decaying, never to be decay'd,

The stationary blasts of waterfalls,
And everywhere along the hollow rent
Winds thwarting winds, bewilder'd and forlorn,
The torrents shooting from the clear blue sky,
The rocks that mutter'd close upon our ears,
Black drizzling crags that spake by the wayside
As if a voice were in them, the sick sight
And giddy prospect of the raving stream,
The unfetter'd clouds, and region of the Heavens,
Tumult and peace, the darkness and the light
Were all the working of one mind, the features
Of the same face, blossoms upon one tree,
Characters of the great Apocalypse.
The types and symbols of Eternity,
Of first and last, and midst and without end.

(The Prelude 6:556–72)

Baudelaire also seeks out "types and symbols of eternity" but he frequently does so on the basis of an intellectual rather than an affective memory. Even in cases where a biographical reading can detect residual traces of specific memories, Baudelaire's language tends to elide them, placing the emphasis more on the transforming power of imagination. Thus, while it may be true that this poem harks back to a youthful poem written in response to an 1836 journey to the Pyrenees, "Elévation" itself transforms the specificity of the earlier piece, refusing to attach to the earthly elements the poetry and the power that he wants to give to the upper regions of freedom and imagination. James McGowan's translation of "Elévation," seeking a rhyme, lends the opening line of the poem a loftier and more specific rhetoric than the original. Baudelaire generalizes by using the everyday terms for ponds and valleys, while McGowan's translation has rills and meres. Norman Shapiro's translation is closer here, drawing on a more familiar lexicon of "valley, mountain, wood, and pond." Earth is summed up as morbid fogs: the upper air as a clear fire, a divine liqueur that brings insight. There is a search here for universality that demands an equally universal language to translate it.

Even in Baudelaire's depictions of exotic Nature, where personal memory does play an important part, what dominates is that transformation of the specific through the imagination. His sea voyage to the Indian Ocean, for instance, left him with a rich compendium of memories not just of the sea and more specifically of sunlight on water and sunsets over the ocean but also of a luxuriant vegetation and an intensity of color, light, and odors. These are the memories that lend a characteristic vibrancy to prose poems like "La Belle Dorothée (Beautiful Dorothy)" where the opening sentence sets up a series of sound patterns that underline the intensity of heat and light: "Le soleil ac*cable* la ville de sa lumière droit et terri*ble;* le *sable* est éblouissant et la mer miroite." To catch something of this pattern of rhythm and sound, I translate this as "the sun p*o*unds the *t*own with its terrible, perpendicular light: the *s*and dazzles and the *s*ea *s*parkles)" (PPP XXV). The reader discovers a similar determination to echo sense with sound a little later, in the assonances and alliteration in the description of the sea pounding on the sand: "La mer, qui b*a*t la pl*a*ge à cent p*a*s de l*à*." Here that sound might be captured in the following way: "The *s*ea b*ea*ts against the b*ea*ch some hundred m*e*ters away" (my emphasis). Smells associated with the tropics waft through this poem, especially in the lines describing the "stew of crab in rice and saffron." But there is nothing in all this that limits the reader's imaginative response, nothing that ties the poem to a specific area in the tropics, no pleasure in naming the trees or telling us precisely what kind of crab is in the stew. Even when he does delight in specific names, as in "Parfum exotique (Exotic Perfume)" with its triumphant closing on the "tamariniers (tamarind trees)," there can be little doubt that the joy he experiences is not that of a botanist but that of a poet exulting at finding so rich a rhyme with the word for sailors, "mariniers" (FM XXII). (In the prose poem "Projets [Plans]" his character dreams of an exotic cabin "overhung by those bizarre, glistening trees whose name has slipped my mind"[PPP XXIV], as if the precise term were of interest only for the rhyme.) His Nature is not just that of the city dweller, but a Nature that is universalized, and thus transformed into a repertory of symbols, a hieroglyphic dictionary (II 59).

Looking back at the Romantic period in 1862, Baudelaire wrote a valedictory sonnet that encapsulates and reflects his response to Nature. Even its title focuses on Nature as symbol: "Le Coucher du soleil romantique (The Setting of Romanticism's Sun)." Richard Howard calls it, more directly, "Romantic Sunset," while Walter Martin seeks, as I do, to seize the link with the Romantic movement in his title "Last Rays of the Romantic Sun." It was written to act as the epilogue for a work by Baudelaire's friend Asselineau, for which Banville had been asked to write a prologue. The central image of Baudelaire's poem offers a rewriting of Hugo's line, which he had quoted from memory in a nostalgic tribute to Romanticism embedded in his essay on Gautier: "Ô splendeurs eclipsées! / Ô soleils descendus derrière l'horizon (O splendors now eclipsed! O suns that have dropped behind the horizon)."[2] Contemporary critics, too, discussed the demise of Romanticism in imagery drawn from Nature. Thus Louis Goudall, writing in the newspaper *Figaro* on February 24, 1856, notes gloomily: "After having described its devastating ellipsis, Romanticism's comet has disappeared from the poetic firmament, and the most we can now glimpse of it is the tail; the rag-picker Realism is on the point of running out of oil to feed his lantern; and black night would be better than those stupid bourgeois

---

[2] Hugo, *Œuvres poétiques*, edited by Pierre Albouy (Paris: Gallimard, 1964), I, 971. This quotation is based on "Passé" from *Les Voix intérieures*: the exact wording of the original is slightly different: "O temps évanouis! ô splendeurs éclipsées! / O soleils descendus derrière l'horizon!" (O vanished times! O splendors now eclipsed! O suns gone behind the horizon!).

glimmers cast around us by the soot of the school of Good Sense." Baudelaire's friend, the poet and art critic Théophile Gautier, had also paid nostalgic tribute to the movement in an 1857 article, later published as part of his book *Histoire du romantisme* (*History of Romanticism*). Like Baudelaire, he creates a landscape that embodies the post-Romantic phase; "the memory is as fresh as if it dated from yesterday. The impression of enchantment still continues. From the land of exile where you travel, gaining glory by the sweat of your brow, through brambles and rocks, along paths bristling with traps, you turn your melancholy face and gaze long and regretfully back at the lost paradise."[3] The prologue Banville wrote for Asselineau's planned but never-published volume captures that same sense of regret for a period of great intellectual excitement, but, for all the virtuosity with which he devotes each four-line verse to summoning up the essence of one great figure, the picture of the dawn remains merely conventional:

Mil huit cent trente! Aurore
Qui m'éblouis encore,
Promesse du destin,
Riant matin!

Aube où le soleil plonge!
Quelquefois un beau songe
Me rend l'éclat vermeil
De ton réveil.

Jetant ta pourpre rose
En notre ciel morose,
Tu parais, et la nuit
Soudain s'enfuit.

La nymphe Poésie
Aux cheveux d'ambroisie
Avec son art subtil
Revient d'exil.[4]

Eighteen thirty! Dawn
That dazzles yet my eye,
Laughing morn,
Promising destiny.

---

[3] Théophile Gautier, *Histoire du romantisme* (Paris: Charpentier, 1882), 86–87.
[4] Banville, *Œuvres poétiques complètes* (Geneva: Slatkine, 1998), V :153–54.

Dawn with its leaping rays!
Sometimes a fine dream
Restores to me those days
In rosy gleams.

Throwing your crimson veil
On skies grim as night
Your rose can still avail—
Puts dark to flight.

The nymph of Poetry
With ambrosial locks
And all her coquetry
Now exile mocks.

Admittedly, Baudelaire's choice of alexandrines within an irregular sonnet form gives him more scope than Banville's stanzas, where three six-syllable lines are followed by one of four syllables, but there is a deeper difference in "Le Coucher du soleil romantique," an awareness of Nature not just as backdrop but as enabling metaphor:

Que le Soleil est beau quand tout frais il se lève,
Comme une explosion nous lançant son bonjour!
—Bienheureux celui-là qui peut avec amour
Saluer son coucher plus glorieux qu'un rêve!

Je me souviens! . . . J'ai vu tout, fleur, source, sillon,
Se pâmer sous son œil comme un cœur qui palpite . . .
—Courons vers l'horizon, il est tard, courons vite,
Pour attraper au moins un oblique rayon!

Mais je poursuis en vain le Dieu qui se retire;
L'irrésistible Nuit établit son empire,
Noire, humide, funeste et pleine de frissons;

Une odeur de tombeau dans les ténèbres nage,
Et mon pied peureux froisse, au bord du marécage,
Des crapauds imprévus et de froids limaçons.

(I 149)

How beautiful the sun when it rises strong and gay,
How its greeting thunders out in salutation!

—But who can find that same exhilaration
When we watch its dreamlike glory fade away?

I remember how I saw them, every flower, every stream,
Swooning in its light, with heart hard beating,
—Now it's late and we must hurry, as the sun is fast retreating
If we're lucky we might catch a fading beam.

But in vain I seek a God that's swiftly fading,
Almighty Night takes back its old domain,
And darkness, cold, and damp alone remain.

My fearful foot along the marsh now wading,
As graveyard stenches through the darkness seep,
Crushes unsuspected toads and slugs that creep.

(I 149)

Baudelaire reworks this imagery in one of his studies for Poe, responding to the criticism that the American's writing represents the "literature of decadence." His response is a caustic boomeranging back of this slur, a forceful riposte that while it might be the destiny of certain writers to belong to an age when a formerly powerful movement was in decline, the fault did not lie with the writers, and that the best they could do was to mirror the setting sun:

That sun which, a few hours ago, crushed everything under its direct, white light, will soon engulf the western horizon in a range of colors. In the games played by that dying sun certain poetic minds will find new delights. There they'll discover glittering colonnades, cascades of molten metal, a paradise of fire, a poignant splendor, the intense pleasure of regret, all the magic of dream, and all the memories of opium. And the setting sun will indeed strike them as a wonderful allegory of a soul freighted with life, dropping behind the horizon with a magnificent provision of thoughts and of dreams.

(II 320)

The allegorical transposition of external reality to literary symbol achieves such power here because it is so firmly anchored in a perceived and familiar reality.

Indeed, this is the kind of Nature the city dweller Baudelaire was familiar with. Paris, set in a bowl around its river, is known for its mists and fogs, which also contribute to its beautiful skies and its sunsets. The animal kingdom is not going to play a large role in the personal mnemonics of Baudelairean Nature. Swans, certainly, like toads and slugs, are part of his experience, but the albatross of his early poem is more likely to have flown in from numerous literary sources, including Coleridge's *Rime of the Ancient Mariner*, and the menagerie of vices set out in "Au lecteur (To the Reader)" is a deliberately disorienting grouping of the exotic, chosen as much for its sounds and for its allegorical value as for any specific image the poet might have of the animals themselves.

We find this kind of device—the taking up of natural motifs merely for rhetorical purposes—elsewhere, too. Thus Baudelaire takes a version of the Malayan *Pantoum*, an elaborate structure formed by a rigid pattern of repeated lines allowing for only two rhymes, to produce a delicate little poem entitled "Harmonie du soir (Evening Harmony)" with about as much feeling for Nature as that usually revealed by an inner-city developer.

> Voici venir les temps où vibrant sur sa tige
> Chaque fleur s'évapore ainsi qu'un encensoir;
> Les sons et les parfums tournent dans l'air du soir;
> Valse mélancolique et langoureux vertige!
>
> Chaque fleur s'évapore ainsi qu'un encensoir;
> Le violon frémit comme un cœur qu'on afflige;
> Valse mélancolique et langoureux vertige!
> Le ciel est triste et beau comme un grand reposoir.
>
> Le violon frémit comme un cœur qu'on afflige,
> Un cœur tendre, qui hait le néant vaste et noir!
> Le ciel est triste et beau comme un grand reposoir;
> Le soleil s'est noyé dans son sang qui se fige.
>
> Un cœur tendre, qui hait le néant vaste et noir,
> Du passé lumineux recueille tout vestige!
> Le soleil s'est noyé dans son sang qui se fige . . .
> Ton souvenir en moi luit comme un ostensoir!

(FM XLVII)

> Now is the hour when trembling on its stem
> Each flower wafts its perfume like a censer.
> The sounds and perfumes circle in the evening air,
> Melancholy waltz and languid vertigo!
>
> Each flower wafts its perfume like a censer.
> The fiddle trembles like a tortured heart,
> Melancholy waltz and languid vertigo!
> The sky is sad and lovely as an altar.

The fiddle trembles like a tortured heart,
A tender heart that hates the vast black void.
The sky is sad and lovely as an altar.
The sun is drowned in blood that clots and sets.

A tender heart that hates the vast black void
Gathers the last shreds of a luminous past!
The sun is drowned in blood that clots and sets.
Your memory glows within me like a monstrance.

This is a finger exercise, the equivalent of scales for a pianist, rather like Auden's sestina "Have a Good Time:"

"We have brought you," they said, "a map of the country;
Here is the lane that runs to the vats,
This patch of green on the left is the wood,
We've penciled an arrow to point out the bay.
No thank you, no tea; why look at the clock.
Keep it? Of course. It goes with our love.

"We shall watch for your future and send you our love.
We lived for years, you know, in the country.
Remember at weekends to wind up the clock.
We've wired to our manager at the vats.
The tides are perfectly safe in the bay,
But whatever you do don't go to the wood." [5]

And so it continues, bringing back the same end words in a different order in each verse, until the love story is told and the country truly known, so that the poet can end with a half-stanza as envoy:

Sees water in the wood and trees by the bay,
Hears a clock striking near the vats:
"This is the country and the hour of love."

The map, in Auden's poem, is above all a map of the poem, not something that can reveal the beauty of the country—its skein of swans above the wood, its moss growing on the vats—which has to be discovered anew and uncharted by each visitor. Baudelaire's evening harmony, where wild Nature is channeled into a corset of pre-

[5] W. H. Auden, *Collected Poems*, edited by Edward Mendelson (New York: Vintage, 1991), 68.

ordained form, can be read as an undercover commentary on the trammeling power of Catholicism, whose rites are thrust into the foreground by the rhymes of his poem. It offers no hope of an eventual liberation, as Auden's sestina does: this pattern is endlessly predictable in ways that Auden's is not.

This is not to say that Baudelaire does not have a profound response to certain aspects of Nature. In his review of the 1846 Salon he includes a quotation from the German romantic writer E. T. A. Hoffmann, whose writings, especially the *Kreisleriana,* had such an influence on him in the period before he encountered the works of Edgar Allan Poe. Baudelaire prefaces the quotation by insisting that it will appeal to all those who sincerely love Nature. It is clear from the quotation itself that those sincere lovers of Nature share his determination to extract from the external world patterns, suggestions, and links that illuminate the inner world:

> It is not just in dreams and in the slight delirium that precedes sleep, but also when I'm awake, when I hear music, that I find an analogy and an intimate connection among colors, sounds and perfumes. It seems to me that all those things have been created by a single ray of light and that they have to combine in a wonderful concert. The smell of brown and red marigolds produces a particularly magical effect on me. It makes me fall into a deep reverie and then it is as if I hear in the distance the deep low tones of the oboe.
>
> (II 425–26)

This sense of correspondences not just linking the physical and the emotional, the concrete and the abstract, but also binding together the different sensations is central to Baudelaire's appreciation of the natural world. It is what infuses, most famously, his sonnet "Correspondances:"

> La Nature est un temple où de vivants piliers
> Laissent parfois sortir de confuses paroles;
> L'homme y passe à travers des forêts de symboles
> Qui l'observent avec des regards familiers.
>
> Comme de longs échos qui de loin se confondent
> Dans une ténébreuse et profonde unité,
> Vaste comme la nuit et comme la clarté,
> Les parfums, les couleurs et les sons se répondent.
>
> Il est des parfums frais comme des chairs d'enfants,
> Doux comme les hautbois, verts comme les prairies,
> —Et d'autres, corrompus, riches et triomphants,

Ayant l'expansion des choses infinies,
Comme l'ambre, le musc, le benjoin et l'encens,
Qui chantent les transports de l'esprit et des sens.

(FM IV)

Nature here is seen both as mnemonic, that is, as a compendium of analogies and allegories, and as a unifying force that allows us to perceive our sensations synesthetically, in terms of each other. Like the Sibyls of antiquity, however, Nature does not speak directly but demands an effort of interpretation. She herself is presented as a symbol in the sonnet's opening lines: a temple, an artificial structure representing a divinity, but not itself divine.

Here, in chronological order, is how some of the translations have dealt with that opening quatrain:

Cornford: In nature's temple living columns rise / Whence issue, sometimes, words confusedly. / Man threads a wood of symbols. Every tree / Watches him passing with intimate eyes.

Campbell: Nature's a temple where each living column / At times, gives forth vague words. There Man advances / Through forest-groves of symbols, strange and solemn, / Who follow him with their familiar glances.

Sturm: In Nature's temple living pillars rise, / And words are murmured none have understood, / And man must wander through a tangled wood / Of symbols watching him with friendly eyes.

Wilbur: Nature is a temple whose living colonnades / Breathe forth a mystic speech in fitful sighs; / Man wanders among symbols in those glades / Where all things watch him with familiar eyes.

Howard: The pillars of Nature's temple are alive / and sometimes yield perplexing messages; / forests of symbols between us and the shrine / remark our passage with accustomed eyes.

Carson: Nature is a Temple: its colonnaded trunks blurt out, from time to time, a verdurous babble; / The dark symbolic forest eyes you with familiarity, from the verge of Parable.

McGowan: Nature is a temple, where the living / Columns sometimes breathe confusing speech; / Man walks within these groves of symbols, each / Of which regards him as a kindred thing.

W. Martin: The colonnades of Nature's temple live / And babble on in tongues half-understood; / Man wanders lost in symbols while the wood, / With knowing eyes, keeps watch on every move.

Shapiro: All Nature is a pillared temple where, / At times, live columns mutter words unclear; / Forests of symbols watch Man pass, and peer / With intimate glance and a familiar air.

However much some of these versions succeed as poems in their own right, however much I'm aware of the difficulties faced, I want here to look at these translations not as independent works of literature, but as mirrors of, and reflections on, Baudelaire's own text. Perhaps precisely because this poem has tempted so many translators, the variety of versions reveals how much is lost in moving from one language to another, even from one person's use of language to another's. That sense of what is lost can however be harnessed to reach a better understanding of Baudelaire's poem and Baudelaire's Nature. The babble that Carson and W. Martin offer, for instance, suggests to me something continuous, a long stream of words, whereas Baudelaire's poem specifies that these words drop only occasionally (*parfois*). Carson gets around it by specifying "from time to time" but Martin's "babble on" misses the point. Shapiro's "mutter" either suggests bad-temper or implies that, if only they had spoken more loudly, we would have understood. You need to watch for these words, Baudelaire advises us, they are rare, and even when you do chance to catch them, deciphering them may prove impossible. The words that these living pillars drop are "*confuses*," literally indistinct, muddled, blending together. Suggesting that they are in a language half understood as Martin does slides around the problem, implying that it is a language that could be learned, rather than that it is a familiar language used in sibylline, unexpected, and ambiguous ways. Cornford transposes the adjective into adverb (confusedly), as though the words were dropped in random piles rather than being intrinsically unclear. Campbell's "vague words" comes closer, since the oracles of the Sibyls were often open to multiple interpretations rather than being bemusing. Wilbur's "mystic" speech is rather more satisfying, as is Howard's "perplexing." Even the simple expression, "l'homme y passe à travers des forêts de symboles," can pose problems, not of course because it is misunderstood, but because of the different degrees of laxity translators will allow in their search for rhythm and rhyme. Thus Cornford's "Man threads a wood of symbols" is attractive, but where Baudelaire's verb is neutral—*passer*—hers can be read as a synonym for linking together. It is certainly better though than either Martin's "wanders lost" (Baudelaire is not suggesting that humanity is lost but rather that we may fail to interpret or even to see these symbols) or, even worse, Campbell's "There Man advances" with its suggestion of the progress Baudelaire so angrily denounced. And to modern ears, the stress on "man" is too limiting, too gender-bound. Shapiro tries rather weakly to sidestep this with a capital, but Howard and Carson are surely right to transform it, respectively to "us" and, less formally, "you." Nevertheless, Howard's "forests of symbols between us and the shrine" works too hard, interpreting rather than translating and trying to get us as readers to see that on the interpretation of the symbols depends our access to the heart of Nature. Despite Baudelaire's reference to Nature as a temple, I am not at all sure that he is arguing that we should worship her, as the use of the word "shrine" seems to indicate—rather that we should attempt to interpret her symbols, attempt to *understand* her.

This brings me to the opening words of the poem. Nature, we are told with typically Baudelairean straightforwardness, is a temple. That this is a cliché of Romantic poetry is part of the challenge he has taken on, cliché being for him an anthill hollowed out by generations of ants, and demanding from the poet an act of creative imagination in order to restore to it something of its potential resonance. Those translators who opt for variants on "Nature's temple" mislead by leaving open the possibility that this is a temple to Nature. Baudelaire invites us rather to see Nature as a temple to something else. That Baudelaire leaves unspecific what that something else might be is characteristic of him, but it also underlines the modernity of his vision. The emphasis here is on contingency, chance, disorder, the "hasard" that no throw of the dice can abolish. Unity can be achieved through the senses, giving the impression of an ordered universe. But the opening quatrain places the emphasis on a source of knowledge and understanding that, like Rimbaud's sorceress in his prose poem "Après le deluge (After the Flood)," watches us but will not guide us. And there is no promise of an ultimate truth. Baudelaire does suggest, however, by binding word (*parole*) and symbol (*symbole*) together through the rhyme, that language is neither transparent, nor purely abstract, but that it carries within it the promise of an ultimately decipherable meaning. Nature is a dictionary, he says in his art criticism, which the painter consults and transforms into the work of art. The temple here is a temple of words, something less to be worshipped than to be interpreted and translated.

The tercets of "Correspondances" also reveal much both about the complexity of Baudelaire's response to Nature and about the difficulty of translation. Here again, for purposes of focusing more closely on the implications and suggestions of the original, is a selection of translations (again, in chronological order):

Cornford: Some scents are cool like children's flesh, some shed / An hautboy's sweetness, some are green as spring, /—Others corrupt and rich triumphing, // And these, like infinite things, have power to spread, / As amber, musk and myrrh and frankincense / Which chant the spirit's marriage with the sense.

Campbell: There can be perfumes cool as children's flesh, / Like fiddles, sweet, like meadows greenly fresh. / Rich, complex, and triumphant, others roll // With the vast range of all non-finite things—/ Amber, musk, incense, benjamin, each rings / The transports of the senses and the soul.

Sturm: Some perfumes are as fragrant as a child, / Sweet as the sound of haut-boys. meadow-green; / Others, corrupted, rich, exultant, wild, / Have all the expansion of things infinite: / As amber, incense, musk and benzoin, / Which sing the sense's and the soul's delight.

Wilbur: Perfumes there are as sweet as the oboe's sound, / Green as prairies, fresh as a child's caress, /—And there are others, rich, corrupt, profound // And of an infinite pervasiveness, / Like myrrh, or musk, or amber, that excite / The ecstasies of sense, the soul's delight.

Howard: There are odors succulent as young flesh, / sweet as flutes, and green as any grass, / while others—rich, corrupt and masterful— // possess the power of such infinite things / as incense, amber, Benjamin and musk, / to praise the senses' raptures and the mind's.

McGowan: Odors there are, fresh as a baby's skin / Mellow as oboes, green as meadow grass, /—Others corrupted, rich, triumphant, full, // Having dimensions infinitely vast, / Frankincense, musk, ambergris, benjamin, / Singing the senses' rapture, and the soul's.

Martin: Some fragrances resemble infant skin, / Sweeter than woodwinds, green as meadow grass— / Others expand to fill the space they're in, // Endlessly rich, corrupt, imperious; / Amber and musk, incense and benjamin / In sense and spirit raptures sing as one.

Shapiro: Perfumes! Some fresh and cool, like babies' skin, / Mellow as oboes, green as meadows; some / Rich and exultant, decadent as sin, / Infinite in expanse—like benzoin gum, / Incense and amber, musk and benjamin—/ Sing flesh's bliss, and soul's delight therein.

These lines are not just important to the sonnet itself. They explore an area—the sense of smell—that is central to Baudelaire's experience, and therefore demand particular attention. Baudelaire is for many the great olfactory poet of France, the one who most keenly and in the most complex ways both responds to the sense of smell and succeeds in conveying it. In comparison with the senses of sight and hearing, the vocabulary of smell is more limited and less precise. Yet, as Marcel Proust insists in a famous passage from *Combray,* the two senses of taste and smell, more fragile but more tenacious than the rest, are those that linger on after all else has gone, supporting what Proust so magnificently calls the "immense edifice of memory."[6] Baudelaire himself, in the poem "Le Parfum (Perfume)," asks us:

Lecteur, as-tu quelquefois respiré
Avec ivresse et lente gourmandise
Ce grain d'encens qui remplit une église,
Ou d'un sachet le musc invétéré?

Charme profond, magique, dont nous grise
Dans le présent le passé restauré!

(FM XXXVIII)

Reader, have you ever breathed in deep,
With ecstasy and greed just held in check,
That grain of incense that can fill a church,
Or known the musk that lingers in a sachet?

Profound and magic charm—intoxicating!—
To find the past restored now to our times!

It is not surprising, therefore, that in "Correspondances" Baudelaire begins with perfumes in his summoning up of the senses. But the link with the "chairs d'enfants," literally children's flesh, has caused problems for the translators. In Belgium, Baudelaire found to his horror that a story he told as a joke in which he presented himself as a cannibal (CII 437) was taken with utter seriousness. Some of the translators hover around such a suggestion themselves, Howard indeed going in unabashed with "odors succulent as young flesh." Martin's "Some fragrances resemble infant skin" strikes the ear strangely, because it leaves out the nub of the comparison, the freshness or coolness, and sets up instead a direct and strangely unsatisfying comparison between perfumes and skin. Wilbur, as so often, finds a beautifully apt version in "fresh as a child's caress," suggesting with apparently effortless simplicity the scent and the touch as well as the affectionate nature of children.

The passage from E. T. A. Hoffmann's *Kreisleriana* quoted above—"The smell of brown and red marigolds produces a particularly magical effect on me. It makes me fall into a deep reverie and then it is as if I hear in the distance the deep low tones of the oboe" (II 426)—hovers behind the next synesthetic connection Baudelaire makes, his bracketing of scent and hearing. Part of the impact of this powerful tercet comes from the simplicity of its language. There is nothing here that is drawn

---

[6] Marcel Proust, *A la recherche du temps perdu*, ed. Pierre Clarac and André Ferré (Paris: Gallimard, 1954), I: 47.

from a lofty diction, no effect created by unusual syntax, no demands made on the reader's knowledge of myth or fable. Yet some translators seem either driven by personal musical preferences or convinced that powerful poetry must also be lofty poetry. Frances Cornford and Frank Sturm, for example, both use "hautboys" which was once the habitual English term for the instrument but was superseded by oboe over the course of the eighteenth century. Howard gives us flutes and Campbell fiddles—even Martin's woodwinds are a little wide of the mark, losing the precise link with the Hoffmann text that is present in the original and that a translation needs to retain.

The final four lines suddenly shift gear and direction, conveying the richness and power of another group of perfumes through a language that is equally rich in its choice of words, especially in that virtuoso list in the penultimate line. Moreover, where the fresh cool perfumes were tied together through the repetition of the sound "air" (*chair, prairie*) and the fricatives f and v (*frais, enfants, verts*), the lines evoking these contrasting scents are linked by nasals: (corro*m*pus, trio*m*pha*n*ts, expa*n*sion, a*m*ber, be*n*join, e*n*cens, cha*n*tent, tra*n*sports, se*n*s). The couplet that closes the sonnet, moreover, thrusts the senses in to prominence. The demands of rhyme and rhythm have forced translators to change this prominence, so that most conclude by emphasizing not the senses but the "esprit" frequently translated by "soul." Howard's suggestion—"mind"—is closer to "esprit," especially in Baudelaire's lexicon, and it could be argued that Baudelaire himself was bullied by rhyme into giving prominence not to understanding but to sensation, where his habitual preference would be for comprehension. But within the parameters of this poem understanding seems a doubtful process, while sensation is given an aura of being beyond question. In part, this is because within *Les Fleurs du mal* the poem is placed early in the poet's evolution, at a point where sensation and emotion prevail over understanding.

The careful architecture of *Les Fleurs du mal* invites us to read this poem not only in the context of those immediately before and after it, but also with the group of poems evoking Nature that come near the end of the first book, *Spleen et Idéal*. This is particularly the case with "Obsession" and "Alchimie de la douleur (Alchemy of grief)" in both of which the tendency to read Nature as allegorical dictionary, together with Nature's power over the poet's senses, are presented in a far bleaker light. Here what Nature seems to offer is not the possibility of ultimately understanding existence but rather a series of terrifying images of decay and death. In that light, "Correspondances" becomes on rereading a poem that is much more ambivalent, much less triumphant than when we first encounter it.

Baudelaire is at his best in evoking those aspects of Nature most familiar to a city dweller, especially the changing quality of the light, the splendor of sunsets, and the shapes made by what he terms in his prose poem "L'Etranger (The Stranger)"—"the clouds, the clouds, the marvelous clouds." In one of his very first letters, when he was not quite 12 years old, he described a sunset he had seen on the way to Lyon: "Day had fallen and I saw a really fine sight, the sunset; that reddish color formed a remarkable contrast with the mountains which were as blue as the deepest pair of trousers" (L 3, CI 4). Already he is both sharply aware of color and contrast, and eager to find a comparison that will clarify his point. These are tendencies that will remain with him.

Among the notes published after his death under the title "Journaux intimes (Intimate Journals)," he notices, for instance, "the green darkness of damp evenings in summer" (I 650) or finds a combination of erotic and esthetic pleasure by having his hero "beg for the right to kiss [his mistress's] leg and [take] advantage of the situation to kiss that lovely leg in such a position that its outline stood out clearly against the setting sun" (I 660). His poems include some glittering evocations of light, all the more powerful for their concision. The prose poem, "Le Fou et la Vénus (The Jester and Venus)," for instance, depicts a beautiful day in which it seems that "an ever increasing light makes the objects sparkle more and more brightly, the excited flowers burn with the longing to rival the blue of the sky through the energy of their colors, and the heat, making the perfumes visible, sent them rising up to the sun like smoke" (PPP VII). And "Confession" beautifully and elliptically suggests moonlight on the Seine.

But he is also able to convey the fogs, vapors and pearlescent light of fall and winter, as he does in "Brumes et Pluies (Mists and Rain)."

Ô fins d'automne, hivers, printemps trempés de boue
Endormeuses saisons! je vous aime et vous loue
D'envelopper ainsi mon cœur et mon cerveau
D'un linceul vaporeux et d'un vague tombeau.

Dans cette grande plaine où l'autan froid se joue,
Où par les longues nuits la girouette s'enroue,
Mon âme mieux qu'au temps du tiède renouveau
Ouvrira largement ses ailes de corbeau.

Rien n'est plus doux au cœur plein de choses funèbres,
Et sur qui dès longtemps descendent les frimas,
Ô blafardes saisons, reines de nos climats,

Que l'aspect permanent de vos pâles ténèbres,
—Si ce n'est, par un soir sans lune, deux à deux,
D'endormir la douleur sur un lit hasardeux.

(FM CI)

O ends of autumn, winters, spring times steeped in mire,
Seasons that lull to sleep, I love you and admire
Your wrapping me like this both heart and thought
In a shroud of mists and in a shadowy vault.

In this great plain where cold wild wind cavorts,
Where through the lengthy nights the weathercock grows hoarse
My soul far better than at the return of spring
Will open wide its mighty raven's wing.

To a heart that's full of grief nothing's so sweet,
A heart long covered with the winter's sleet,
O pallid seasons, you who rule our airs,

Than knowing we'll always see your pale gloom,
—Unless it's on a moonless night, in pairs,
To rock our grief asleep in a prostitute's room.

(FM CI)

It is a theme to which he lends a more disturbing tone in *Spleen et Idéal* when one of the "Spleen" poems (FM LXXV) summons up a far nastier image of winter. Here the feeling of profound disgust with life is given shape and bleak color through a series of metaphors and images whose apparent lack of connection increases the sense of pointless malice. The god of rain pouring his pitcher full of dark and cold on the inhabitants of the cemetery, and dripping mortality onto the foggy suburbs sets the poet's cat nervously twisting and turning in search of a comfortable position. The rain in the gutters seems to give voice to the soul of an old poet, chilly and melancholy. Outside, a huge bell tolls in lamentation. Inside, the smoking fire and the clock, hoarse from coughing, sing a sad duet while the handsome jack of hearts and the queen of spades from a grubby pack of cards talk in sinister tones of their dead loves. This again is Nature urbanized and modernized, but no less powerful for that. The closing image of the pack of cards, described as "a fatal inheritance of a dropsical old woman," offers us an enigmatic key. Autumnal Nature, like a woman suffering from dropsy, swollen and heavy with liquid, leaves us a pack of images that both demand and defy interpretation. Baudelaire gathers together here a series of images—the pitcher, the cat, the bell—and sounds—the dripping gutter, the smoking log, the ticking clock—that lack logical connections in the same way that cards in the Tarot pack appear in no logical order but are able to suggest multiple possibilities without defining any.

However much the poet-protagonist of *Les Fleurs du mal* might seem towards the end of his journey to long only for something beyond all comprehension, the desire to find in Nature allegories and analogies that would allow its dictionary to be fully understood remains a nostalgic temptation. The prose poem "Le *Confiteor* de l'artiste (The Artist's Profession of Faith)," which may well have been written (as Robert Kopp suggests) after a visit to his mother's Honfleur home in 1859, conveys the complexity of Baudelaire's response to Nature, while highlighting his constant desire to equal its creative power and variety. For all its histrionics, this poem does seem to pull together the essential elements of Baudelaire's vision of Nature: sunlight, sea, the sense of an ending that autumn brings, the contrast between the transience of the individual and the permanence and vastness of the cosmos. In admiring Nature's creation, it is also an exploration of the creative process, and an intensely pessimistic admission of inadequacy.

THE ARTIST'S PROFESSION OF FAITH.

How penetrating is the close of day in autumn! Oh! penetrating to the very point of pain, for there are certain delicious sensations, which, while imprecise, are not without intensity, and no blade has a keener tip than that of Infinity.

How great a delight it is to drown one's gaze in the vastness of sky and sea! The solitude, the silence, the incomparable chastity of all that azure! a small sail trembling on the horizon, imitating in its minuteness and its solitude my own irremediable existence, the monotonous melody of the surge, all these things think through me and I through them (for in the grandeur of reverie, the sense of self soon fades!); they think, as I say, but in music and pictures, without quibbles, without syllogisms, without deductions.

And yet, these thoughts, whether they come from me or spring from objects, soon become too intense. When energy combines with sensual delight it creates a mental malaise and positive pain. My over-stretched nerves now produce only clamorous and painful vibrations.

And now the depth of the sky fills me with consternation; its clarity exasperates me. The insensitivity of the sea and the immutability of the spectacle revolt me. . . . Oh! must one endlessly suffer or endlessly flee from beauty? Nature, merciless enchantress, ever-victorious rival, let me be! Tempt no more my desires and my pride! The study of beauty is a duel in which the artist screams with fear before being defeated.

(PPP III)

Although the artist is condemned in advance to fail in this struggle with Nature, and more generally with beauty, the struggle itself is what defines him or her. As Baudelaire affirmed in his preface to the study of the artificial paradises, "it is clear that [. . .] the natural world penetrates the spiritual world, provides it with its nourishment, and thus helps to bring about that indefinable amalgam that we call our individuality" (I 399). Moreover, while Nature might defeat the artist, Baudelaire presents art itself as greater than Nature, since it projects on to the world the power of the intellect and of memory. Thus, in his "L'Invitation au voyage (Invitation to a journey)," he evokes a "singular land, superior to others just as Art is superior to Nature, where Nature is reformed by dream, where it is corrected, embellished and forged anew" (PPP XVIII). This is Baudelaire's Nature—not Nature experienced for herself but Nature reformed by dream and re-created through art.

CHAPTER TEN

The Art of Transposition

"Glorify vagrancy and what might be called Bohemianism, the cult of multiple sensations, finding expression in music. Use Liszt as a reference" (I 701).[1] Wandering through Paris, drawing on the multiple sensations offered by a large city, twining together the permanent and the ephemeral, as the rod and the flowers are bound together to represent the thyrsus Baudelaire dedicates to Franz Liszt: all this offers an allegory not just of the poet's exploitation of Paris as motif but also of his magpie appropriation of esthetic theory and practice. There is nothing static or rigid about either Baudelaire's passions or his esthetics. They shift, evolve, transform themselves in response to political, social, and personal events. In so doing, they reflect a growing cynicism and pessimism that crystallize in the poems as images of passionate intensity. Running through these shifting patterns, however, are two everpresent but evolving threads: there is the Dandy's determination to make of himself and his life a work of art, and there is the cult of painting, which he terms his great, unique, and primitive passion (I 701).

The Dandy, Baudelaire argues, is not, as is commonly believed, preoccupied above all with clothes and material elegance, but with something far deeper, more intellectual and spiritual, a cast of mind that makes him the "last flush of heroism in times of decadence" (II 711). Dandyism is above all an attitude of mind, a discipline of the soul and of the will, based on an esthetics of life: "The Dandy must aspire to be unremittingly sublime, living and sleeping in front of a mirror" (I 678). The Dandy is one who gives him or herself[2] to be read and seen as a work of art, constantly recreated, offering an element of permanence, regardless of fluctuations in health or social position. This is performance art raised to the level of high culture.

Underpinning that concept of the self is the cult of images, itself a central feature

---

[1] In 1859 Liszt reciprocated Baudelaire's dedication to him of the prose poem "Le Thyrse (The Thyrsus)" by sending the poet a copy of his piece "The Bohemians" inscribed: "To Charles Baudelaire in devoted and admiring sympathy."

[2] In an entry in the *Journaux intimes* (*Intimate Journals*), Baudelaire does seem to envisage the possibility of a female dandy (I 664), although in *Mon cœur mis à nu* (*My Heart Laid Bare*) he asserts: "Woman is the opposite of the Dandy" (I 677).

not just of Baudelaire's esthetics but also and more generally of his perception of human values. Baudelaire's experiences as a young child taken by his father to visit artists in their studios, his own artistic gifts, revealed in the drawings he scribbled down in the margins of his manuscripts, and his early friendships with painters have all left their mark on much of his writing, from his letters to his poetry, from his personal notebooks to his art and literary criticism.

Even as an adolescent, he was forming and expressing his views on painting, writing to his step-father after a visit to Versailles and its pictures:

> I don't know if I'm right, since I know nothing of painting, but it seemed to me that there were very few good pictures there. Perhaps what I'm saying is stupid but apart from some paintings by Horace Vernet, two or three by Scheffer, and Delacroix's *Battle of Taillebourg* I don't remember any of them, except, too, a canvas by Regnault on some marriage or other of the Emperor Joseph, but this painting stands out for an entirely different reason. All the paintings made during the Empire, which are supposed to be very beautiful, often seem so regular, so cold. The people in them are frequently arranged like trees, or minor characters in an opera. It's probably very silly of me to talk in this way of paintings that have been so highly praised. Perhaps I'm talking nonsense, but I'm only giving my own impressions—perhaps it's also the result of reading *La Presse* that praises Delacroix to the skies?
>
> (L 15–16, CI 58)

The art critic whose praise of Eugène Delacroix (see figure 13) had so attracted the 16-year-old's attention was Théophile Gautier (see figure 7). Gautier had originally hoped to become a painter, but his shortsightedness had forced him to abandon that ambition and concentrate instead on writing. As an art critic, therefore, he had the double advantage of practical experience as a painter and a superb gift for description. Baudelaire tells us that when he first went to meet Gautier, the latter asked him if he liked reading dictionaries, and when he affirmed that from boyhood he had been a lexico-maniac, he was told that *"every writer who cannot say everything, every writer who is left speechless by an idea, however strange, however subtle one might imagine it to be, however unforeseen, falling like a stone from the moon, every writer who does not have the wherewithal to give form to such an idea, is no writer"* (II 108). Fierce words, and ones that stuck in Baudelaire's memory. So much in fact that when at one point Thomas de Quincey talks about something as inexpressible, Baudelaire leaves the word "inexpressible" out of his translation. Gautier's sense of color and shape, and his exuberant vocabulary, as well as his enthusiasm for artists whose work reflected the passions and predilections of Romanticism, exercised an important influence over the young Baudelaire, who, after all, was only twenty-four when his review of the 1845 Salon was published in the form of a small book. He was also influenced by the art criticism of the eighteenth-century writer Denis Diderot, whose accounts of the annual painting salons were being published in the 1840s, that of the salon of 1759, for instance, appearing in *L'Artiste* just before the opening of the first salon that Baudelaire would review.[3] In May 1845, knowing that his friend Jules Champfleury was planning to publish a review of his account of the 1845 salon, Baudelaire sent a brief letter begging him to "write a few serious lines, and SPEAK about the *Salons* of Diderot" (CI 123). Champfleury responded in his article for *Le Corsaire-Satan* of May 27, 1845: "M. Baudelaire-Dufaÿs [Baudelaire incorporated his mother's name in signatures of his early work] is as bold as Diderot, but leaves out the paradox" (quoted II 1265). In addition, Stendhal's explorations of Italian art and his ability to convey a passionate response to painting in dry, often acerbic, tones also attracted Baudelaire's enthusiasm. But however important Gautier, Stendhal, and Diderot might be in helping shape the ways in which Baudelaire conceived of the art critic's task, the letter to his stepfather already shows one of its vital components, the determination, whatever others might think, to focus on his own impressions.

The best criticism, he argues in his account of the 1846 salon, is amusing and poetic, reflecting the works of art through the intelligence and sensitivity of the critic, and therefore passionate, political, and partial. In saying that, Baudelaire insists, however, that although he is adopting an exclusive point of view, it is a point of view chosen to open the widest horizons (II 418). It is this passionate partiality that not only so wonderfully explores the painting of the time but that also reflects so intensely and so fascinatingly Baudelaire's own personality. It is also what makes his art criticism so different from that of his contemporaries, especially in the way in which he extends the frontiers of criticism, and reformulates—better, rejects—the boundaries between critical and creative writing. His criticism includes poems, maxims, and digressions on the relationships between artists and writers, and explorations of esthetic matters that pertain not just to the visual arts but also to literature.

Baudelaire lacked the discipline, or perhaps more precisely, the willingness to follow those routines required of a regular journalist. Meeting deadlines and writing on demand were not for him, the result being that he wrote reviews of only three of the annual salons—those of 1845, 1846, and 1859. Nevertheless, he did also publish studies of laughter, focusing particularly on the comic in the plastic arts, both French and foreign. He described the World Fair of 1855, offered a study of Constantin Guys as painter of modern life that is also a study of himself (see figure 14), summed up Delacroix's life and work in a remarkable article mourning the artist's death, and produced a handful of shorter articles on engravers, the sale of a private collection, and the museum of the Bonne Nouvelle Bazaar. All these articles demonstrate, often in very different ways, Baudelaire's determination to transform delight into knowledge, to understand his own reactions to what he observed, but also to

---

[3] Jean Pommier, *Dans les chemins de Baudelaire* (Paris: Corti, 1945).

translate them into words. There is a double translation taking place here: that of moving from emotion to comprehension; and that of finding a language that will convey both the response and the work that created it. Modern critics have the advantage of talking about works that most of their readers have seen, if not in the original, then at least in reproductions, and probably in color reproductions. Baudelaire's contemporaries faced a quite different challenge, that of summoning into the reader's imagination the colors and tones and shapes of a work they may never have seen. And it is a challenge to which he responds with all the more enthusiasm and joy—a palpable joy in many cases, belying the frequent groans we hear in the correspondence about work waiting to be done—in that it is yet another aspect of the *transposition d'art* in which Baudelaire, like many of his contemporaries, found such a source of inspiration.

The transposition of a theme, an image, a technique from one form of art—say the theatre—to another—say painting—can frequently be detected in Romantic and post-Romantic works. Delacroix draws inspiration from Shakespeare or Walter Scott, Gautier devotes a poem to a statue ostensibly depicting a woman bitten by a snake but whom he recognizes as swooning in sexual rapture, Banville transforms into a sonnet Narcisse Diaz de la Peña's painting of Diana or Jean-Jacques Feuchère's *Amazon Mastering a Horse,* and Claude Debussy answers the challenge of finding a musical equivalent for the sounds and images he found in Mallarmé's sonnets or the "L'Après midi d'un faune (The Afternoon of a Faun)." It is both an active critical response and a finger exercise that lets them test out certain practices, motifs, or structures. "The best review of a painting could be a sonnet or an elegy," Baudelaire affirms in his 1846 Salon, only apparently to turn away from that possibility by acknowledging that "this kind of criticism is destined for volumes of poetry and readers of poetry" (II 418). But of course that acknowledgement is just a form of retreating the better to advance. Both his critical studies and his creative writing are rich in just such tributes.

Partly what is at issue here is the kind of challenge Gautier threw down to the young Baudelaire. Build on your love of dictionaries to develop a vocabulary rich and varied and subtle enough to allow you to convey any idea, any sensation. Partly it is the same kind of stimulating struggle that Baudelaire suggests in a reference to translating: "What glory for an intelligent translator willing to pit his skill against this great poet!" (II 151). The great poet he refers to in this quotation is Victor Hugo, but the exclamation casts light on what tempted Baudelaire himself to devote so much time to both Poe and De Quincey. There is of course in the latter cases a sense of fraternity, the feeling that in these English-language writers he has found unknown brothers, whose thinking reflects and parallels his own. In Delacroix and Guys, too, he seems to have encountered kindred spirits whose experiments, although carried out in a different medium from his, nevertheless illuminate and add meaning to his own—or at least can be read as if they do. But this sense of fraternity is also a sense of rivalry, a driving urge to show that in his own way and on his own terms he can do just as well as these soul brothers. His art criticism is rich in passages where a sudden sense of recognition sparks the desire to transpose an idea or a technique from the medium of painting into that of words. Equally, there are passages where irritation with a concept poorly realized or talents misdirected have goaded Baudelaire into showing how it could be done—a transposition here not of what was achieved, but of what could have been achieved. It is characteristic not just of his art criticism but also and perhaps even more so of his literary criticism. But there is a third element to this desire to transpose from painting to poetry: it parallels and exemplifies the need for the spectator to translate what is seen into his or her own idiom. The World Fair of 1855 provides a telling example of this essential step, while at the same time acknowledging and demonstrating its difficulty. In reviewing the Fair, Baudelaire considers the role of the European who is faced unexpectedly and without preparation with a Chinese work of art, "a strange product, bizarre, its shape ungainly and its color intense," he suggests, adding in a remarkable and highly original twist to his sentence, "and yet occasionally delicate enough to make you swoon" (II 576). Yet, Baudelaire goes on to claim, in an extraordinary passage that reveals how open and flexible his mind was: "This is an example of universal beauty; but for it to be understood, critics or spectators must themselves perform a transformation that is close to a miracle and, through a phenomenon of will-power acting on imagination, learn by themselves what gave birth to that curious flowering" (II 576). There is in much of Baudelaire's writing a determination to find a way of translating the exceptional and the alien, not in order to reduce its quintessential strangeness, but to make that strangeness more approachable. It is also one of the ways in which he works on making the strangeness of experience and emotion in modern existence more approachable when he transposes it into poetry.

Wandering through the salons and the artist's studios, Baudelaire often battens onto aspects of the works that throw down the gauntlet to the wordsmith. Skies and clouds, the only things that the outsider of the first prose poem will admit to loving, frequently attract Baudelaire's attention when he explores an artist's skill. Here he is conveying in words the sense of peace and the visual pleasures of Delacroix's fresco devoted to the meeting of Virgil and Dante: "The clouds, diluted and stretched hither and thither, like gauze unraveling, seem to weigh almost nothing; and that deep, luminous azure vault flies up to a prodigious height" (II 438–39). Looking at Eugène Boudin's pastel sketches of sea and sky he writes:

All those clouds with their fantastic and luminous shapes, those chaotic shadows, those immense extents of green and pink, each hanging from or heaped on the others, those gaping furnaces, those firmaments of black or violet satin, crumpled, rolled or torn, those horizons in mourning or streaming with molten metal, all those depths, all those splendors, ended by going to my head like an intoxicating drink or like the eloquence of opium.

(II 666)

Profound perception is itself a source of intoxication, a turn of mind that enables the recognition of similarities between disparate elements, and creates the kinds of chains of comparison and analogies that Baudelaire offers in his finest poems. Here the bracketing of profound darkness and intense burning light, of great heights and measureless depths is kept—but only just—from flying off into the supernatural by the two somewhat more homely terms, "furnace" and "satin." When Baudelaire translates Théodore Rousseau's skies into prose, he wants to suggest something quite different from this fantastic freewheeling imagination that is building on the clouds in order to conjure up immensity and violence. In Rousseau's case it is more that the sky evokes a mood of melancholy that as writer and critic Baudelaire is eager to reveal: "He loves landscapes infused with bluish lights, the twilight of dusk or dawn, strange sunsets steeped in moisture, heavy clouds traversed by breezes, the great play of shade and light. His color is magnificent but not dazzling. His skies are incomparable in their fluffy softness. [. . .] Much of his soul goes into his land-scapes" (II 484–85). Perceiving the painter's own temperament through his or her depictions of nature, deciphering their metaphorical and metonymical suggestions is, Baudelaire argues here, a central part of the critic's task, but it also has as its necessary parallel the task of the reader. This is the kind of critical approach that both seeks, and invites readers themselves to find in representations of the outer world, a key to understanding the artist's inner world. "What is pure art according to the modern conception?" Baudelaire asks in his unfinished article on philosophical art. "It is the act of creating a suggestive magic containing at once object and subject, the world outside the artist and the artist himself" (II 598). It points forward to what Virginia Woolf would later demand from novelists in the remarkable essay that contends that "on or about December 1910 human nature changed"[4] and challenges novelists to find new ways of responding to that transformation.

One more example of Baudelaire's transcription of painting's ability to capture light is worth quoting for its complexity and intensity. This time Baudelaire is considering Alexandre-Gabriel Decamps, a painter attempting to convey the intensity of North Africa's dry and burning sunlight: "What pleased him above all," writes Baudelaire, "was the most bizarre and improbable play of shade and light. In a canvas by Decamps, the sun literally burns the white walls and the chalky sand. All the colored objects have an intense and lively transparency. The waters have incredible depth. The deep shadows that cut through the sections of houses and that doze

[4] Virginia Woolf, "Character in Fiction," in *Essays*, ed. Andrew McNeillie, III:1919–1942 (New York: Harcourt Brace Jovanovich, 1989).

sprawled out across earth or water have the indefinable indolence or the *far niente* that belongs to shadows" (II 450). What is remarkable here is the intensity of Baudelaire's description and the sense we get of his determination to take Decamps's burning heat even further in forging a language for it. The pleasure he takes in transposing the essence of Decamps's art into words leads him to create an exuberant synesthetic comparison: "The most appetizing dishes, the most thoughtfully produced culinary jests, the most intensely seasoned food was less complex and exciting, gave off less wild pleasure for the nose and palate of a food-lover than M Decamps's paintings for an art-lover" (II 449). There is nothing academic or bloodless about Baudelaire's art criticism, and in moments like this it sheds a sudden and intense light on the poet's temperament, his pleasures, and his sources of inspiration.

Not surprisingly, given Baudelaire's fascination with the city as source of allegory and inspiration, artists who paint cityscapes also stimulate him to rival them in words. Baudelaire's response to Delacroix's painting *The Capture of Constantinople by the Crusaders,* now in the Louvre, insists on the ways in which the evocation of sky and sea and architecture has captured the sense of tumult now calmed, the awareness of a great event that has just been brought to completion. One has the sense here of a great wind blowing, a metaphorical representation of change:

> What a sky and what a sea! Everything here is tumultuous and tranquil, like the aftermath of a great occasion. The city, rising up behind the crusaders who have just traversed it, spreads out with an impressive verisimilitude. Everywhere you look there are those glittering, undulating flags, unfolding and clacking their luminous folds in the transparent atmosphere! Everywhere you look the crowd surges, alarmed, there is the tumult of arms, the pomp of garments, the emphatic truthfulness of gestures made in the great moments of life!
>
> (II 592)

The passage is remarkable for its ability to convey movement and color, sound and the play of light, and to set it within the heightened dramatic framework of a decisive historical turning point. That turning point, one feels, is not just the taking of Constantinople. It is even more vitally the radically new way in which Delacroix has conveyed his subject. Baudelaire does not, however, deny the importance of precedents, revealing Delacroix's achievement all the more clearly by tying it to the beauty of Shakespeare. It is a comparison that might strike the unwary modern reader as banal, but the French had been slow to acknowledge the essentially alien genius of Shakespeare, whose theatre had not really begun to find an appreciative audience in Paris until the 1830s. (Shakespeare's blend of comedy and tragedy, his rejection of the classical unities, and the variety of stylistic register he deploys all shocked a French audience used to the classical purity of Racine and Corneille.) What Baudelaire suggests, moreover, shows the specific nature of his own vision of the English playwright: "No one, after Shakespeare, excels as Delacroix does in molding drama and reverie into a mysterious unity" (II 592). In Delacroix's painting the drama is suggested by the wildly flapping flags with their billowing, clacking movements, while the reverie—a reverie focused on the implications of this victory in the development of human civilization—stems from the ways in which clothes and gestures conjure up the pomp and high seriousness of the moment.

And just to show that he can indeed find words for whatever he is called upon to describe, he even sketches for us the romantic landscapes whose absence from the 1859 salon he laments. But whereas the cityscapes recall those of Baudelaire's poetry, this romantic landscape is not at all the landscape we might find in his creative writing, with its exotic trees and light, its suggestions of the harsh cry of parrots and its scents of tropical fruits and spicy seafood. This is quite simply Baudelaire insisting that he could produce such landscapes if he wanted to: "I miss those great lakes that represent the immobility in despair, the immense mountains, stairways the planet sends up to the sky, from which everything that seemed big seems small, the fortresses (yes, my cynicism will even go that far), the crenellated abbeys reflecting themselves in mournful ponds, the gigantic bridges, the Ninivite constructions inhabited by vertigo—in a word everything you would have to invent if it did not already exist!" (II 667). This is Baudelaire transforming the task of the critic into that of the poet: "in describing what is, the poet degrades himself and descends to the rank of teacher; by telling what is possible, he remains faithful to his function; he is a collective soul who questions, who weeps, who hopes, and who sometimes divines" (II 139).

That power of insight in addition to mere portrayal also underpins a constant theme in Baudelaire's art criticism, a theme that, of course, illuminates in turn his creative writing. In exploring and translating for us the works of art the salon offers or indeed should offer he is driven by a deeper urge, that of seizing the themes and methods demanded by the contemporary world, blown toward us by the wind of modernity. His conclusion to the review of the 1845 Salon throws down the gauntlet in resounding style: "To the wind that will blow tomorrow no one lends an ear; and yet the heroism *of modern life* surrounds us and presses against us. [. . .] The true painter will be the one who is able to wrest the epic side from contemporary life, make us see and understand, with color or line, how great and poetic we are in our cravats and polished boots.—May the true seekers give us next year that singular joy of celebrating the arrival of the *new*" (II 407).

For Baudelaire, Romanticism was the expression of modern society, the vehicle of modern art, which he defined as "intimacy, spirituality, color, aspiration to the infinite, expressed by all the means that the arts contain" (II 421). Romanticism is also an integral part of that great sense of melancholy that Baudelaire sees pervading modern life, a "high and serious melancholy" conveyed for instance in Delacroix's paintings and Weber's melodies (II 440), reflected in the fashion for black coats that he saw as the outward sign of universal mourning for an unspecified loss.

The modern is also to be found in apparently trivial objects or episodes that reflect the transitory and contingent but that the artist forges with the eternal and the immutable to create the masterpiece. That need to seize the ephemeral leads to a focus on, for instance, the changing fashions and materials that modern women choose to wear. To illustrate his image of the modern artist, he chooses Constantin Guys, whose watercolors offer what seem to be rapidly created impressions of contemporary city life. In this exploration, we find Baudelaire both transposing Guys's watercolors and supplying an implicit commentary on the modernist vision reflected in some of his own poems, poems such as "Avec ses vêtements ondoyants (With her undulating clothes)" and "A une passante (To a woman passing by)." The draperies of Rubens and Veronese, he notes, cannot teach us how to represent the materials and dresses worn today, materials that are lifted and oscillated by the crinoline or the starched muslin petticoats: "The cut of a skirt and of a blouse is absolutely different in our days, the pleats are draped according to a different system, the gesture and the bearing of contemporary woman give her dress a life and a physiognomy that are not those of the woman of antiquity" (II 695). That gesture and bearing, that swing of the skirt and the subtle sounds it makes can be seen and heard in the opening quatrain of "A une passante": "Une femme passa, d'une main fastueuse / Soulevant, balançant le feston et l'ourlet (A woman walked past, her luxurious hand / raising and swinging the hem and festoons of her dress)" (FM XCIII). Baudelaire captures it even more voluptuously in the open lines of sonnet twenty-seven: "Avec ses vêtements ondoyants et nacrés, / Même quand elle marche en croirait qu'elle danse (With her undulating, shimmering clothes, / Even when she walks she seems to dance)" (FM XXVII). He takes the motif up again in his study of Guys, warming to his theme as he transposes Guys's watercolors, mingled with memories from his own experience, and creates this pen picture, becoming so carried away with the challenge that he walks a narrow line between the miraculous and the bathetic:

> Woman is no doubt a light, a glance, an invitation to happiness, sometimes a word; but she is above all a general harmony not only in her walk and the movement of her limbs, but also in the muslins and gauzes, the vast, glimmering clouds of materials she wraps around herself, which are like the attributes and the pedestal of her divinity; in the metal and mineral that snake around her arms and her neck, that add their sparkle to the fire of her gaze, or that chatter gently in her ears.

> (II 714)

Guys is all but forgotten here as Baudelaire's own predilections and personality grow to dominate his description, transforming the critical article into something far more creative, shifting the gaze from the object to the subject. This is the reverse of what is happening in the final tercet of sonnet twenty-seven, where the poet becomes so involved in transforming the woman into a work of art, made of steel, light, and diamonds that he concludes by recognizing the sterility of what he has done. When he closes on a line whose alliterations and rhythms border on the precious, he is acknowledging, I would argue, that while his art may have succeeded in sterilizing woman, woman—real life, natural woman, made of flesh and blood rather than minerals—has escaped him. This is Pygmalion in reverse, dourly noting that all he has been able to create is "la froide majesté de la femme stérile (the cold majesty of the sterile woman)" (FM XXVII).

The point Baudelaire is making most powerfully and most subtly in the study of Guys is that works of art—paintings, poetry, music—and also works of criticism must reproduce the intimate thought of the artist, a thought that dominates the subject in the same way that any creation is dominated by its creator. The subject of the work of art fades into the background as the critic, gazing into the heart of painting or poem, statue or novel, seeks out that intimate thought. It is not of course that every work is a self-portrait, but more that Baudelaire is hunting for the symbolic dimension of the work of pure art. This is why realism strikes him as so spurious, such a "farce" as he puts it in his draft for a never completed study of the movement, and it is why poetry is what is "completely true only in *another world*" (II 59).

As we have seen, Baudelaire's openness of mind when seeking out that intimate thought makes him not only receptive to Chinese art, at a time when very few had any sensitivity to a beauty we now take for granted, but also enabled him to challenge his own prejudices and question his own assumptions. Why is sculpture tiresome? he had asked in the account of the Salon of 1846.[5] Part of the problem for him is that unlike the painter, the sculptor is unable to control the viewpoint adopted by the spectator. We can move all around a sculpture and view it at all angles, except the one that sets off its beauties best; or a trick of the light can reveal to us a beauty the artist did not intend (II 487). Yet Baudelaire was to change his mind about sculpture in time for his review of the 1859 Salon. In part, this change of heart or mind is brought about by the work of Ernest Christophe, and specifically by statues of his that gain their meaning precisely through the viewer's liberty to walk around them. In part, it is as if the suggestive qualities of sculpture find a deeper rapport with the growing melancholy of the older Baudelaire's state of mind than it did with the greater optimism and brashness of the poet in his twenties. Moreover, there is an increasing tendency in his writing to admire the monumental.

[5] My grateful thanks to Sandy Hamrick for the translation of *ennuyeuse* here as *tiresome* rather than the more usual *boring,* and for the suggestions she made about this exclamation at the Nineteenth-Century French Studies Conference in October 2000.

But there is also a sense of the desire to meet a rhetorical challenge, for the section devoted to sculpture in the 1859 review has a poetics all its own.

The sculpture passage in the Salon of 1859 uses none of the traditional opening gambits. There is no general commentary on sculpture, no survey of the works exhibited. Instead it sets sculpture in a specific physical environment and more remarkably and arrestingly still gives us a series of contexts that seem part of Baudelaire's imaginary universe. Where painting opens an imaginary space independent of the wall on which a particular canvas happens to be hanging, sculpture demands a pre-existing space if its promise is to find fulfillment. Or better, it demands that the viewer imagine that space and set the museum-bound statue within it.

Baudelaire offers us five contexts, which are also five examples of sculpture's artistic role—the word Baudelaire uses to describe that role is "divine." We are deep within an ancient library, "in that propitious half-light that caresses and suggests long meditations," enjoined to silence by a statue of Harpocrate, the name under which the Greeks and Romans worshipped the Egyptian sun god Horus. Apollo and the Muses watch over our thoughts and encourage us to create the sublime. Or we are walking in a copse—this is Baudelaire, so one must imagine a manicured wood on the edge of the city—when we come across "eternal Melancholy reflecting her noble face in the waters of an ornamental pond, waters as motionless as she herself. And the dreamer who walks by, saddened and charmed, contemplating this great figure whose robust limbs are weakened by secret suffering, says: 'There's my sister!'" (II 669). More powerfully still, in chapel or cemetery, sculptures act as powerful reminders of our own mortality. We catch sight of "an emaciated and magnificent phantom discretely raising the enormous cover of its sepulcher to remind us, ephemeral creatures that we are, to think of eternity" or in the alley of a cemetery leading to a tomb housing the remains of those dear to us we encounter "the prodigious figure of Mourning, prostrate, disheveled, drowning in floods of tears, crushing under its heavy desolation the dusty remains of a famous man" (II 669). Or you are in an old-fashioned garden, delighting in the music of falling water, when you come across a statue of Venus or Hebe, "playful goddesses who sometimes presided over your life" and who now stretch out their charming limbs under alcoves of foliage. And these, moreover, are limbs to which the furnace has given "the rosy glow of life"—statues made, in other words, of terra cotta, a material now "unjustly" abandoned for marble. We are back here with the Venus and Pomona of the little garden Baudelaire remembers from childhood, but imbued now with memories of the real women he had loved in his youth. Or we are walking through a city whose history goes far back into antiquity and whose public squares are marked by "motionless people, larger than those passing by on foot, who narrate for you in a silent language the solemn legends of glory, war, scholarship or martyrdom." These stone phantoms—the allusion to Molière's *Dom Juan* is undeniable—seize us and order us, "in the name of the past, to think of things that are no longer of this world" (II 670). Learning, morality, love, the melancholy of the present, and the teachings of the past: these are the domains that belong to what Baudelaire calls the magnificent program of sculpture. And there are close links between that program and that of poetry. "Just as lyric poetry ennobles everything, even passion, so sculpture, real sculpture, solemnizes everything, even movement" (II 671). In exploring sculpture, therefore, Baudelaire is also looking more closely into the heart of poetry. And he is also looking at how subjects are transformed, transposed, from one art medium to another. Thus, for instance, sculpture shows how "the undulating and glittering dream of painting is transformed into a solid and obstinate meditation" (II 671). Obstinate is one of those key words in Baudelaire's writing, suggesting perseverance, a determined gathering of spiritual and intellectual resources, a quality allowing the poet oppressed by the demands of the everyday to keep his eyes and mind on what really matters.

That kind of obstinate meditation leads Baudelaire to offer transpositions both in prose and in poetry of the few sculptures he sees that live up to what he demands of the medium. Two statues by Ernest Christophe achieve that accolade, one exploring the possibilities for sculpture to suggest both appearance and reality, the other representing what Coleridge characterized as the nightmare life in death. The first is "The Mask," now in the Musée d'Orsay, although it long stood, as its replica still stands, in the Tuileries gardens. Here is Baudelaire's exploration of it in his review of the 1859 Salon:

> . . . a naked woman, whose large and vigorous form recalls Florentine art [. . .], who, seen front on, presents the spectator with a smiling, pretentiously sweet face, a theater face. A light cloth, skillfully twisted, acts as a suture between that pretty, conventional head, and the robust chest on which it seems to be leaning. But, as you take a step to left or right, you discover the secret of the allegory, the moral of the fable, I mean the real head, thrown back and swooning in tears and agony. What at first had enchanted your eyes was a mask, the universal mask, your mask, my mask, the pretty fan that a clever hand uses to hide from the world's eyes grief or remorse.
>
> (II 678)

In other words, what made sculpture tiresome in the eyes of the Baudelaire who reviewed the 1846 Salon, the ability of the viewer to move around the statue, selecting the viewpoint according to preference or caprice, is exactly what gives meaning to this statue. Here is how he conveys those ideas in poetry, leading the viewer through the process by the use of the first person plural, picking up the link to Florentine mannerism through a lexicon marked by its preciosity, deploying a series of alliterations bordering on the exaggerated, and drawing his conclusion through a dialog between reader (forced, as in "Le Voyage" for instance, to ask the silly insensitive question) and the poet, who expresses the moral of the fable in alexandrines of great suppleness and movement, and in a vocabulary that now has nothing of the archaic or the pretentious about it.

LE MASQUE

(Statue allégorique dans le goût de la renaissance)

Contemplons ce trésor de grâces florentines;
Dans l'ondulation de ce corps musculeux
L'Élégance et la Force abondent, sœurs divines.
Cette femme, morceau vraiment miraculeux,
Divinement robuste, adorablement mince,
Est faite pour trôner sur des lits somptueux,
Et charmer les loisirs d'un pontife ou d'un prince.

—Aussi, vois ce souris fin et voluptueux
Où la Fatuité promène son extase;
Ce long regard sournois, langoureux et moqueur;
Ce visage mignard, tout encadré de gaze,
Dont chaque trait nous dit avec un air vainqueur:
"La Volupté m'appelle et l'Amour me couronne!"
A cet être doué de tant de majesté
Vois quel charme excitant la gentillesse donne!
Approchons, et tournons autour de sa beauté.

O blasphème de l'art! ô surprise fatale!
La femme au corps divin, promettant le bonheur,
Par le haut se termine en monstre bicéphale!

—Mais non! ce n'est qu'un masque, un décor suborneur,
Ce visage éclairé d'une exquise grimace,
Et, regarde, voici, crispée atrocement,
La véritable tête, et la sincère face
Renversée à l'abri de la face qui ment.
Pauvre grande beauté! le magnifique fleuve
De tes pleurs aboutit dans mon âme soucieux:
Ton mensonge m'enivre, et mon cœur s'abreuve
Aux flots que la Douleur fait jaillir de tes yeux!
—Mais pourquoi pleure-t-elle? Elle, beauté parfaite

Qui mettrait à ses pieds le genre humain vaincu,
Quel mal mystérieux ronge son flanc d'athlète?

—Elle pleure, insensé, parce qu'elle a vécu!
Et parce qu'elle vit! Mais ce qu'elle déplore
Surtout, ce qui la fait frémir jusqu'aux genoux,
C'est que demain, hélas! il faudra vivre encore!
Demain, après-demain et toujours!—comme nous.

(FM XX)

THE MASK

(Allegorical Statue in Renaissance Taste)

Let's gaze on this treasure of Florentine grace;
In the curves of her muscular body abound
Elegance and Strength, those sisters divine.
This woman, a truly miraculous piece,
Divinely robust, and adorably slim,
Deserves pride of place on sumptuous beds,
Charming the leisure of princes and popes.

—Gaze, too, on that subtle, voluptuous smile
Where complacency shows its rapturous pleasure;
That long, sly, languorous, mocking gaze,
That pretentiously sweet face, with its frame of soft gauze
Whose every line tells us with conquering air:
"Pleasure invites me, Love grants me its crown!"
And see just how much her kindness increases
The rousing charm of this majestic creature.
Come closer, let's wander around her great beauty.

O blasphemy of art! O fatal surprise!
This glorious body that promises such joy
Ends at the top in a two-headed monster!
—No! it's only a mask, a trick of deception
This face that an exquisite grimace lights up,
And, look here, you'll see in horrible contortion
The head that is true and the face that's sincere,
Thrown back, and protected by the face that deceives.
Poor mighty beauty! The magnificent flood
Of your tears pours into my compassionate heart.

Your lie goes to my head and my soul drinks its fill
In the rivers Grief sends in torrents from your eyes!

—But why does she weep? She, whose beauty is perfect,
Who could set her foot on mankind's conquered neck,
What strange evil gnaws at her athletic flank?

—O fool, she is weeping, because she has lived!
And because she lives now! But what she decries
More than anything else, what sets her knees trembling
Is, alas, that tomorrow, she'll still have to live!
Tomorrow and the next day and always!—Like us!

A second statue by Christophe also finds itself doubly transposed in the review. Here we have another female skeleton, this time dressed for a party. She is now merely "that horrible thing that once was a beautiful woman," but her bust, desiccated by the passage of time, still thrusts against her blouse, and she still wears a crinoline and carries a bouquet. Baudelaire moves rapidly from the prose description to the rhymes, in which, as he argues, he has "attempted, not to *illustrate,* but to explain the subtle pleasure" (II 679) that he feels on contemplating the statue. Here is one of the many instances when we find him moving away from the standard view of the differences between critical and creative writing, as he embeds in his critical study lines from his poetry. And in one of the many suggestions about how to read that he scatters through his critical writing, he compares this transposition to the way in which "a careful reader scribbles in pencil in the margins of his book." There is nothing exceptional, he appears to be claiming, in explaining pleasure in this way—you, reader, do the same thing in your own fashion.

Baudelaire's openness to works of the plastic arts, his cult of images, his friendships with artists, particularly his relationship with Delacroix, and above all his determination not just to understand his reactions to works of art but to give those reactions a resonant written equivalent—this is what makes him the most powerful and suggestive art critic of his time. He clearly knew less about music, was rather less exposed to it, and perhaps was less moved by it. He did know the music of Carl Maria von Weber and Hector Berlioz, and he presents Ludwig van Beethoven as one of the great innovators who made Romanticism possible, by "beginning to stir up the worlds of incurable melancholy and despair amassed like clouds in humanity's internal sky" (II 168). When he evokes music in his prose poems, it is mainly to suggest open-air concerts that interest him more for their audience than for their intrinsic value. Yet he dedicated to Franz Liszt a prose poem that offers a poetic exploration of the nature of inspiration, and, as he reveals in his enthusiastic and powerful essay on the performance, *Richard Wagner et Tannhäuser à Paris* (*Richard*

Wagner and Tannhäuser in Paris), he was one of the very few to recognize Wagner's greatness when the German composer at the beginning of his fame presented *Tannhäuser* to a largely uncomprehending French public in 1860 (see figure 11). He read Liszt's analysis of *Tannhäuser*, which, together with a study of *Lohengrin*, he published in volume form in 1851 (they first appeared in the *Journal des débats* in 1849).

Certainly some of his friends could have shared with him their enthusiasm for music in general and their impressions of Wagner. Nerval attended a performance of *Lohengrin* conducted by Liszt as part of the celebrations for the inauguration of Goethe's statue at Weimar in August of 1850. In one of the articles inspired by these celebrations he described the libretto of *Lohengrin* as written in majestic verse that, in French terms, raised the alexandrine to the third power.[6] Moreover, Gautier had traveled to Wiesbaden in 1857 to hear *Tannhäuser* in a performance he had reviewed in *Le Moniteur* at the end of September 1857, concluding on the wish that the opera might be performed in Paris. Of all Baudelaire's close acquaintances, Champfleury was certainly the one most familiar with music and the one who was most enthusiastic about Wagner. (The journalist Allyre Bureau ghosted many of Gautier's music reviews.) In January 1860, inspired by the concert that both he and Baudelaire had just heard, he devoted a sixteen-page pamphlet to defending the new German music, dedicating it to Charles Barbara, the friend who had first introduced Baudelaire to the writing of Poe. The program of that concert is worth reproducing for its ambitious nature and the range of Wagner's music that it revealed. The first half consisted of the overture to the *Flying Dutchman,* followed by four selections from *Tannhäuser*: the march and chorus, the introduction to the third act, the pilgrims' chorus, and the overture. The second half opened with the prelude to *Tristan and Isolde,* followed by three selections from *Lohengrin* (the overture, the wedding march, the introduction to the third act). Champfleury's pamphlet in response to Wagner's music is made up of short vibrant paragraphs rather than a coherent argument. His enthusiasm and his musical sensitivity are striking, especially given the atmosphere of hostility, summed up in Flaubert's entry in his dictionary of received ideas: "Wagner: sneer at the sound of his name and make jokes on the music of the future." Here is Champfleury, clearly deeply moved: "Wagner's music takes me back to far off days when alone in a little Normandy village lying on the wild broom above a cliff, I watched, defying boredom, the sea in its constant beauty, its constant novelty and its constant suggestion of great thoughts." And he adds, "How can one convey, except by analogies based on the senses, the mystical language of those intoxicating sounds?"[7]

Baudelaire's imagination is above all visual and rhythmical. Indeed, for him, music, rhythm, and space are closely intertwined: "Music," he jotted down in his notebooks, "conveys the idea of space. All the arts do, more or less, since they are

[6] See Robert Kopp, *Richard Wagner et Tannhäuser à Paris* (Paris: Belles Lettres, 1994).
[7] Ibid., 117.

number and number is a translation of space" (I 702). There is a tendency in Baudelaire to attach a kind of mystical significance to numbers. His early reading of the social philosopher Fourier, who obsessively divided society into carefully numbered types, may have shaped that fascination, which we find reflected again in a desire, never apparently followed through, to write on the thinker and mathematician Hoeni Wronski whose obituaries had apparently fired his imagination (CI 231). But in communicating his response to music, Baudelaire seems more eager to suggest the link with space than any connection with numbers. The paragraph that summons up Liszt in the prose poem, "Le Thyrse (The Thyrsus)", for instance, is an ebullient attempt to draw parallels between music and landscapes. "Dear Liszt, through the haze, beyond the rivers, beyond the towns where pianos sing your glory, where the printing press translates your wisdom, wherever you may be, in the splendors of the eternal city or in the fogs of dreaming lands consoled by Cambrinus [the god of beer], improvising songs of delight or ineffable grief, or entrusting to paper your abstruse meditations, singer of eternal Pleasure and Anguish, philosopher, poet and artist, I greet you in immortality!" (PPP XXXII).

His sonnet on music ("La Musique," FM LXIX) is above all concerned with mood and rhythm. It might be best to approach it by remembering a line from the letter he wrote to Richard Wagner: "In hearing [your music] I frequently experienced a rather odd emotion, which could be described as the pride and joy of comprehension, of allowing myself to be penetrated and invaded—a truly sensual pleasure, recalling that of floating through the air or rolling on the sea" (L 146, CI 673).

LA MUSIQUE

La musique souvent me prend comme une mer!
Vers ma pâle étoile,
Sous un plafond de brume ou dans un vaste éther,
Je mets à la voile;

La poitrine en avant et les poumons gonflés
Comme de la toile,
J'escalade le dos des flots amoncelés
Que la nuit me voile;

Je sens vibrer en moi toutes les passions
D'un vaisseau qui souffre;
Le bon vent, la tempête et ses convulsions

Sur l'immense gouffre
Me bercent. D'autres fois, calme plat, grand miroir
De mon désespoir!

(FM, LXIX)

MUSIC
Music sometimes takes me like a sea!
Towards my pale star,
Under a ceiling of fog or in a vast ether,
I set sail;

Chest out and lungs filled full
Like canvas sails,
I clamber over the backs of mountainous waves
That night keeps hidden;

I feel vibrating in me all the passions
Of a vessel tormented;
A following wind, the tempest and all its convulsions

On the vast abyss
Rock me. At other times, dead calm, great mirror
Of my own despair!

Music, this sonnet suggests, is more likely to intensify than to change his moods. It is less capable of tearing him out of depression than is art, more apt to leave him unmoved in moments of despair. The unusual structure of the sonnet, with its twelve syllable lines alternating with lines of five syllables, intensifies the importance of rhythm, for even the shape on the page shows the wave-like crests and troughs of emotion. Moreover, the triumphant opening line, with its joyous forward movement, however delighted the exclamation that closes it, however much one might feel it stops only through excess of happiness, nevertheless seals the poem's fate. Once the long line has been chosen for the opening, the sonnet is condemned to end on that bleakly abrupt five-syllable line. In this poem, one might say, rhythm is destiny.

Rhythm, space, and color all play a role in Baudelaire's attempt to convey the excitement of hearing Wagner's music. There is something analogous here to the unusually open-minded approach he adopted to Chinese art, when almost none of his contemporaries was capable of detecting its beauties. Although there were certainly more Parisians who shared his enthusiasm for Wagner, Baudelaire was surrounded by ardently hostile critics and unenthusiastic friends. For instance, Asselineau, despite his knowledge of music, did not attend the Wagner concerts, "because" (at least according to Baudelaire in a letter to his friend and publisher Poulet-Malassis) "they were *so far away, so far from his house* and because someone had told him that Wagner was a *Republican*" (L 144, CI 670). "I dare not speak of Wagner any more," he confided to Poulet-Malassis. "People are too fed up with me. That music was one of the great pleasures of my life. It's a good fifteen years since I've felt so swept off my feet" (L 144, CI 671). The letter was written in 1860. Fifteen years before, Baudelaire was in his early twenties, surrounded by friends, living a carefree Bohemian existence, and with his ambitions, his hopes, and his humor still intact. Something akin to that intensity was recreated for him by Wagner's music, and his essay, like the letter he wrote to the composer, strove not only to find verbal equivalents for that emotion but also, as always, to explain it, to transform pleasure into knowledge (II 786).

He is eager to explore the limitations and the potential for music to translate emotions or ideas, just as he is eager to suggest that music conveys them in its own way, and that just like painting and poetry, music demands an active participation from the listener, an imaginative response that fills in the inevitable gaps. He is leading up here to an affirmation of the idea of correspondences between sensations—between sound and color, scent and touch, for instance—of the kind he reveals in a very different way in the poem entitled "Correspondances." Here, as in all his criticism and in the works he chooses to translate, it is less that Baudelaire gives us reflections of his personality, than that he is indicating the ways in which a personal response is also likely to offer profound analogies with the personal responses of other people; he thus suggests to the recalcitrant or to the timid ways of approaching these works that will open up the widest horizons and lead to the most intense pleasure. Seeing music in terms of color is one such technique, as he suggests in the letter he wrote to Wagner in February 1860. "Your music," he tells him,

> is full of something that is both uplifted and uplifting, something that longs to climb higher, something excessive and superlative. To illustrate this, let me use comparisons borrowed from painting. I imagine a vast extent of a somber red spreading before my eyes. If this red represents passion, I see it change gradually through all the shades of red and pink until it reaches the incandescence of a furnace. It would seem difficult, even impossible, to render something more intensely hot and yet a final flash traces a whiter furrow on the white that provides its background. That, if you will, is the final cry of a soul that has soared to a paroxysm of ecstasy.
>
> (L 146, CI 673–74)

Baudelaire's essay on Wagner reveals that for him one way of responding most deeply to music is to find analogies between it and works with which he is already familiar. The meditations on De Quincey that had led to his adaptation of the *Confessions* in the previous year are clearly key to part of his understanding of the German composer. The ability to convey space and depth, Baudelaire argues, is paramount in Wagner: "It sometimes seems, when you listen to that ardent and despotic music, that you can find painted on the depths of darkness, torn asunder by reverie, the vertiginous conceptions of opium" (II, 785). "Obsession," a poem he sent to his publisher in the same month that he wrote to Wagner, reflects a similar grouping of images:

Mais les ténèbres sont elles-mêmes des toiles
Où vivent, jaillissant de mon œil par milliers,
Des êtres disparus aux regards familiers.

(FM LXXIX)

But the darkness itself is made of paintings
Where live, leaping by their thousand from my eyes,
Beings now gone whose gaze is known to me.

"Un Fantôme (A Phantom)," sent a few weeks later, in March 1860, offers similar images:

Dans les caveaux d'insondable tristesse
Où le Destin m'a déjà relégué;
Où jamais n'entre un rayon rose et gai;
Où, seul avec la Nuit, maussade hôtesse,

Je suis comme un peintre qu'un Dieu moqueur
Condamne à peindre, hélas! sur les ténèbres.

(FM XXXVIII)

In the caverns of immeasurable sorrow
Where Destiny has sent me already,
Where never enters a gay, rosy beam,
Where, alone with the Night, sullen hostess,

I'm like a painter that a mocking god
Has condemned, alas!, to paint on the darkness.

But he also finds analogies with Poe, whose theoretical writings he had translated and whose works had inspired him with their sense of seeking to create a total, unified effect (II 329, 332). Everything in Poe's short stories, Baudelaire insists, is included in view of creating the overall effect: nothing is extraneous, nothing allowed to interfere with or dilute that overall impression. What he seizes on in reading Wagner's pamphlet, entitled *Letter on Music*, is almost identical:

That absolute, despotic taste for a dramatic ideal, where everything, from a declamation noted and underlined by the music with so much care that it is impossible for the singer to leave it for so much as a single syllable, a true arabesque of sounds sketched by passion, right to the most minute care taken over the scene and the staging, in which all these details, as I say, must constantly work towards a totality of effect, have formed the destiny of Wagner.

(II 790)

If Poe and De Quincey are there to guide him through Wagner, so also is Baude-laire's own experience. *Tannhäuser,* in which he stresses above all the struggle of the principles of good and evil for possession of the human heart, is a staging of his own twin postulations, analyzed in various forms in the notebooks: "There is in each person, at each hour, two simultaneous postulations, one towards God, the other towards Satan" (I 682). Listening to *Tannhäuser* he finds himself thinking along sim-ilar lines: "Every properly fashioned brain carries within it two infinities, heaven and hell, and in every image of one of these two infinities the mind will suddenly recognize half of itself" (II 795). Above all, as he asserted in his letter to the German composer, he felt on listening to Wagner's music that it was his own. "At first it seemed to me," he confessed, "that I knew your music already, and later, in thinking it over, I understood what had caused this illusion. It seemed to me that the music was *my own,* and I recognized it, as we all recognize those things we are destined to love" (L 145 CI 672–73). This is one of Baudelaire's great gifts, or great skills. In his novella, *La Fanfarlo,* he might mock the protagonist Samuel Cramer for his eager-ness to appropriate works he enjoyed or admired: "After a passionate reading of a fine book, his involuntary conclusion was: now there's something fine enough to be by me!—and from that to thinking so it is by me!—there is only the space of a dash" (I 554). But by the time he came to his great critical pieces on art and music, that power of appropriation, coupled with an active and creative attempt to do some-thing just as fine in his own way and in his own terms, had become a method, a means of entering into the mind of the other and using it both as a mirror reflecting himself and as a telescope letting him see far further.

CHAPTER ELEVEN

The Old Captain Death

In January 1860 the *Revue contemporaine* published Baudelaire's adaptation and analysis of Thomas De Quincey's *Confessions of an English Opium Eater.* The final sentence, which Baudelaire adds to De Quincey's text, is not only typical of a cast of mind that had long contemplated the unpredictability of human life, but is also movingly prescient. Baudelaire, meditating on a footnote in which De Quincey announces his plans to extend his work *Suspiria de profondis,* remarks: "But Death, whom we do not consult about our projects and whose consent we cannot request, Death, who allows us to dream of happiness and fame, and who says neither yea nor nay, suddenly steps out from his ambush, and with a wing beat sweeps away our plans, our dreams, and the architectures of fantasy in which we imagine we can protect the glory of our closing days!" (I 517).

Two years later, a comment jotted down in his notebooks brings that elaborate metaphor abruptly down to earth.

> Mentally as well as physically, I have always been aware of the abyss, not just that of sleep, but the abyss of action, dream, memory, desire, regret, remorse, beauty, number, and so forth. I cultivated my hysteria with delight and terror. Now, I constantly suffer from vertigo, and today, 23 January 1862, I had a remarkable warning—I felt pass over me *the wing beat of imbecility*.
>
> (I 668)

That remarkable warning was not quite the first indication of the paralysis that would descend upon him. In January of 1860 he had already suffered what he identifies in a letter to his mother as a minor stroke (CI 660). The increasing seriousness of his illness seems belied by the wonderful burst of productivity that marks the period from 1858 to 1862, years that saw him dramatically revising *Les Fleurs du mal,* translating and adapting De Quincey, reviewing the salon of 1859, writing articles of literary criticism devoted to his contemporaries, completing his *Paradis artificiels,* producing his studies of Eugène Delacroix and Constantin Guys, responding to the music of Richard Wagner, and preparing his translation of Edgar Allan Poe's philosophical piece, *Eureka.*

Moreover, he had, in a gesture incomprehensible except in the light of his insistence on the right to contradict himself, embarked on a bid to be elected to the French Academy. The attempt was doomed to failure from the start, and it is hard to imagine why someone who spoke so contemptuously about public and traditional honors would even contemplate trying to achieve them. "Anyone who demands the cross [of the Légion d'honneur] looks as if he is saying: if you do not decorate me for having done my duty, I shall never do my duty again," he snorts in one journal entry, adding: "If a man has merit, what is the point of decorating him? If he has none, *then* you can decorate him, because that will at least give him some reputation" (I 677–78). Sour grapes? Perhaps, but Baudelaire's disdain for the bourgeoisie whom such honors might dazzle is so profound that it is difficult to see him ever seriously valuing a place in the Academy, so many of whose seats at that time were occupied by nonentities. What would he have found to say to them? But there was, of course, his mother, and in his longing to make her see him as successful he must have been willing to swallow much of his pride. The outcome was of course predictably humiliating, although Baudelaire withdrew his candidature in February 1862 before the vote took place. By that time, he had, as tradition demanded, visited most of the members of the Academy. The poet Alfred de Vigny, who himself was gravely ill from cancer at the time, was one of the few who received him with dignity. The meeting left a luminous memory with Baudelaire, a sense of having met someone with whom he was truly in tune. Vigny's diary entry for December 22, 1861 notes: "I received M. Baudelaire. Interview from 2 till 4. He is very erudite, knows English well, at 17 lived in India and knows it well." Why did Baudelaire continue with this myth of a voyage all the way to India, and above all why tell it in circumstances and at a time when it could do him no good? Had he come to believe it himself? Had it become so much a part of the essential myth of his personality that removing it or even just failing to refer to it would seem a kind of amputation? Vigny continues: "Seems to exist literarily only as the translator of this philosophical novelist [he means Poe]. Has the distinguished and unhealthy look of a studious and hard-working person. He has been given some bad advice, and acted incorrectly—as I told him—by officially declaring his candidature at such an early stage" (quoted in Pichois 294). The critic Abel François Villemain, who was the Academy's secretary, and whom Baudelaire detested, gave him a predictably rough ride, as the *Revue anecdotique* related, while the attempt to storm the Academy was still in progress. According to this satirical paper, the following conversation took place between these two men, who were poles apart in their conception of literature:

Villemain: "So you're applying to the Academy, Monsieur. How many votes do you have?"

Baudelaire: "The perpetual secretary knows as well as I do that the rule forbids the Academicians to promise their votes. I shall therefore have no vote until that day on which, no doubt, I shall receive none."

Villemain, *insistently*: "*I*, Monsieur, have never been an original."

Baudelaire, *with innuendo*: "Monsieur, what do *you* know about that?"

(Pichois 295)

In which, of course—if anything like this actually took place, but if so, who told? and with what embellishments?—Baudelaire simultaneously wins and loses. Charles-Augustin Sainte-Beuve, who according to Baudelaire himself had been the one to advise him to make the attempt, wrote condescendingly in the official newspaper *Le Constitutionnel*:

> It is not so easy as one might think to prove to these Academicians and statesmen that there are, in *Les Fleurs du mal,* poems revealing a very remarkable talent and artistry; to explain to them that the author's prose poems, "Le Vieux Saltimbanque" and "Les Veuves," are two jewels, and that in sum M. Baudelaire has found the means of building in the far reaches of a tongue of land considered uninhabitable and beyond the confines of known Romanticism, a bizarre kiosk, highly ornamental and contorted, but truly stylish and mysterious, where one reads Edgar Poe, where one recites exquisite sonnets, where one gets high on hashish in order to philosophize afterwards, where one takes opium and a thousand abominable drugs in goblets of perfect porcelain. This singular kiosk made in marquetry of a deliberate and complex originality, which for some time has been drawing eyes to the furthest point of Romanticism's Kamtschatka, I call Baudelaire's folly.[1]

Perhaps this piece of analysis was driven less by literary judgment—in which Sainte-Beuve was certainly not deficient—than by the propulsion of metaphor itself. Could it be that the desire to express Baudelaire's extension of Romanticism, particularly in terms of language, spawned the geographical equivalent of a tongue of land jutting off the far edge of Russia? If so, what else could he imagine as the architectural equivalent of Baudelaire's poetry than an elaborate and intricate kiosk filled with the pleasures and pitfalls of the artistic Bohemia? Even Théophile Gautier, in an assessment of the progress of French poetry written shortly after Baudelaire's death, stresses the strangeness and exoticism he finds in the *Fleurs du mal*: "They have grown on the black soil of corrupt civilizations, these flowers that seem to have been carried back from India or Java."[2]

These were also years marked by increasingly severe financial problems. The

---

[1] Sainte-Beuve, *Nouveaux Lundis* (Paris: Michel Lévy, 1863), I:401.
[2] Théophile Gautier, *Histoire du romantisme* (Paris: Charpentier, 1882), 347. The Academy awarded its chair in due course to Albert de Broglie, a conservative journalist.

risky and elaborate system Baudelaire and his friend and publisher Auguste Poulet-Malassis had worked out to shuttle the responsibility for his mounting debts from one to the other had collapsed, leading in large part to Poulet-Malassis' bankruptcy. Desperate letters from Baudelaire to his mother beg, demand, and cajole her to send him money to tide him over.

Professing himself weary of Paris, tired of seeking fame and fortune in a city that seemed determined to belittle him, increasingly concerned with the state of his health, Baudelaire decided to go into a form of voluntary exile in Belgium. His aim was to write a book of personal impressions of his time there, and in particular of the art museums and galleries. He planned a series of lectures, designed to found his reputation in a country where his name held no particular associations. He wanted to establish relationships with Lacroix and Verboeckhoven, the printing company that published the works of Victor Hugo (see figure 6). But in the months leading up to his departure, things in Paris went from bad to worse. On July 1, 1862, he had sold everything he had written so far, and indeed the rights on works still to be written, to Poulet-Malassis. Four months later Poulet-Malassis was forced to declare bankruptcy. The prose poems were appearing in *La Presse,* but publication of them was suspended in September 1862. On November 1, 1863 Baudelaire sold the publisher Michel Lévy absolute ownership of his five volumes of translations of Poe, forced by increasing financial difficulties to prefer the immediate payment of 2,000 francs to the long-term revenues they would have brought him. Claude Pichois has established that in 1864 the total amount that Baudelaire had earned from all his publications was a meager nine thousand nine hundred French francs, half of which came from his translations. (Remember he had inherited a hundred thousand francs.) Small wonder that when he left for Brussels in November of 1863, he wrote to his mother: "I suffer greatly from the lack of *friendship* and *luxury.* I'm so crushed by solitude and laziness" (C II 332). Small wonder, too, that he should tell her he held out little hope for this voyage, expecting to be poorly paid for his lectures, and fearing (correctly) that he might fail to sell his three volumes of criticism to Lacroix and Verboeckhoven.

The six weeks he told his mother he planned to spend in Belgium dragged out to eighteen months. The lectures proved a disaster. Suffering horribly from stage fright, Baudelaire mumbled his way through his written text, while his audience, small to begin with, slowly wandered away. He hated Brussels, despised its inhabitants, found the beer insipid, the people ugly, and the weather depressing. The notes he took during this period reflect his impotent rage, shot through only occasionally with the wit and intelligence of his earlier writings. "The Belgian character is not very well defined. It floats between the mollusk and monkey" (II 845); "The most brilliant nature would fade away here in the universal indifference" (II 848); "Spirit of conformity, even in joy" (II 859); "No Latin. No Greek. Professional studies. Produce bankers. Hatred of poetry. A Latin specialist would be a very poor business man" (II 873). In the pages of notes he accumulated, there is little that would have enabled Baudelaire to write the book of impressions he hoped would establish his wider reputation. Perhaps he could have made something of notes jotted down under the heading "Physiognomy of the Street" where the great poet of scents evokes the characteristic smells of different towns:

It is said that each town, each country, has its own odor. Paris, so they say, smells or at least used to smell of old cabbages. The Cape smells of lamb. There are tropical islands that smell of roses, musk, and coconut oil. Russia smells of leather. Lyon smells of coal. The Orient in general smells of musk and carrion. Brussels smells of black soap. The hotel rooms smell of black soap. The beds smell of black soap. The towels smell of black soap. The sidewalks smell of black soap. Façades and sidewalks are always being washed, even when the rain is bucketing down.

(II 822–23)

The architecture of certain churches alone excited his admiration. The stained glass windows of Sainte Gudule brought him briefly out of his self-destructive vindictiveness: "Beautiful, intense colors," he wrote, equally beautifully, "like those a profound soul projects over all the objects of life" (II 942). There are notes for a study of Jesuit architecture that might have led to something like the splendor of passages in the 1859 salon—"the majesty of all these Jesuit churches, inundated with light"—just as some of the comments on Bruges suggest the possibility of poems capturing the beauty of this little, canal-rich medieval city: "A phantom city, mummified, almost completely preserved. It smells of death, of the Middle Ages, of Venice, but in black, of routine specters and tombs" (II 952–53). But it was not until Georges Rodenbach's poetic novel, *Bruges-la-morte,* of 1892 and Stéphane Mallarmé's beautiful sonnet in remembrance of his Belgian friends, "Remémoration d'amis belges (Remembering Belgian Friends)," first published in 1893, that Bruges found its transformation into great French literature.

One other Jesuit church filled Baudelaire with special admiration. This was the church of Saint Loup in Namur, the church he describes as "the masterpiece of the Jesuits' masterpieces" (II 950), a "sinister and gallant marvel" whose interior is that of a "catafalque embroidered in black, pink, and silver" (II 952). It was in the church of Saint Loup around the middle of March 1866 that Baudelaire collapsed on to the floor. It became increasingly obvious that his brain was affected, and on July 2 his mother took him back to Paris, where, aphasic and paralyzed, he entered a nursing home. He died on August 31st, 1867, after having been given the last rites.

It has been argued, most cogently perhaps by John E. Jackson, that much in Baudelaire's thinking gains its force and pathos from his meditations on death.

There is ample justification for such a belief. Think for instance of that extraordinary passage in "Une mort héroïque (A Heroic Death)" when the clown Fancioulle, condemned to death but allowed to perform one more time, does so with such authority, genius, and inspiration as to justify the narrator's exclamation: "The intoxication of art is more effective than any other at veiling the terrors of the abyss" (PPP XXVII). Art as a veil the mind places between itself and the fear of death offers a powerful lens for reading Baudelaire. Certainly his notes contain various statements along the lines of the following: "The taste of death has always reigned in me, conjointly with the taste for life. I enjoyed life with bitterness" (I 592). Of course, it has to be admitted that such a formula closely recalls the atmosphere of certain more extravagant French Romantics, of Pétrus Borel and Théophile Dondey and others who took a macabre delight in drinking out of skulls and affecting a fascination with gothic visions of the fantastic.[3] Baudelaire's meditations on death, however, were shaped both by his profoundly Catholic sensitivity, and by the equally profound absence of any belief in redemption. His depiction of modern man in the *Paradis artificiels,* which is often seen as a self-portrait, stresses a "taste for metaphysics, a knowledge of the various hypotheses philosophy has made about human destiny." Certainly Baudelaire's writing is deeply marked by a fascination with such ideas— among them, those of Honoré de Balzac in *Séraphîta* and *Louis Lambert,* those of Poe in the tales "Mesmeric Revelation" or "The Facts in the Case of Mr Valdemar," those of Goethe (whom Baudelaire could have read in various translations, including that of Gérard de Nerval) and Hoëné Wronski, on whose search for absolute truth Baudelaire contemplated writing an article (CI 231 and 836–37, and NL 13). But these are all speculations either on universal destiny or on the fate of the individual after death. Grieving for another, the sense of losing a close friend or simply an admired predecessor, is absent from Baudelaire's poetry. Victor Hugo's later poetry is unthinkable without the loss of his daughter Léopoldine, just as much of Mallarmé's thinking and writing is profoundly shaped by his mourning for his son Anatole and for friends who died before him. Mallarmé's letters show him more deeply moved by the illness and death of Baudelaire, whom he did not know personally, than Baudelaire himself seems to have been for any one. The loss of his father when he himself was seven years old is the only bereavement he records: there seem to be no close friends, no great poets whose loss he laments. The artist, Emile Deroy, with whom he had enjoyed a close friendship in the 1840s and who died, very young, in 1846, seems to have left no detectable trace in Baudelaire's writing (see figure 1).[4] When Baudelaire spoke to a Belgian audience on Delacroix a few months after the latter's death in 1863, the language he used was a strange mixture of the conven-

---

[3] On this, see for example Enid Starkie, *Petrus Borel* (London: Faber and Faber, 1954).

[4] For Asselineau's moving tribute to Deroy see Crépet and Pichois, *Baudelaire et Asselineau* (Paris: Nizet, 1963), 68–69. Deroy left a remarkable portrait of Baudelaire, together with a painting of the red-haired beggar girl who inspired Baudelaire's poem, "A une mendiante rousse (To a red-haired beggar girl)."

tional, the emotional, and the personal. He talks, banally enough, of an "unexpected catastrophe" (II 773), but then tells his audience, with much more typical intensity, that he experienced the news as one does a profound wound, the seriousness of which is realized only a few minutes after it has been received. He rushed over to the studio and spent two hours weeping with Delacroix's companion, thinking: "I will never, never, never again see the man I loved so much, the man who deigned to love me and who taught me such a lot" (II 774). Perhaps it was the constant self-control of the Dandy that led to this strangely muted and disturbingly self-centered response. No doubt it seemed to him an unprecedented piece of soul-baring, to discuss his tears so openly before strangers, yet to us, reading it now, what is striking is not just the emphasis on the "me" but even more the uncharacteristic failure to analyze and understand the experience of grief. But it seems of a piece with the nature of his poems on death, which are not about loss and mourning so much as attempts to imagine an afterlife.

"Dreams on Death, and warnings," Baudelaire jots down in his notebooks (I 672). From his mid-twenties on he contemplates suicide, whether seriously or in order to draw his mother's attention to him, one cannot be sure. But both *Les Fleurs du mal* and the prose poems seem to reflect such dreams, waking or sleeping, on death, and he uses the image of decaying flesh to chastise his mistresses and to give meaning and amplitude to the poems in which, in contrast to the transience of the beauty those mistresses possess, he can offer them an after-life in poetry. "Remords postume (Posthumous remorse)" imagines the tomb punishing his mistress in the sleepless watches of the night and depicts worms gnawing at her flesh like remorse, while "Je te donne ces vers (I give you these lines)" accepts her with all her faults, and promises that she will remain linked forever to his lofty rhymes, traveling in his ship to the remote ages when posterity's dreams will be shaped by his poems.

The closing section of *Les Fleurs du mal* is dominated by the theme of death, by meditations on what an afterlife might be, on what kinds of death await certain types of people—lovers, who hope to attain perfect union in death, artists, who hold out hopes that death may encourage their creations to flower, and the poor, to whom death offers an elixir that will heal them of their illnesses, protect them from the cold, provide the key to the mystical granary of the after-life. The 1857 edition had ended with "La Mort des artistes (The Death of Artists)" which at least left open the optimistic possibility that the works might achieve fame after the artist's death. The 1861 edition is more pessimistic, more ambiguous too, in the juxtaposition of "Le Rêve d'un curieux (The Dream of a Curious Man)" with its deliberately dull and chilling affirmation of monotony even after death, and "Le Voyage," with its lingering hope for novelty, even if all thoughts of fame are abandoned.

"The Dream of a Curious Man" brings together several central motifs—the fascination with the theater, the sense of being different from others, the dull weight of spleen bearing down on everything. He dedicated it to his friend, the photographer

Félix Tournachon, who worked under the name of Nadar, whom the poet had known since 1844, and whose superbly revealing portraits of Baudelaire might lead one to think that there was some depth of understanding between the two men (see figure 12). But Nadar, when Baudelaire showed him the poem in manuscript form, announced that he could not understand it, although, perhaps wrung by pity, he added that this might be because the handwriting was hard to decipher and once it was printed he might see what it meant. (I cannot help thinking of Mallarmé sending prose poems to his close friends Monet and Berthe Morisot, with a request that they illustrate the poems. They professed themselves "flabbergasted" and clearly had no notion what the poems they were meant to illustrate might mean or suggest or imply.) Baudelaire's poem is, however, clear enough:

LE RÊVE D'UN CURIEUX

Connais-tu, comme moi, la douleur savoureuse,
Et de toi fais-tu dire: "Oh! l'homme singulier!"
—J'allais mourir. C'était dans mon âme amoureuse,
Désir mêlé d'horreur, un mal particulier;

Angoisse et vif espoir, sans humeur factieuse.
Plus allait se vidant le fatal sablier,
Plus ma torture était âpre et délicieuse;
Tout mon cœur s'arrachait au monde familier.

J'étais comme l'enfant avide du spectacle,
Haïssant le rideau comme on hait un obstacle . . .
Enfin la vérité froide se révéla:

J'étais mort sans surprise, et la terrible aurore
M'enveloppait.—Eh quoi! n'est-ce donc que cela?
La toile était levée et j'attendais encore.

(FM CXXV)

"THE DREAM OF A CURIOUS MAN"

Do you know, as I know, the pleasure of pain?
Do people say of you: "What a singular man?"
—I was about to die. My amorous soul was full
Of longing and of horror, a strange infirmity;

Anguish and sharp hope, no mocking mood,
And as the fatal sand slipped slowly through

My torture grew more bitter and more sweet;
My heart tore thread by thread from all I knew.

A child eager for the curtain's rise,
Where now the show lies hidden from his eyes . . .
At last the icy truth was all laid bare:

Death had already seized me unsurprised, and that dread
Dawn enveloped me.—You mean, that's all it is?
They'd raised the curtain and yet I waited there.

That sense of the boredom of life continuing unchanged in death, of infinite sameness as the afterworld's main characteristic, has already formed part of the world evoked by *Les Fleurs du mal*. In the poems on Paris, skeletons return to take part in balls, and in one of the bookseller's booths on the quays the narrator catches sight of an engraving showing a skeleton digging like a laborer. The poet asks the inevitable question:

Voulez-vous (d'un destin trop dur
Epouvantable et clair emblème!)
Montrer que dans la fosse même
Le sommeil promis n'est pas sûr;

Qu'envers nous le Néant est traître;
Que tout, même la Mort, nous ment,
Et que sempiternellement,
Hélas! il nous faudra peut-être

Dans quelque pays inconnu
Ecorcher la terre revêche
Et pousser une lourde bêche
Sous notre pied sanglant et nu?

(FM XCIV)

Here is my translation, striving above all for accuracy and faithfulness:

Are you attempting (harsh fate's
Dread explicit emblem!)
To show that even in the grave
The sleep that's promised is not sure?

To show the Void betrays us;
That even Death deceives us,
And that forever and forever
Alas! we may be forced

In some unknown land
To scratch the surly soil
And drive a heavy spade
With bare and bleeding foot?

Which, in Seamus Heaney's inspired adaptation in his collection, *North,* becomes:

[. . .] are you emblems of the truth,
Death's lifers, hauled from the narrow cell
And stripped of night-shirt shrouds, to tell:
"This is the reward of faith

In rest eternal. Even death
Lies. The void deceives.
We do not fall like autumn leaves
To sleep in peace. Some traitor breath

Revives our clay, sends us abroad
And by the sweat of our stripped brows
We earn our deaths; our own repose
When the bleeding instep finds its spade."[5]

That image of the afterlife as repeating earthly life finds a curious metaphorical reflection in the prose poem, "Déjà (Already)," in which the narrator, after a long sea voyage, contemplates with deep unhappiness the prospect of reaching land. All around him, those who had sailed with him are filled with joy, while he alone is "sad, unimaginably sad":

Like a priest whose divinity has been torn from him, I could not, without a sense of overwhelming bitterness, detach myself from a sea so monstrously seductive, from that sea which has such infinite variety in its terrifying simplicity, and which seems to contain within itself and represent in its games, its movement, its anger and smiles, the moods, the agonies, and the ecstasies of all the souls that have lived, that are living, and that are yet to live!

[5] Seamus Heaney, *North* (London: Faber and Faber, 1975), 25–26.

In bidding farewell to this incomparable beauty, I felt myself crushed to the point of death, and this is why when each of my companions said: "At last" I could only cry: *"Already!"*

Yet it was the earth, the earth with its noises, its passions, its commodities, its festivals; it was a land that was rich and magnificent, full of promise, from which wafted a mysterious perfume of rose and musk, and from which the music of life reached us in an amorous murmur.

(PPP XXXIV)

What Baudelaire's narrator seeks, and this is true of both *Les Fleurs du mal* and the prose poems, is something new, no matter what its nature, the infinite variety of the sea rather than the familiar comforts of the land.

Yet, however present the motif of death might be, Baudelaire's treatment of it lacks the resonance, the intensity, and the originality of his handling of love or jealousy, the city or dream, boredom or escape. There is something too mechanical in the macabre, too facile in the fantasies. Many of these poems are from early in his career. "Le Rêve d'un curieux" was written later on, and its power stems from understatement. Those poems devoted to decay—"Une charogne (Carrion)" and "Remords postume (Posthumous Remorse)" would be good examples—lack something of the profound humanity that makes, say "Le Cygne (The Swan)" or "Les Petites Vieilles (The Little Old Women)," so arresting. In terms of the macabre, Borel and the early Gautier rival Baudelaire in imagination if not in rhetoric. When Baudelaire wrote his article on Borel for Eugène Crépet's anthology of contemporary writers, he depicted him as "one of the stars of Romanticism's somber sky" (II 153), a representative of that later Romanticism in which "melancholy assumed a more striking, more savage, more earthly tone" (II 155). Borel's vast, somewhat rambling, but occasionally astonishingly intense gothic novel, *Madame Putiphar,* together with the prefatory poem, offered Baudelaire an image of what a French Lord Byron or Charles Robert Maturin might be. Gautier—not so much the poet associated with art for art's sake, but the earlier Gautier, the devotee of Romanticism who attended the turbulent first performance of Victor Hugo's play *Hernani* wearing a pink waistcoat—is also mentioned as filling a gap in what Baudelaire terms the new literature through his ability to convey laughter and "the sentiment of the grotesque" (II 110).

Other poets also better Baudelaire in suggesting death in poetry. Hugo's chillingly powerful "I Am Made of Shadow and Marble" for instance, is more imaginative and more suggestive at least than the first four poems in the *Fleurs du mal* book entitled "La Mort (Death)," perhaps because it turns its focus away from questions of individual fate and onto the relationship between the poetic voice and posterity:

Je suis fait d'ombre et de marbre.
Comme les pieds noirs de l'arbre,

Je m'enfonce dans la nuit.
J'écoute; je suis sous terre;
D'en bas je dis au tonnerre:
Attends! ne fais pas de bruit.

Moi qu'on nomme le poëte,
Je suis dans la nuit muette
L'escalier mystérieux;
Je suis l'escalier Ténèbres;
Dans mes spirales funèbres
L'ombre ouvre ses vagues yeux.

I am made of shadow and marble.
Like the black roots of a tree
I thrust into the night,
I listen; I am underneath the earth;
Down there I say to the thunder:
Wait! Make no sound.

I who am called the poet,
In the silent night I am
The mysterious stairway;
I am the stairway of the Dark;
In my funereal spirals
The shadow opens uncertain eyes.[6]

Mallarmé, in his tribute to Poe, finds a more telling expression than Baudelaire in "La Mort des artistes (The Death of Artists)" for the way in which a poet's glory is achieved after his or her death. In Mallarmé's poem, Poe becomes his true self through a transformation effected by eternity. Only then can his age discover that "death triumphed in that unfamiliar voice." Or one might think of the understated power of Wilfred Owens's war poems, or the chilling fantasy of Elizabeth Bishop's "The Weed."

T. S. Eliot spoke both eloquently and rather disparagingly of Baudelaire's "morbidity of temperament,"[7] yet it seems to me that morbidity in Baudelaire is less an element deeply rooted in his psyche and more a mask adopted by a young poet seeking his way. A passage in the 1856 preface to his translation of certain Poe short stories

---

[6] Victor Hugo, *Choix de poèmes,* ed. Jean Gaudon (Manchester: Manchester University Press, 1956), 64–65. The poem originally appeared in the 1881 collection entitled *Les Quatre Vents de l'esprit.*
[7] T. S. Eliot, *Selected Prose,* ed. Frank Kermode (London: Faber and Faber, 1975), 231.

sheds light on this tendency. Baudelaire is of course analyzing Poe here, but he is also, as so often, using his literary criticism to reach a deeper understanding of himself. Poe, in any case, attracted him because of profound similarities he perceived with his own personality, his own literary ambitions, and his own gifts. In his preface to the collection of Poe's stories he had called *Histoires extraordinaires,* he writes:

> The very ardor with which he throws himself into the grotesque for love of the grotesque, and into the horrible for love of the horrible, allows me to confirm the sincerity of his work and the harmony between the man and the poet.—I have already remarked that in several men that ardor was often the result of a vast vital energy that remained untapped, or at times of a stubborn chastity and a profound but repressed sensitivity. The supernatural pleasure a man can feel at watching his own blood flowing, the sudden, violent, pointless movements, the great cries hurled into the air when the mind has not ordered the throat to act, are phenomena to be included in the same order.
>
> (II 317)

The grotesque and the horrible that are loved for themselves, the sudden outbursts of passion or movements or cries, are all familiar territory to readers of Romantic texts, from Chateaubriand to Hugo. The analysis here points forward to Freud with that suggestion of the sudden return of the repressed, but all of this seems dominated by emotions that while certainly not alien to Baudelaire are not those that lead either to his most original or his most creative writing.

Where Baudelaire comes into his own is less in his experiments with the grotesque and the macabre than at those points when his powerful imagination fuses with his exceptional rhetorical powers to reveal the complexity of the human experience of the passing of time. "Le Voyage," the closing poem of *Les Fleurs du mal,* derives its extraordinary power not from its attempt to suggest the nature of any afterlife, but from its dense and evocative summarizing of all that has gone before, both in life and in the book. And much that has gone before is in part or in full shaped and driven by a sense of time passing, never to be regained.

As early as 1845, in a witty little prose piece entitled "How you pay your debts if you're a man of genius," Baudelaire is already suggesting the awareness of time galloping by. Here he is describing Balzac, up to his eyes in debt and desperately trying to work out a way of writing quickly enough to earn the money he needs:

> The great man's sorrow was a common sorrow, down to earth and ignoble, shameful and ridiculous; he found himself in that mortifying situation we all often experience, where every minute that flies by carries off on its wings the chance of salvation; where, one eye fixed on the clock, the genius of invention feels the need to increase his strength two-fold, three-fold, ten-fold, in pro-

portion to the decrease in time available and the approaching speed of the fatal hour.

(II 7)

It is a motif that recurs with exasperating frequency in the *Hygiène* section of Baudelaire's note books, a section in which the poet desperately whips himself on, taking time out to berate his procrastination, and seeking means of urging himself to confront the tasks awaiting him. "At every moment," Baudelaire reminds himself, "we are crushed by the idea and sensation of time. And there are only two ways of escaping this nightmare,—two ways to forget it: Pleasure and Work. Pleasure drains us. Work fortifies us. The choice is ours" (I 669).

Les Fleurs du mal is rich in images evoking the idea and the sensation of time, even in the opening poems, where the poet-hero is young and existence might seem to stretch before him. The ninth poem, for instance, "Le Mauvais Moine (The Bad Monk)," the manuscript of which dates back to 1842, ends with the following exhortation: "When will I then turn / The living spectacle of my sad destitution / Into the work of my hands and the love of my eyes?" (FM IX), while the tenth poem, "L'Ennemi (The Enemy)," ends with an equally regretful but more macabre tercet: "O sorrow! O sorrow! Time chews on our lives / And the hidden enemy who gnaws at our hearts / From the blood draining from us grows larger and stronger" (FM X). "Le Goût du néant (The Taste for the Void)," which was written for the second edition, introduces a different image, one in which the horror is increased through the protagonist's insensibility: "Time engulfs me minute by minute / As expanses of snow cover a body grown rigid; / I contemplate from on high the globe in its roundness / And no longer seek out the shelter of a cabin" (FM LXXX). Most chilling, perhaps, is the poem "L'Horloge (The Clock)," which was written in 1860 to provide a fitting closure for *Spleen et Idéal*. Reading this poem leaves a strong sense of an intense personal experience that surges up from the haunting rhythms and the way in which the images transform the banal and everyday into the exceptional.

Horloge! dieu sinistre, effrayant, impassible,
Dont le doigt nous menace et nous dit: "*Souviens-toi!*
Les vibrantes Douleurs dans ton cœur plein d'effroi
Se planteront bientôt comme dans une cible;

Le plaisir vaporeux fuira vers l'horizon
Ainsi qu'une sylphide au fond de la coulisse;
Chaque instant te dévore un morceau du délice
A chaque homme accordé pour toute sa saison.

Trois mille six cents fois par heure, la Seconde
Chuchote: *Souviens-toi!*—Rapide, avec sa voix
D'insecte, Maintenant dit: je suis Autrefois,
Et j'ai pompé ta vie avec ma trompe immonde!

Remember! Souviens-toi, prodigue! *Esto memor!*
(Mon gosier de métal parle toutes les langues.)
Les minutes, mortel folâtre, sont des gangues
Qu'il ne faut pas lâcher sans en extraire l'or!

Souviens-toi que le Temps est un joueur avide
Qui gagne sans tricher, à tout coup! c'est la loi.
Le jour décroît; la nuit augmente; souviens-toi!
Le gouffre a toujours soif; la clepsydre se vide.

Tantôt sonnera l'heure où le divin Hasard,
Où l'auguste Vertu, ton épouse encor vierge,
Où le repentir même (oh! la dernière auberge!),
Où tout te dira: Meurs, vieux lâche! il est trop tard!"

(FM LXXXV)

Clock! sinister god, impassive and terrible,
Whose threatening hand says always: "*Remember*
That soon I'll hurl into your terrified heart
My accurate darts and their quivering pains.

The false wraith of pleasure will head for the hills,
As a sylph disappears in the theatre's wings;
Each instant devours a parcel of the pleasure
That's all we will get for the whole of our lives.

Three thousand six hundred times an hour,
The Second whispers: *Remember!*—The swift insect voice
Of the Moment announces: I'm Time that's passed by
And my horrible snout has sucked out your life.

Esto Memor, wastrel, *vergiss nicht!*
(My metal throat speaks all earthly tongues.)
The minutes, rash mortal, are all precious lodes
You should never let go till the gold's all extracted!

Remember that Time is a passionate gambler
Who wins without cheating, every hand! that's the law.
Daylight dims; night increases; remember!
The abyss always thirsty, the water clock draining dry.

The hour will soon strike when the goddess of Fortune,
And dignified Virtue, your still-virgin bride,
When Repentance itself (oh! the last inn of all!)
Will all say: Old coward, your moment is up!

Time as the net fighter in the gladiatorial games, time as the insect sucking away our substance, but time, too, as the skein of wool slowly, too slowly, unwinding: throughout his poetry, the richness and variety of Baudelaire's images and their ability to suggest the complexity of his responses make this motif not only more intricate but also more powerful than those associated with death itself. Above all, perhaps, this is a theme that gains its poignancy from Baudelaire's sense that those very states when he is least able to act are those when he is most aware of time slipping by. "Do not forget," he notes at one point, "that drunkenness is the negation of time, like any violent state of mind, and that consequently all the results of that loss of time must file past the drunkard's eyes without destroying in him the habit of putting his conversion off until tomorrow, resulting in the complete perversion of all his feelings, and the final catastrophe" (I 592). It is under such circumstances that "poetic memory, once an infinite source of delight, becomes an inexhaustible arsenal of torments" (I 483). No one knew the infirmity of procrastination better than Baudelaire, whose letters to his mother so frequently include promises along the following lines: "I promise you that I'll work unceasingly, not only to pay off the debts that make my situation so ambiguous and painful, but also to create for myself a daily regulator that will diminish the influence of all the follies and passions that constantly bubble away within us" (CI 174).

Of course, the theme of time rushing past has a long and distinguished history, from Horace's "Eheu fugaces, Postume, Postume, labuntur anni" through Villon's "Où sont les neiges d'antan?" And from the poets of the Baroque era to Poe whose protagonists frequently express the terror of their lives slipping away, revealing, as Baudelaire cogently puts it in one of his studies of the American writer, "hysteria usurping the place of will-power" (II 317). But Baudelaire finds metaphors, analogies, and allegories for this theme that give it a distinctly modernist flavor. Moreover, these images are to a large extent preparatory, stage-setting suggestions for the yet more original images that mark Baudelaire as one of the founding poets of modernism. He sees the city as a parchment on which each inhabitant has scraped off earlier writings and has imposed his or her own, creating a palimpsest containing layer upon layer of experience. The images Baudelaire seizes on are those that suggest not just the fleeting nature of time but more vitally the multiplicity of levels of time within a city—a palimpsest he so powerfully reveals in "Le Cygne"—and within individuals, either by perceiving in the shrunken forms of little old women the beauties, actresses, and lovers they were in earlier days, or by confronting individuals with their future manifestations, as happens in the prose poem, "Le Vieux Saltimbanque (The Old Mountebank)." The city whose labyrinthine streets—both those that now shape Haussmann's Paris and those destroyed to make that vision possible—figure a spider's web of associations across space and time. The inhabitants of those streets, those who walk them now, together with those who walked them in the past, are presented in ways that point forward to and indeed make possible Proust's unforgettable images of people walking on stilts of time and concealing, like a fan ready to be unfolded, multiple aspects of themselves across time. Thus Baudelaire's poet sees in the old women "suffering mothers, courtesans or saints, whose names were once on everyone's lips" (FM XCI), detects the passions, vices, or virtues that shaped their young womanhood, and appears to read through the aspects they now present the multiple figures that have also been theirs through time. Walking through a showground on a holiday, he catches sight of an old mountebank, now too old to perform, destitute and abandoned, yet retaining that pride and that certainty of his own talents and worth that mark him as a projection of the poet's own future: "And as I went home, obsessed by this vision, I tried to analyze my sudden grief, and I said to myself: I have just seen the image of the old man of letters who has outlived the generation he so brilliantly amused; the image of the old poet who has no friends, no family, no children, degraded by his poverty and by public ingratitude, and into whose booth the forgetful world no longer wishes to enter!" (PPP XIV). Baudelaire despised those unable to distinguish between the poet and the individual, those who saw every poem as a personal confession to be interpreted only as such, those whose limited imagination diminished the imaginative possibilities of poetry to transform individual experience into the universal. But he would not deny the power any work derives from being rooted in the personal, and here the expression "degraded by his poverty and public ingratitude" takes on a particular resonance, recalling his complaints of suffering "from the lack of friendship and luxury" and his outbursts of rage against the city that refused to acknowledge him.

The richness of Baudelaire's concept of time is also revealed in the opening stanza of "Le Voyage" where the child's image of a world infinitely large, and the adult's sense of a world woefully shrunken, exist simultaneously within the voyager. The adult's intellectual perception gives a particular poignancy to the child's wondering and confident optimism, but it does not destroy or ridicule that optimism:

Pour l'enfant, amoureux de cartes et d'estampes,
L'univers est égal à son vaste appétit.

Ah! que le monde est grand à la clarté des lampes!
Aux yeux du souvenir que le monde est petit!

(FM CXXVI)

For the child, enamored of prints and of maps,
The universe is as vast as his own boundless dreams.
How mighty the world in the light of the lamps!
To memory's gaze how modest it seems!

This is why, although the traveler knows that all one extracts from travel is the bitter knowledge of the world's monotony and pettiness, the final stanzas show him setting off again, incurably determined to:

Plonger au fond du gouffre, Enfer ou Ciel, qu'importe?
Au fond de l'Inconnu pour trouver du nouveau!

(FM CXXVI)

Plunge into the abyss, be it Heaven or Hell
To the depths of the unknown in search of the new!

Charles Taylor, in his study of the development of the sense of self, argues: "The modernist multi-leveled consciousness is [. . .] frequently 'decentered.'"[8] Baudelaire's modern city-dwellers are certainly multiple, living in a palimpsest of places and times, but they are also decentered, since the connections become apparent to them only at those elusive moments when, for totally incomprehensible reasons, "the moral world opens its vast perspectives, full of new light" (I 401). It is at such moments, when time is perceived not as a one-directional arrow, but as a series of layers like those in a cliff built by millennia of accumulated sediments, that Baudelaire is at his most arresting and most modern. This is the source of that fecundity he perceives in Parisian life: "The wonderful envelops us and rains down upon us, like the atmosphere," he asserts, adding: "But we do not see it" (II 496). Baudelaire did see it, and more than his meditations on death, it is his sensitivity to the combination of the eternal and the fleeting in life that makes him the great poet of modernity. As he says of the painter, Constantin Guys, in a passage that confirms yet again that he took the artist as a mirror in which to explore himself: "He sought out everywhere the ephemeral and fleeting beauty of present life, the character of what the reader has allowed us to call *modernity*. Often bizarre, violent, excessive, but always poetic, he was able to concentrate in his sketches the bitter or heady flavor of the wine of Life" (II 724).

[8] Charles Taylor, *Sources of the Self* (Cambridge, Mass: Harvard University Press, 1989), 481.

The Tip of the Iceberg

Baudelaire is an iceberg, remarks Claude Pichois, and what we know of his readings, what we know of the works of art he saw or the pieces of music he heard, represents only the tantalizing tip of that iceberg. For all the spleen his letters exhale, for all the sense of frustration and rage that builds up in him over the years of poverty and neglect, no one can read much of his writing without glimpsing enormous reserves of curiosity and ambition. There are frequent references to him attempting to track down specific books or manuscripts, eager not just to read and see and hear, but also to transform that experience into the analysis of criticism or the synthesis of lyricism. His contemporaries often depict him carrying books and notebooks. We catch a tempting glimpse of him, on arrival at Reunion Island, making his way down a swaying rope ladder hanging from a gigantic scaffold, and clutching books under each arm as he does so (Pichois 76). Champfleury presents him entering casinos with "a plump note book under his arm,"[1] or describes him with a volume of Swedenborg, soon to be replaced by a "fat volume of algebra."[2] And then there are those portraits by Courbet, with Baudelaire lost in a dog-eared volume whose identity it is tempting to try to guess.

Certain stars in our galaxy, so we are told, are so faint that none of our instruments can detect them, yet their presence can be inferred from the way in which their gravity tugs on the visible stars. In similar ways, Baudelaire's reading, both its substance and perhaps more vitally still the very act of reading itself, like experiences in his life, leaves a trace, so faint as to be barely detectable in much of his writing. And not just in the works he published, for there are tempting lists of projects, titles of prose poems never completed, drafts for plays. In the early 1860s he contemplated writing on "imaginary museums" and "lost museums," an idea his compatriot, André Malraux, would take up a century later and that Lydia Goehr has more recently extended to music. What might have figured in these imaginary mu-

---

[1] Champfleury, *Souvenirs et portraits dejeunesse* (Paris: Dentu, 1872), 144.
[2] Ibid., 132–33.

seums and how might he have presented them? Perhaps as a series of critical ekphrases, written descriptions of purely imaginary works of art? Or as a group of poems like those in *Les Fleurs du mal* that draw their inspiration from statues, paintings, or engravings—"L'Amour et le crâne (Eros and the Skull)," for instance, with its transformation of an etching by Hubert Goltzius, or "Une gravure fantastique (A Fantastic Engraving)" with its transposition of John Mortimer's illustration of a passage in the book of Revelation depicting the arrival of death on a pale horse? Or might he have invented a completely new genre?

In particular, the published prose poems seem just the tip of the iceberg of what he thought of doing. There are long lists of titles under such headings as "Parisian Topics" or "Dream Worlds" or "Symbols and Moralities." While one can guess at the main outlines of "From the Heights of the Buttes Chaumont" or "Cholera at the Opera" or "The Seductive Undertaker" or "Filial Ingratitude," other titles seem more opaque: what about the tempting title "The Black Hen," for instance, or "Prisoner in a Lighthouse" or "The Mouse Trap"? Some of these headings are fleshed out, though left incomplete. One, which takes its inspiration from a painting, suggests the rapid notation of a Constantin Guys:

THE COURTYARD OF THE POST OFFICE

In the middle a group of various people getting down from a stagecoach, a woman surrounded by her children throws herself into the arms of a traveler wearing a cotton bonnet. A cold Paris day. A child stands on tiptoe to be kissed. Further off, another traveler loads his parcels onto a delivery boy's pack. In the foreground, on the left a beggar holds out his hat to a soldier with a yellow plume, a mercenary, thin as Bonaparte, and a member of the national guard tries to embrace a succulent flower-seller carrying a basket; she defends herself half-heartedly. On the right, a gentleman, hat in hand, talks to a woman carrying a child; near this group, two dogs are fighting.[3]

A jotted note tells us that this scene is inspired by Louis-Léopold Boilly's canvas, *The Arrival of the Coach in the Courtyard of the Post-Office*. One wonders what Baudelaire would have done with it. Pick up on one of those stories? Reveal similar interests to those in his prose poem "Les Bons Chiens (The Good Dogs)" and follow the fighting dogs? Or suddenly turn away from this already slightly old-fashioned scene (Boilly died in 1845) to suggest a contemporary equivalent?

"Symptoms of Ruin" is another project that Baudelaire had begun to flesh out and that suggests a starting point in the visual arts, especially in paintings like those of the Italian artist much admired by Gautier, Giovanni Battista Piranesi:

[3] Baudelaire, *The Prose Poems*, trans. Rosemary Lloyd (Oxford: Oxford University Press, 1991), 116.

Symptoms of ruin. Vast buildings. Several, one on top of the other, apartments, rooms, here and there a temple, galleries, stairways, cul-de-sacs, viewpoints, lanterns, fountains, statues.—Fissures and cracks. Dampness resulting from a reservoir situated near the sky.—How to warn people and nations? Let us whisper warnings into the ears of the most intelligent.

High up, a column cracks and its two ends are displaced. Nothing has collapsed as yet. I can no longer find the way out. I go down, and then climb back up. A labyrinth tower. I never succeed in leaving. I live forever in a building on the point of collapsing, a building undermined by a secret malady.—I work out in my mind, for my own amusement, whether such a prodigious mass of stones, marbles, statues, walls, which are about to collide with each other, will be greatly sullied by that multitude of brains, human flesh, shattered bones.—I see such terrible things in my dreams that sometimes I wish I would sleep no more, if I could be sure not to feel too weary.[4]

This reads like a condensation of many of Baudelaire's central themes: the sense of decay and imminent danger; the awareness that all this is taking place in a vast city, with all its architectural complexity; the curious sensation of time held in abeyance—nothing has collapsed yet—and then having passed with immense speed—"I live forever;" the conviction that there is some ineradicable flaw in everything that surrounds him, a flaw depicted in terms of a human illness, a "secret malady" like his own venereal illness. Equally typical are his responses: the need to warn, as his poems warned, of the power of evil; the decision that only a select few can be saved; the intellectual analysis of what the result of this threatened collapse will be. And then there is that pulling back from the intensity of the vision, what looks like a deliberate weakening of it in the assimilation of that vision to a dream, something much more banal than the description that first meets us.

The most unexpected of these projects is perhaps the notes for an elegy on hats. Although Manet depicts him wearing top hats, there is little else that suggests the passion for head wear that these lines convey, and little in his writing that corresponds to this exuberant delight in listing objects. Some of it is an elated pleasure in the riches of language, a degree, too, of showing off his knowledge of hats, as he evokes the differences between a Mary Stuart and a Marinière, a Longueville and a Lavallière. But the exultant and energetic start suddenly halts abruptly as the image of hats in a milliner's shop promptly spawns the thought that the heads that wore them have been guillotined. Baudelaire the moralist steps in and brings it all plummeting down to earth in the somewhat curmudgeonly response of an elderly Dandy to a superficial focus on mere appearance:

[4] Ibid., 116.

A hat. Smooth surface.

A cap. Folded or bubbling surface.

The pass (from the spot which no longer sits on the head.)

That part at the back that is called the crown or dome, or the lining, when it is fluted.

Bonnet strings. Fasteners or little ribbons.

Feathers, marabous or aigrettes.

Headbands, of feathers and flowers.

A *Maintenon,* a kind of lace snood, fitted onto the hat and tied on above the ribbons.

A *Mary Stuart,* a form in which the peak is very low, a Sarrasin or ogival shape.

A *Lavallière* (gone out of fashion) with two feathers meeting behind.

Russian hat. An aigrette.

The little toque has a pompon or a wing.

A flower (rose) placed on a *Marie-Louise.*

A *Marinière* hat, with a bouquet.

A *Longueville* hat is a Lavallière with a single feather which floats and flaps in the wind.

A Scottish hat, in poplin with squares, has a rosette, a silver clasp, and an eagle's or a raven's feather.

Ornaments: puffs, ruffs, bias cuts, borders.

The furnishing of a fashion shop.

Curtains in muslin or silk of a uniform white color. Divans. Looking glass, a smooth, mobile surface. Oval, inclined mirrors. Large oval table, with a long-legged hat stand. A fairies' laboratory. A clean task.

General appearance: coolness, light, whiteness, and the sparkling colors of a flowerbed. Ribbons, frills, tulle, gauze, muslin, feathers etc . . .

The hats inspire thoughts of faces, and look like a gallery of faces, since each hat, because of its character, evokes a face and lets the mind's eye see it. Guillotined heads.

What sadness there is in this solitary frivolity! A distressing feeling of foolish ruin. A monument to gaiety standing in a desert. Frivolity in abandon.

The suburban milliner, pale, anemic, milk coffee-color, like an old tobacconist.

A distressing feeling.[5]

This description suggests that Gustave Flaubert's wonderfully elaborate description of Charles Bovary's cap at the beginning of *Madame Bovary* may well have inspired Baudelaire, but if so, what he would have done would have been very different. "A

[5] Ibid., 115–16.

monument to gaiety standing in a desert" is distinctly Baudelairean, slippery in its irony and caught ambiguously between the sardonic and the defiant.

And then there are the ideas and projects for plays—like many of his contemporaries, Honoré de Balzac, Flaubert, and Stendhal among them, Baudelaire thought of the stage as a means to fame and fortune. He draws on his friendship with the arch-Catholic novelist Jules Barbey d'Aurevilly to jot down notes for a play presenting a Catholic dandy—Tartuffe in reverse, he suggests. There is a list of possible titles: "The Women Kept without Knowing it," "A Story of Brigands during the Directorate," "A Roman Drama (of the Republic or the Empire)," "The Cuckolds' Club." Much more fleshed out are two envisaged plays, "Idéolus" written in 1843 with his friend, Ernest Prarond, and "The Marquis of the First Hussars." There are tempting notes and suggested titles for novels and short stories. "Write to Malassis," he enjoins himself at one point, mysteriously enough, "to ask him for books on Drivers, Brigands, Sorcerers, especially during the Revolutionary time" (I 593), and he adds, on the same sheet, "a novel on the *Last Men*. The same vices as before," and then: "On war, marriage, politics etc. . . . among the last men" (I 593). There is a project for a novel to be called "The Rational Madman and the Beautiful Adventuress:"

> Sensual pleasure in the Society of Extravagants.
> What horror and what pleasure in loving a female spy, a female thief, etc . . . !
> The moral reason for this pleasure.
> You always have to go back to De Sade, that is to say to *Natural Man,* to explain evil.
> Begin with a conversation, on love between finicky people.
> Monstrous feelings of friendship or admiration for a depraved woman.
> All of the Sisina is in this.
> Find strange and horrible adventures, through the capital cities.
>
> (I 595–96)

The Sisina was Elisa Gnerri or Neri, a friend of Mme Sabatier. Baudelaire was inspired to write a sonnet dedicated to her, and refers to her in a marginal annotation to the manuscript of that sonnet as "the Diana who drank Orsini's health in Van Swieten water" (I 938). Felice Orsini was the terrorist who had attempted to assassinate Napoleon III, using a bomb whose shape is reproduced in Antoni Gaudi's Cathedral to the Holy Family in Barcelona. Van Swieten water was reputed to have prophylactic and anti-syphilitic qualities. It is hard to imagine this schema providing a sufficient framework for a novel. Part of it seems to have fed into one of the prose poems, "Portraits de maîtresses (Portraits of Mistresses)" (PPP XLII), which does indeed focus on a conversation on "love between finicky people," and that connection casts some light on why loving a female spy or thief might cause such pleasure and such horror. In all four cases related in the prose poem, the finicky lover has encountered a woman out of the ordinary: one experimented in chemistry, a second was completely insensitive to sexual pleasure, another was a gluttonous eater, and a fourth was so perfect that her lover found himself forced to murder her. Women, it seems, at least for these men, should not possess a strong personality of their own or differ from a standard model in any way. As a result, the prose poem ends with the four men turning to a different source of pleasure, the wine that allows them to "kill Time which clings so fiercely to life, and to accelerate Life, which passes so slowly" (PPP XLII). Loving someone so outside the norms as a female spy or thief would, within the terms set down in this vision, be both a great source of pleasure (in killing time and speeding life up), and a source of horror, because it runs so much counter to established conventions and sexual stereotypes. Hence the need for the protagonist to be both rational and mad. But what might be sustainable in a prose poem—and "Portraits de maîtresses" is not one I would list among the most successful—might well not suffice for a novel. Baudelaire had neither the temperament nor the leisure to devote to such a lengthy form: his art lies in pithiness, suggestion, and implication rather than in the kind of detailed analysis that seems to be demanded of a novel, or at least that is indicated by his note to himself: "The moral reason for this pleasure."

Trying to imagine the submerged iceberg of Baudelaire's reading and of his plans leads to a series of haunting *what ifs?*, none of which, of course, has much intrinsic value except to reinforce a sense of his immense appetite for the curious and his boundless ambitions. That appetite is something readers of his poetry need to share, especially, perhaps, if they are reading him in translation. His writing draws so much on patterns of sound, on echoes across his production as a whole, on the connotations as well as the denotations of words, that it frequently seems, if not to defy translation, at least to throw the power of translation into question. The solution seems to be a kind of multiple reading, following the original where possible and exploring its suggestions through several different translations. Only the kind of multiple vision I have been suggesting in exploring various translations of "Le Cygne," or "Correspondances," for example, would enable readers to select elements from a variety of translations that might together convey rather better the complexity of the original. Above all, we need to think of Baudelaire not just as the poet of *Les Fleurs du mal* but also of his art and literary criticism, his study of Wagner, his prose poetry, and his explorations of the artificial paradises.

In February 1861, Baudelaire published a poem that pays tribute to that vast world of reading and the imagination whose presence can frequently be detected in his work, even in those pieces most steeped in spleen. It seems to provide a kind of summary of his intellectual life, slightly saccharine perhaps in comparison with other Baudelaire poems, but nonetheless illuminating in the light it projects on his poetic personality. In translating it, I shall need to keep in mind several important threads. The rhymes are both playful and revealing, and I want to convey that element. In Baudelaire's poem, for instance, *in-folio,* the large book format, rhymes with *fabliau,* a narrative genre popular in the Middle Ages. Since the word *fabliau* will not be familiar to many English-speakers, I'll need to find some kind of equivalent for this playful rhyme. Through his rhymes, moreover, Baudelaire ties together the idea of the dream (*songe*) and that of the lie (*mensonge*), echoing at the same time a La Fontaine fable with which every French reader would be familiar, that of the astrologer so busy gazing at the stars that he fell into a hole. Here it may be more important to find a correspondingly familiar English saying or allusion rather than to try to link dream and lie through a rhyme. But above all, I'll want to keep Baudelaire's stylistic register, avoiding archaisms and slang, allowing what he is saying about the two voices and his personal preference for one over the other to retain the unpretentious clarity of the original.

La Voix

Mon berceau s'adossait à la bibliothèque,
Babel sombre, où roman, science, fabliau,
Tout, la cendre latine et la poussière grecque,
Se mêlaient. J'étais haut comme un in-folio.
Deux voix me parlaient. L'une, insidieuse et ferme,
Disait: "La Terre est un gâteau plein de douceur;
Je puis (et ton plaisir serait alors sans terme!)
Te faire un appétit d'une égale grosseur."
Et l'autre: "Viens! oh! viens voyager dans les rêves,
Au delà du possible, au delá du connu!"
Et celle-là chantait comme le vent des grèves,
Fantôme vagissant, on ne sait d'où venu,
Qui caresse l'oreille et cependant l'effraie.
Je te répondis: "Oui! douce voix!" C'est d'alors
Que date ce qu'on peut, hélas! nommer ma plaie
Et ma fatalité. Derrière les décors
De l'existence immense, au plus noir de l'abîme,
Je vois distinctement des mondes singuliers,
Et, de ma clairvoyance extatique victime,
Je traîne des serpents qui mordent mes souliers.
Et c'est depuis ce temps que, pareil aux prophètes,
J'aime si tendrement le désert et la mer;
Que je ris dans les deuils et pleure dans les fêtes,
Et trouve un goût suave au vin le plus amer;

Que je prends très souvent les faits pour des mensonges,
Et que, les yeux au ciel, je tombe dans des trous.
Mais la Voix me console et dit: "Garde tes songes:
Les sages n'en ont pas d'aussi beaux que les fous!"

(I 170)

THE VOICE

My cradle used to rock against a library wall,
A somber Babel, where novels, science, tales and all,
Where Latin ash and Grecian dust twined in an imbroglio.
All this, when I stood just as tall as an in-folio.
Two voices spoke. The first, insidious and obdurate, said:
"The earth is like the very sweetest bread.
The gift I have is one of boundless pleasure,
You've but to make the earth your appetite's fair measure."
The other said: "Come, o come traveling in the mind,
Beyond what's possible, beyond what scholars find!"
Coming from who knows where, caressing the ear,
A wailing phantom that yet fills us with fear,
This voice sang like the wind on the strand.
I answered: "Sweet voice! I'm yours to command."
And thus began my flaw and my fatality.
In the vast distance behind the scenery
In the darkest point of the deep abyss
I see strange worlds distinctly in my bliss.
Ecstatic victim of my visionary grace,
Foul serpents bite my shoes as on I pace.
It's since that time I share the prophets' taste,
For empty seas and for the sandy waste;
Since then I laugh at funerals and weep at feasts,
And wine most men find gall to me tastes sweet;
Since then I think men lie when truth they utter,
And, gazing at the moon, fall in the gutter.
The Voice consoles me saying: "Let dreams rule;
The wise man dreams less richly than the fool."

In reading Baudelaire's spleen poems, or the letters in which he complains to his
mother of his poverty and his suffering, it is easy to think of him crushed by apathy
and misfortune, someone for whom, as he puts it in "Le Goût du néant (The Taste
for the void)," "adorable Spring has lost its perfume" (FM LXXX). But that is only
part of the story. Despite the assertion in the final poem of *Les Fleurs du mal* that all

we gain from traveling—physically and mentally—is a "bitter knowledge," the undertone running through all Baudelaire's writing is an extraordinary appetite for life. It is this appetite that combines with a love of language and a determination to listen to the wind of modernity to ensure that while his poetry may make us angry or melancholy, ecstatic or shocked, it can never leave us indifferent.

Bibliography of Translations

Aggeler, William. *The Flowers of Evil.* Fresno, Calif.: Academy Library Guild, 1954.

Ashbery, John. *A Wave.* New York: Viking, 1984.

Barnard, Patrick. *The Language of Silent Things.* Dunvegan, Ont.: Quadrant Editions, 1983.

Bernstein, Joseph M. *Baudelaire, Rimbaud, Verlaine: Selected Verse and Prose Poems.* New York: Citadel Press, 1947.

Cameron, Norman. *Intimate Journals.* New York: Syrens, 1995.

——. *My Heart Laid Bare and Other Prose Writings.* Edited by Peter Quennell. London: Weidenfeld and Nicolson, 1950.

Campbell, Roy. *Poems of Baudelaire.* New York: Pantheon Books, 1952.

Carson, Ciaran. *The Alexandrine Plan.* Loughcrew, Ireland: Gallery Press, 1998.

——. *First Language.* Loughcrew, Ireland: Gallery Press, 1993

Clark, Carol, and Robert Sykes, eds. *Baudelaire in English.* Harmondsworth: Penguin, 1997.

Cornford, Frances. *Fifteen Poems.* Edinburgh: Targa Press, 1976.

Crowley, Aleister. *Little Poems in Prose.* Paris: E. W. Titus, 1928.

Davis, Dick. *The Covenant.* London: Anvil Press Poetry, 1984.

Dillon, George, and Edna St. Vincent Millay. *Flowers of Evil.* New York: Harper and Brothers, 1936.

Egan, Beresford, and C. Bower Alcock. *Flowers of Evil in Pattern and Prose.* New York: Sylvan Press, 1947.

Fitzgerald, Robert. *Spring Shade.* New York: New Directions, 1971.

Flecker, James Elroy. *Forty Two Poems.* London: J. M. Dent, 1911.

Ford, Charles Henri, ed. *The Mirror of Baudelaire.* Norfolk, Conn.: New Directions, 1942.

Fox, Ellen. *Artificial Paradise.* New York: Herder and Herder, 1971.

Hamburger, Michael. *Twenty Prose Poems.* London: Cape, 1968.

Heaney, Seamus. *North.* London: Faber and Faber, 1975.

Howard, Richard. *Les Fleurs du mal.* Boston: David R. Godine, 1982.

Hyslop, Lois Boe, and Francis E. Hyslop. *Baudelaire as a Literary Critic.* University Park: Pennsylvania State University Press, 1964.

Isherwood, Christopher. *Intimate Journals.* Boston: Beacon Press, 1957.

Kaplan, Edward. *The Parisian Prowler.* Athens: University of Georgia Press, 1997.

Kitchin, Laurence. *Baudelaire's Paris.* London: Forest, 1990.

Lappin, Kendall. E. *Baudelaire Revisited.* Annapolis, Md.: K. E. Lappin, 1981.

Leakey, F. W. *Selected Poems from "Les Fleurs du mal."* Greenwich: Greenwich Exchange,

1997.

Leclercq, Jacques. *Flowers of Evil*. Mount Vernon, N.Y.: Peter Pauper Press, 1958.

Lloyd, Rosemary. *Baudelaire's The Prose Poems and La Fanfarlo*. Oxford: Oxford University Press, 1991.

——. *The Conquest of Solitude. Selected Letters of Charles Baudelaire*. Chicago: University of Chicago Press, 1986.

Lowell, Robert. *Imitations*. New York: Farrar, Straus and Cudahy, 1961.

——. *The Voyage and Other Versions of Poems by Baudelaire*. New York: Farrar, Straus and Giroux, 1961.

MacIntyre, C. F. *One Hundred Poems from Les Fleurs du mal*. Berkeley: University of California Press, 1947.

Martin, Dorothy. *Sextette: Translations from the French Symbolists*. London: Scholartis Press, 1928.

Martin, Walter. *The Complete Poems of Baudelaire*. Manchester: Carcanet Press, 1997.

Mathews, Marthiel, and Jackson Mathews. *The Flowers of Evil*. New York: New Directions, 1955.

Mayne, Jonathan. *Art in Paris, 1845–1862*. London: Phaidon, 1965.

——. *The Painter of Modern Life*. London: Phaidon, 1964.

McGowan, James. *The Flowers of Evil*. Oxford: Oxford University Press, 1993.

Moore, Nicholas. *Spleen*. London: Menard Press, 1990.

Moore, Thomas Sturge. *Poems*. London: Macmillan, 1932.

Paul, David. *Poison and Vision: Poems and Prose of Baudelaire, Mallarmé, and Rimbaud*. Salzburg: Salzburg University, 1996.

Richardson, Joanna. *Selected Poems*. Harmondsworth: Penguin, 1975.

Roseberry, Patricia. *Artificial Paradise*. Harrogate, U.K.: Broadwater House, 1999.

Scarfe, Francis. *The Complete Verse of Baudelaire*. London: Anvil Press, 1986.

Shapiro, Norman R. *Selected Poems from "Les Fleurs du mal."* Chicago: University of Chicago Press, 1998.

Stang, Maurice. *Hashish, Wine, Opium*. London: Calder and Boyars, 1972.

Sturm, Frank Pearce. *His Life, Letters, and Collected Work*. Edited by Richard Taylor. Urbana: University of Illinois Press, 1969.

Wallis, Glenn. *Les Fleurs du mal*. Baltimore: Contemporary Poetry, 1955.

Walton, Alan Hull. *Selections from Baudelaire*. London: Fortune Press, 1942.

Wilbur, Richard. *L'Invitation au voyage*. Boston: Little, Brown, 1997.

Selected Bibliography

Auden, W. H. *Collected Poems*. Edited by Edward Mendelson. New York: Vintage, 1991.

Balzac, Honoré de. *La Cousine Bette*. Paris: Gallimard, 1972.

Bandy, W. T., and Claude Pichois. *Baudelaire devant ses contemporains*. Paris: Editions du Rocher, 1967.

Banville, Théodore de. *Œuvres poétiques complètes*. 7 vols. Edited by P. J. Edwards et al. Geneva: Slatkine, 1992–2001.

———. *Petit Traité de Poésie française*. Paris: Les Introuvables, 1978.

———. *Petites Etudes. Mes Souvenirs*. Paris: Charpentier, 1882.

Barlow, Norman. *Sainte-Beuve to Baudelaire*. Durham, N.C.: Duke University Press, 1964.

Baudelaire, Charles. *Correspondance*. 2 vols. Edited by Claude Pichois and Jean Ziegler. Paris: Gallimard, 1973.

———. *Les Fleurs du mal*. Edited by Jacques Crépet and Georges Blin. Paris: Corti, 1942.

———. *Nouvelles Lettres*. Edited by Claude Pichois. Paris: Fayard, 2000.

———. *Œuvres complètes*. 2 vols. Edited by Claude Pichois. Paris: Gallimard, 1975–1976.

———. *Petits Poëmes en prose*. Edited by Robert Kopp. Paris: Corti, 1969.

———. *The Conquest of Solitude: Selected Letters of Charles Baudelaire*. Translated and edited by Rosemary Lloyd. Chicago: University of Chicago Press, 1986.

———. *Un Mangeur d'Opium*. Edited by Michèle Stäuble. Neuchâtel: A la Baconnière, 1976.

Benjamin, Walter. *Charles Baudelaire: A Lyric Poet in the Era of High Capitalism*. Translated by H. Zohn. London: NLB, 1973.

Brewer, Ebenezer Cobham. *Dictionary of Phrase and Fable*. London: Cassell, 1968.

Burton, Richard. *Baudelaire in 1859: A Study in the Sources of Poetic Creativity*. Cambridge: Cambridge University Press, 1988.

———. *Baudelaire and the Second Republic: Writing and Revolution*. Oxford: Clarendon Press, 1991.

Champfleury [Jules Husson]. *Souvenirs et portraits de jeunesse*. Paris: Dentu, 1872.

Chesters, Graham. *Baudelaire and the Poetics of Craft*. Cambridge: Cambridge University Press, 1988.

Citron, Pierre. *La Poésie de Paris dans la littérature française de Rousseau à Baudelaire*. 2 vols. Paris: Minuit, 1967.

Crépet, Jacques, and Claude Pichois. *Baudelaire et Asselineau*. Paris: Nizet, 1953.

Delacroix, Eugène. *Correspondance générale*. Edited by André Joubin. Paris: Plon, 1938.

———. *Journal*. Edited by André Joubin. Paris: Plon, 1932.

Eliot, T. S. *Selected Prose*. Edited by Frank Kermode. London: Faber and Faber, 1975.

Esquiros, Adolphe. *Les Hirondelles.* Paris: Renduel, 1835.

Fairlie, Alison. *Baudelaire: Les Fleurs du mal.* London: Edward Arnold, 1960.

Ferguson, Priscilla Parkhurst. *Paris as Revolution. Writing the Nineteenth-Century City.* Berkeley: University of California Press, 1994.

Gautier, Théophile. *Histoire du romantisme. Suivie de Notices romantiques et d'une étude sur la poésie française 1830–1868.* Paris: Charpentier, 1882.

——. *Mademoiselle de Maupin.* Paris: Garnier-Flammarion, 1966.

Gilman, Margaret. *Baudelaire the Critic.* New York: Columbia University Press, 1943.

Hannoosh, Michele. *Baudelaire and Caricature: From the Comic to an Art of Modernity.* University Park: Pennsylvania State University Press, 1992.

Hemmings, F. W. J. *Baudelaire the Damned: A Biography.* New York: Scribner, 1982.

Hiddelston, James. *Baudelaire and "Le Spleen de Paris."* Oxford: Clarendon Press, 1987.

——. *Baudelaire and the Art of Memory.* Oxford: Clarendon Press, 1999.

Houssaye, Arsène. *Poésies complètes.* Paris: Charpentier, 1850.

Howells, Bernard. *Baudelaire: Individualism, Dandyism and the Philosophy of History.* Oxford: Legenda, 1996.

Hugo, Victor. *Choix de poèmes.* Edited by Jean Gaudon. Manchester: Manchester University Press, 1956.

——. *La Légende des siècles.* Edited by Jacques Truchet. Paris: Gallimard, 1950.

——. *Œuvres poétiques.* Edited by Pierre Albouy. Paris: Gallimard, 1964.

Hyslop, Lois Boe, and Francis Hyslop. "Baudelaire and Manet." In *Baudelaire as a Love Poet and Other Essays,* 87–103. University Park: Pennsylvania State University Press, 1969.

Hyslop, Lois Boe. *Baudelaire, Man of his Time.* New Haven: Yale University Press, 1980.

Jackson, John E. *La Mort Baudelaire: essai sur Les Fleurs du mal.* Neuchâtel: La Baconnière, 1982.

Jenkyns, Richard. *Virgil's Experience.* Oxford: Clarendon Press, 1999.

Jones, Percy Mansell. *Baudelaire.* New Haven: Yale University Press, 1952.

Jong, Alex de. *Baudelaire, Prince of Clouds: A Biography.* New York: Paddington Press, 1976.

Jouve, Pierre-Jean. *Tombeau de Baudelaire.* Paris: Editions du Seuil, 1958.

Kopp, Robert, ed. *Richard Wagner et Tannhäuser à Paris.* Paris: Belles Lettres, 1994.

Lawler, James R. *Poetry and Moral Dialectic: Baudelaire's "Secret Architecture."* Madison, N.J.: Fairleigh Dickenson University Press, 1997.

Leakey, Felix. "Baudelaire and Kendall." *Revue de Littérature comparée* (1956): 53–63.

——. *Baudelaire and Nature.* Manchester: Manchester University Press, 1969.

Lloyd, Rosemary. *Baudelaire's Literary Criticism.* Cambridge: Cambridge University Press, 1981.

——. "Le Latin sans pleurs: le vocabulaire illustré de François Baudelaire." *Essays in French Literature* 32–33 (November 1995–1996): 22–40.

——. " 'Le Réseau mobile de quelque toile d'araignée': Banville et la conversation poétique." In *Poésie et Poétique en France: 1830–1890,* edited by Peter J. Edwards, 185–204. New York: Peter Lang, 2001.

MacInnes, John W. *The Comic as Textual Practice in "Les Fleurs du mal."* Gainesville: University of Florida Press, 1988.

Mallarmé, Stéphane. *Œuvres complètes.* Edited by Henri Mondor and G. Jean-Aubry. Paris: Gallimard, Pléiade, 1945.

——— *Œuvres complètes.* Vol. 1. Edited by Bertrand Marchal. Paris: Gallimard, Pléiade, 1998.

Morgan, Edwin. *Flower of Evil, a life of Charles Baudelaire.* New York: Sheed and Ward, 1943.

Mossop, D. *Baudelaire's Tragic Hero.* Oxford: Oxford University Press, 1961.

Nerval, Gérard de. *Œuvres.* Edited by Albert Béguin and Jean Richer. Paris: Gallimard, 1974.

Pichois, Claude. *Auguste Poulet-Malassis.* Paris: Fayard, 1996.

———. *Baudelaire.* Translated by Graham Robb. London: Hamish Hamilton, 1987.

Poe, Edgar Allan. *Works.* New York: Walter J. Black, 1927.

Pommier, Jean. *Dans les chemins de Baudelaire.* Paris: Corti, 1945.

Proust, Marcel. *A la recherche du temps perdu.* Edited by Pierre Clarac and André Ferré. Paris: Gallimard, 1954.

———. *Contre Sainte-Beuve.* Edited by Pierre Clarac. Paris: Gallimard, Pléaide, 1971.

Raser, Timothy. *A Poetics of Art Criticism: The Case of Baudelaire.* Chapel Hill: University of North Carolina Press, 1989.

Richardson, Joanna. *Baudelaire.* New York: Saint Martin's Press, 1994.

Robb, Graham. *La Poésie de Baudelaire et la poésie française 1838–1852.* Paris: Aubier, 1993.

Sainte-Beuve, Charles-Augustin. *Nouveaux Lundis.* Vol. 1. Paris: Michel Lévy, 1863.

———. *Vie, Poésies et Pensées de Joseph Delorme.* Edited by Gérald Antoine. Paris: Nouvelles Editions latines, 1956.

Sartre, Jean-Paul. *Baudelaire.* Translated by M. Turnell. London: Hamish Hamilton, 1964.

Scott, Clive. *Translating Baudelaire.* Exeter: University of Exeter Press, 2000.

Starkie, Enid. *Baudelaire.* Harmondsworth: Penguin, 1971.

———. *Petrus Borel The Lycanthrope. His Life and Times.* London: Faber and Faber, 1954.

Stephens, Sonya. *Baudelaire's Prose Poems: The Practice and Politics of Irony.* Oxford: Oxford University Press, 1999.

Taylor, Charles. *Sources of the Self.* Cambridge: Harvard University Press, 1989.

Tennyson, Alfred Lord. "The Lotus Eaters." *In Memoriam, Maud and Other Poems.* Edited by John D. Jump. London: J. Dent and Sons, 1974.

Turnell, Martin. *Baudelaire.* New York: New Directions, 1954.

Verlaine, Paul. *Œuvres poétiques complètes.* Edited by Y. G. Le Dantec and Jacques Borel. Paris: Gallimard, 1962.

Williams, R. L. *The Horror of Life.* Chicago: University of Chicago Press, 1980.

Woolf, Virginia. *The Essays of Virginia Woolf. 1919–1924.* Vol. 3. Edited by Andrew McNeillie. New York: Harcourt Brace Jovanovich, 1989.

Wright, Barbara and David Scott. *"La Fanfarlo" and "Le Spleen de Paris."* London: Grant and Cutler, 1984.

Index of Works by Baudelaire

General Index